Springer Books on Professional Computing

Edited by Henry Ledgard

Springer Books on Professional Computing

Peter P. Silvester

The Unix™ System Guidebook

Guidebook

An Introductory Guide for Serious Users

Springer-Verlag
New York Berlin Heidelberg Tokyo

Peter P. Silvester
Department of Electrical Engineering
McGill University
Montreal, Quebec
Canada H3A 2A7

Series Editor
Henry Ledgard
Human Factors Ltd.
Leverett, Massachusetts 01054
U.S.A.

With 6 Figures.
Unix is a trademark of Bell Laboratories.

Library of Congress Cataloging in Publication Data
Silvester, Peter P.
    The Unix system guidebook.

    (Springer books on professional computing)
    Bibliography: p.
    1. UNIX (Computer system) I. Title. II. Series.
QA76.6.S564   1983   001.64′25   83-16846

Media conversion by Science Typographers, Inc., Medford, New York.
Printed and bound by R. R. Donnelley & Sons, Harrisonburg, Virginia.
Printed in the United States of America.

9 8 7 6 5 4 3 2 (Second printing, 1985)

ISBN 0-387-90906-0 Springer-Verlag New York Berlin Heidelberg Tokyo
ISBN 3-540-90906-0 Springer-Verlag Berlin Heidelberg New York Tokyo

Preface

Well suited to medium-scale general purpose computing, the Unix time-sharing operating system is deservedly popular with academic institutions, research laboratories, and commercial establishments alike. Its user community, which until recently was made up mostly of experienced computer professionals, is now attracting many people concerned with computer applications rather than systems. Such people are mainly interested in putting Unix software to work effectively, hence need a good knowledge of its external characteristics but not of its internal structure. The present book is intended for this new audience, people who have never encountered the Unix system before but who do have some acquaintance with computing.

While helping the beginning user get started is a primary aim of this book, it is also intended to serve as a handy reference subsequently. However, it is not intended to replace the definitive Unix system documentation. The Unix operating system as it now exists at most installations (popularly, though somewhat inaccurately, called Version 7 Unix) is substantially as described by the Seventh Edition of the system manuals. This book emphasizes Version 7 and systems closely related to it, but it does also describe some other facilities in wide use.

Many people have been instrumental in shaping this book and the author wishes to express his gratitude to them all. Particular thanks are due to David Lowther, for our many helpful discussions; and to the many students whose suggestions enlivened the task.

PETER P. SILVESTER

Contents

Chapter 1

Introduction

The Unix time-sharing system is rapidly becoming one of the most popular computer operating systems ever designed. Its unique popularity may be the result of portability; Unix systems are available for various different computers, while practically all other operating systems are tied to specific machines. Whether for this reason or any other, the Unix system is becoming universal, much as Fortran became the universal language in its day. And just as Fortran influenced the style of other programming languages, so Unix software characteristics are becoming visible—both by emulation and deliberate avoidance—in other operating systems. For computer users, some acquaintance with the Unix system is therefore taking on increasing importance.

A Multimachine Operating System

Although it was originally intended for the PDP-11 family of computers, Unix software has been recreated for use on many other machines, both smaller and larger. There now exist versions of the Unix system, or other operating systems which very closely resemble it, for many widely used small computers based on 16-bit microprocessor chips. Upmarket from the PDP-11, Unix systems (in some cases several) exist for the Interdata 8/32, the PERQ, the VAX-11 family, and other large minicomputers. Other versions run on large mainframe computers like the Amdahl. At the opposite end of the computer spectrum, Unix-like operating systems are available for several eight-bit microprocessors.

System Characteristics

Three main reasons are usually cited for the current popularity of Unix and Unix-like operating systems with users. First, they provide a simple and logically almost consistent command language through which the user can interact with the system; a language easy to learn, fairly easy to understand, and not very easy to forget. Second, Unix systems provide a very wide variety of software tools and services, so that program development can progress rapidly. Third, and perhaps most important, both system services and user programs are insured against too rapid obsolescence, by being nearly machine-independent. Programs can be moved to new computers along with the operating system, while new system services become available on practically all versions of the Unix system at once.

Traditionally, many computer manufacturers have regarded operating system software as an unpleasant hurdle to be overcome before a new machine could be marketed. The relative portability of the Unix system has endeared it to hardware makers, for computers can be designed to run under this operating system by investing only a modest amount of software effort. New hardware can be made ready for the market not only quickly, but with all the sureness of an already accepted product. To the user, a knowledge of Unix software structure and command language is of long-term value, for it is very likely that his next computer will employ a variant of the same system or one of its close cousins. Relative machine-independence also enriches the range of general utility programs available; because programs can migrate to new computers along with the operating system, development of new general-purpose programs becomes attractive.

Not surprisingly, the Unix operating system is not quite perfect. Its major shortcomings include, first of all, that it assumes a friendly user community. The file security provided, for example, is not nearly good enough to make it attractive in such sensitive applications as banking or finance. Secondly, many of its command structures and conventions bear the marks of having been developed by a circle of friends, without much regard for subsequent distribution to others. For instance, many commands are abbreviated to very short forms and appear easy to confuse with others. Finally, protection against operator error is imperfect; certain users can even accidentally destroy all files on the system, including the operating system itself. This latter disadvantage can be very serious, especially in commercial or financial applications. But fortunately it only matters to very experienced users, who have gradually acquired a knowledge of pretty well everything the system can do. Novices are very unlikely to have access to quite so much destructive power.

Portability

Because Unix programs are almost entirely written in a high-level programming language called C, this system is practically guaranteed to become available on many future computers as well as quite a few more already existing ones. To install a Unix system on yet another computer, two main things are necessary: a C compiler and a modest amount of machine-dependent coding. A compiler for the C language is always required, so that the Unix operating system itself can be translated to the native language of the new machine. Construction of such a compiler generally takes a few man-months or perhaps a man-year of programming effort. In addition to the compiler, transporting Unix to another machine requires a few machine-dependent input-output hardware service routines. These must necessarily be written in the native language of the new machine, so that they are strictly locked to that computer. Fortunately, they are usually quite short, so that much programming effort is not needed. Usually, a matter of man-weeks or, at worst, man-months, is involved. These amounts of time are tiny when compared to the investment required to design and write a new operating system. The initial effort that produced the Unix kernel amounted to two or three man-years, but the addition of the many utility programs that make Unix systems useful has taken much, much more.

The great majority of Unix system services available—editors, compilers, file sorting and merging programs, and others—are written in high-level languages, with C the most widely used language by far. New utility programs constructed by the now quite wide Unix user community are also written in high-level languages, C being again the most frequent choice. As a result, the new programs can be incorporated in almost any Unix installation without alteration.

Past and Future

Although it has gained wide popularity only recently, the Unix system is mature software which has undergone years of testing and rewriting. To assess its probable future, its history may deserve at least brief mention.

Ancient History

The first Unix system was written by D. M. Ritchie and K. Thompson at Bell Laboratories, around 1969 or 1970, to run on the now all-but-forgotten PDP-7 and PDP-9 computers. Their primary objective was to produce a system convenient for inexperienced users, and they succeeded at least well enough to be encouraged to construct a second version to run on a PDP-11/20. Because the PDP-11 family of computers became enormously popular in the decade of the seventies, a third version, again fully rewritten, appeared in due course; it supported the PDP-11/34, /40, /45, /60, and /70. By 1973, the system authors had abandoned assembler language coding, for it was becoming evident that transportability from machine to machine would be greatest if a very large part (ideally but impossibly, all) of the system were written in a high-level language. A language called C was developed for the purpose. C is well suited to writing operating systems while retaining most other characteristics of good high-level languages, and it remains the principal language of the Unix operating system. C resembles Pascal in many respects, but it does allow programming a little closer to the machine register level—as if Pascal were to recognize the existence of registers and bits! The structure and capabilities of C thus allowed building the Unix system in a fashion which made it largely independent of the machine hardware structure: at least transportable, if not actually portable.

A paper on the Unix operating system was published by Ritchie and Thompson in 1974 in the *Communications* of the Association for Computing Machinery. This paper quickly became a defining landmark for the system. It outlined the basic system structure and methods of work; although these have been refined considerably since that time, the basic notions have remained almost unchanged. What has changed, to be sure, is the range of system services and utilities available. Unix probably contains a better selection of software tools than any other operating system. Not only is their range wide, but they have for the most part been written to go together well.

The Unix system is currently available on all computers in the PDP-11 family, including the PDP-11/23, /24, /44, and other recent additions. It represents a fourth broad rewriting of the system, although it is popularly (though not quite correctly) called Version 7. The number 7 in fact refers to the seventh edition of the *Unix Programmer's Manual*, the document which describes the operation of the current system version. Very few people, incidentally, possess a complete copy of that document—not because it is secret, but because it is about the size and shape of the Manhattan telephone directory!

A significant influence on the course of Unix software development came in the late 1970s, when a major development project at the University of California, Berkeley, began to bear fruit. The Berkeley Unix system adhered closely to the spirit and objectives of its Bell Laboratories cousin, but it introduced substantial extensions and improvements. Many of the improvements were internal, invisible to the casual user. Others, like the Berkeley vi text editor, are immediately visible.

The Modern Age

Unix systems for computers other than the PDP-11 started appearing in the late seventies. A version for the Interdata 8/32 computer became available around 1978, and one for the VAX-11/780 came soon thereafter. Several versions for other processors, notably the model 68000 and Z8000 16-bit microprocessor chips and thus for the many computers built around them, followed. Between 1978 and 1982, other operating systems also appeared, developed independently but with a remarkable similarity to Version 7 (and its predecessor Version 6) Unix systems. Some resemble Version 7 only in what the system looks like to the user at the terminal. In others, the similarity extends to such internal details as file formats, so that not only programs but even disk or tape files can be moved between systems. Most of the look-alikes are intended for computers that employ 8-bit or 16-bit microprocessor chips, but at least one is available on the commercial market for the PDP-11 series of machines.

Until 1980–1981, the creation and marketing of look-alike Unix systems was lent strong encouragement by the fact that the Bell Laboratories Unix system itself was, for all practical purposes, available for academic research and teaching use only. Look-alike systems therefore appeared to fill the commercial gap. For example, the Idris and Unix systems are independent but look similar to the user, and they are compatible with each other. Since about 1981, Unix has been made available commercially through retail vendors, under various names such as Xenix, Unisis, or Unity. These are not look-alikes, but Unix itself dressed in a commercial suit. They are not only entirely compatible with Unix systems; they *are* Unix systems. Most such derivative systems are enhanced, modified, or adapted to perform well in particular environments.

Both the independently developed systems and the licenced variants of Version 7 appear on the market under names other than Unix. Different names are used for both commercial and legal reasons, among which trademark protection probably ranks high. With Unix systems coming into widespread use and commercially available almost everywhere short of drugstore counters, Bell Laboratories are presumably concerned lest their trademark pass into the public domain through excessively great success—along with aspirin, bakelite, and many others. At present, there is no generic name to cover Unix, Xenix, Coherent, Zeus, Cromix, Flex, Qunix, ... and much of the computer press refers to them all as "Unix-like operating systems."

Through a Glass Darkly

Will the Unix operating system prove sufficiently long-lived and sufficiently universal to merit study and practice? No one can tell for sure, but the answer is more likely yes than no. This system is no longer new; it has been seasoned by more than a decade of development, through several stages, and has settled down. The prospect for its commercial success is excellent, and the future of Unix systems in the 1980s may easily resemble that of the Fortran language in the sixties. Both were initially developed with particular computer systems in mind, but they quickly outgrew their original hosts. Both suffer from structural and logical deficiencies which seemed minor or unimportant at the outset but became irksome after the first decade. Both seem better suited to their tasks (warts and all) than any currently available competitor. Both may therefore live on long after better languages and more portable systems became available. Like the English language, with its constrictive syntax, difficult grammar, incomprehensible spelling, ... and two or three billion people who continue to use it simply because they all understand it.

Things to Read

Until recently, very little has been available by way of a simple introduction to the Unix operating system. Most beginners have been expected to cut their teeth on photocopies of the admittedly excellent brief articles that survey the system characteristics—and by perusal of the *Unix Programmer's Manual*, which in its seventh (current) edition is a large volume some ten centimeters thick. Indeed it is the definitive work, but hardly easy for the beginner.

With the growing popularity of Unix systems, textbooks and articles of a tutorial nature have begun to appear. These tend to be a good deal more readable than the full manual and should constitute the major reference point for the beginner. A brief bibliography listing most of these, annotated to give some idea of their contents, appears at the end of this book.

The *Unix Programmer's Manual* is the defining document of the system and is furnished both as paper copy and in machine-readable form. Provision is made in Unix systems for keeping much of the user documentation available as disk files, so that users can read particular portions of the manual without having access to a printed copy, or without even needing one. Keeping the system manuals in computer-readable form and therefore easy to modify is vital for most Unix installations, for there are probably no two installations exactly alike. While every system manager strives to keep documentation current for his system, in many places no up-to-date paper manual exists; the disk-file version is the only true version.

Typographic and Lexical Curios

The words used in Unix system commands, the way words are abbreviated, and occasionally the ways they are spelled are a bit idiosyncratic. Presumably this is the result of having been developed initially within a circle of friends prepared to put up with each other's foibles. Some users take to the strange habits of Unix like a duck takes to water; others show enthusiasm more appropriate to a cat. There is no choice; Unix commands come the way they come.

Lowercase letters are used almost exclusively in Unix system commands, programming languages, and naming conventions. Although they are rare, exceptions do exist; it is not simply a matter of using lower case instead of upper. Both are used, but for some reason capital letters occur much less frequently than they do in English. A particularly irksome idiosyncrasy to some is the failure to accept initial capitals even where the conventions of English demand it. The author, for example, will probably never grow quite accustomed to identifying himself as *silvester*, without a capital S.

The almost, but not quite, total use of lower case causes certain problems when documentation is written in natural languages. For example, the Unix text editor program is called **ed**, and the phototypesetter program has the name **troff**. (Not unreasonably, some users would have preferred mnemonically more useful names, e.g., *Editor* and *Phototype*.) They are never called **Ed** and **Troff**, because the system regards the letters **E** and **e** as simply two different, unrelated, characters. But what should one do when a sentence begins "**troff** is a program for ..."? In this book, the Unix program naming convention is followed strictly: program names exist in lower case only, they do not acquire capitals even if they occur at the beginnings of sentences. But much Unix system literature, occasionally even including the definitive manual, is somewhat inconsistent about usage in this matter.

Word usage in the Unix system shows up a lot of curious details rooted in history, but it is often difficult for the newcomer to master. For example, the verb "print" is used almost everywhere in the manuals to imply that output is to be sent to the user terminal. That verb may have been accurate at some past time, but today few users employ printing terminals; display screens are much more common. (The verb "print" to most computer users implies use of a line printer, not the user terminal.) As another example, the verbs "move" and "remove", when referring to files, are employed to mean "rename" and "delete". The reference here is to the software methodology employed: deletion is achieved by removing a linking pointer.

Using This Book

The best way of learning to use an operating system is to use it. To allow the beginner to learn in this natural way, the first (short) part of this book contains an introduction to the system and its use, in quite brief and very simple form. It is sufficiently concise to be usable while sitting at the terminal, trying out the commands. The main part of this book is longer. It is intended for reading away from the terminal, and for reference; it therefore consists of a few explanatory chapters, followed by a summary description of the more important system commands.

Chapter 2

Getting Started

The Unix operating system is generally considered easy to learn and easy to use. But even the easiest operating system takes a little getting used to, especially at the very start when nothing looks even remotely familiar and every response from the system appears vaguely ominous—if indeed the system responds at all! Most computer users dislike the first hour or so spent with a new operating system, when the initial difficulties of a new command language, new name conventions, and new protocol rules all appear together. This chapter is intended to provide a launching pad for the novice user and to help him overcome the problems of that first hour. It is brief enough to be read at the terminal, trying out the various commands on the spot or it can be read at another time and place, in preparation for that first hour.

Communicating with the System

Several users can be logged in to the same computer at the same time under the Unix timesharing multi-user operating system. Learning to use the Unix system therefore begins with becoming an authorized system user, then acquiring familiarity with the procedures for using a terminal.

User Names and Numbers

To keep track of users and their needs, every Unix system has a human *system manager*. In large computing centers, the system manager may well consist of a whole office establishment with receptionists and secretaries to cater to the needs of milling thousands. In small installations, he is most often another user who happens to be particularly knowledgeable about the system, and who is prepared to undertake the management chore. Whoever he may be, this individual authorizes users, issues passwords and user identification numbers, creates file directories, and takes care of the many other administrative needs that always arise when numerous people attempt to share the same computer. The first requirement is therefore a visit to the system manager, so as to obtain the necessary authorization.

The Unix system manager issues every user a *login name* (also called the *user id*) and (on most systems) a password. Both are composed of lower case characters only. The login name is simply a name and is publicly known. In small installations, it is frequently simply the user's first name. The password is known only to the user. Users can change their passwords at will, and sometimes even the system manager may have difficulties finding out what the new password is. All password-based operating systems ultimately present the user with an irresolvable dilemma: it seems desirable to write down the password in lots of accessible places (to avoid forgetting it), yet it is undesirable to have it written down at all (to keep it secret).

Many Unix systems also have the system manager assign a *user group number* to each user. User groups are generally just what the word implies: groups of people associated in a common goal or common administrative framework. In industrial programming environments, groups are usually people working on the same project. In an educational setting, a user group might be all the students in a particular course. Groups are generally people needing access to a common pool of files.

Internally, Unix system software keeps track of users by means of user identification numbers and group identification numbers. The novice user really has no need to be concerned with these; he logs in and generally identifies himself by his login name.

Logging In and Out

When a Unix system is started up, all the terminals connected to it display a login prompt, and wait for users to log in. The prompt is displayed at the left margin of the terminal. It may take different forms in different systems, sometimes even including a message for the day or recent system news. In the simplest version, it consists of the request

`login:`

To log in, a valid user name is typed, all lower case (it does look strange, but it works), followed by a carriage return. The system will then ask for the password, which is also typed in lower case and followed by a carriage

return. On most terminals the password will refuse to show on the screen or
paper, so as to guard its secrecy, but it will be received by the system all the
same. If the password is correct, the login attempt is accepted, and the user's
terminal is permitted access to the system itself. Unix signals the user that it
is ready to accept commands, by prompting with the *shell prompt* character
at the left margin. (Its strange name comes about because the program
which actually sends out this character is called *shell*). The shell prompt
character can be changed by the Unix system manager and therefore varies
from installation to installation. The dollar sign **$** is commonly used, and
the percent sign **%** is another though less popular choice. In this book the
dollar sign is used, for the sake of consistency.

To log out, it suffices to type control-D in response to the shell prompt,
i.e., to type the character D while holding down the CONTROL key on the
terminal. Users not thoroughly conversant with terminal keyboards should
note that, unlike normal typewriter keyboards, computer terminals have two
different types of shift keys, called SHIFT and CONTROL, respectively.

Curiously, no way is provided for the user to log out, except by means of
the control-D character; there is no command such as "logout". Choosing
the control-D character as a logout signal may seem irrational at first
glance, but it makes sense after a certain fashion. The control-D character
(ASCII octal 004) is employed everywhere in Unix software as an end-of-file
mark, so that sending a control-D from the terminal is taken to mean "end
of terminal activity". Nevertheless, some users find this scheme a little
strange, and certainly not very easy to remember. Hence quite a few Unix
installations provide a (locally provided) logout command, which may be
"logout", "off", "goodbye", "arrivederci", or whatever the imagination of
the local programming support staff dictates.

When the user has logged out, the system will declare itself ready for the
next user, and will ask for another login. In fact, if an immediate change of
users is desired, it is possible to issue a login command in response to the
shell prompt without logging out first. Typing

   $ login *newuser*

where *newuser* is the new user login name, is all that is required; the old user
is automatically logged out as the new user is logged in. The new user's
password will be requested next. If the new user then wishes to verify
whether the login worked correctly, the **who** command (see below) may be
employed to check who is logged in at the moment.

Just to complicate matters, Unix internal software maintains a record of
the characteristics of each terminal. This record can be changed by users
and in some circumstances by programs. Normally, it is possible to communicate with a terminal only if the characteristics which the system has on
record actually correspond to those of the terminal. If a terminal refuses to
log in, there is very likely some disagreement between the operating system

and the terminal as to what to expect. Sending a control-D should reset the internal records and allow logging in to proceed.

The Terminal

There is one immediately striking and unusual fact about Unix commands: this operating system insists on working with lowercase characters, even where the normal conventions of English clearly demand capitals (user names, initial words of command sentences). However, uppercase characters are used in some cases. A terminal capable of using lowercase characters is therefore essential. Some versions of the Unix system do provide for automatic character conversion from upper to lower case, so that "uppers-only" terminals can be used; but these are rather messy at best. Anyhow, there are not many modern terminals incapable of handling lowercase characters!

Practically every terminal is equipped with a whole row of little switches for setting the various terminal characteristics: communication speed (baud rate), full/half duplex communication, upper/lower case characters, treatment of line terminators, tab characters, and a host of other matters. Of course the switches must be set up in precisely the way the system expects. If they are not, logging in may be impossible or may result in incomprehensible strings of apparently random characters on the screen. Because there are many types of terminals and many variations on the acceptable switch settings for each, it is almost impossible to give any firm rules—except that if the terminal is used only for communicating with the Unix system, it is likely to be set up correctly and to remain so, since nobody has an interest in altering the switch settings. Problems ordinarily arise only in computer installations where the same terminal is used with several different operating systems.

Sometimes it happens that resetting the terminal switches has no effect at all. This happens most often if the terminal is new, modern, and microprocessor-controlled. In such terminals, the switches do not control any electronic circuits directly. Instead, the microprocessor reads the switch settings when it is first turned on, and subsequently controls all terminal functions in accordance with the switch settings as they were at the time they were read. Changing switch settings alters nothing at all, unless the microprocessor is forced to read the switch settings again—for example, by turning the terminal power off and on again after a few seconds, whenever any switch setting is altered.

Typing at the Keyboard

Characters entered at the keyboard are not immediately acted upon, they are merely stored until a carriage return is typed (with the RETURN key) to signify termination of the line. The Unix system only attempts to read and understand a keyboard line once it has been terminated. This allows typing mistakes to be corrected on the spot.

If a wrong character is typed at the keyboard, it can be corrected by means of the BACKSPACE key, which works in the obvious way on screen-type terminals. But when printing terminals are used, there is no way of erasing a character once it has been printed. When such terminals are used, a character is considered to have been erased if it is followed by a special character, the *erase character*. Most usually, the # character is employed for this purpose. When decoding, any character will be ignored if it is immediately followed by the erase character. Thus la#of#gim#n is interpreted as login, the characters a, f, and m having been "erased" by the # sign. Similarly, a *kill character*, usually but not always @, is used to "kill" everything typed since the beginning of the line, so that kif@login is interpreted as login. If either of the characters # or @ is actually wanted as part of a line, it must be preceded by the backslash character \ in order to avoid erasure. In other words, A\#B is decoded as A#B not AB.

Because typed characters are not decoded on the spot but merely stored for decoding when a carriage return is sent, it is both possible and permissible to "type ahead," i.e., to keep typing even though the screen echo of the typed characters does not keep up. (It will come eventually). But this practice is not generally good because typing without an immediate screen echo can leave typing errors unnoticed, with possible unexpected consequences to come!

Like many other computer operating systems, Unix employs all the printable ordinary keyboard characters, as well a set of *control characters*, which are not printable. The latter are formed by striking the appropriate key while holding down the CONTROL key. The CONTROL key works in a manner similar to the SHIFT key, i.e., it alters the meanings of the other keys. Simply striking the CONTROL key by itself produces nothing whatever, just exactly like striking the SHIFT key. Consequently, it is normal to press and hold down the CONTROL or SHIFT key, as appropriate, before striking the character key required. Control characters are unprintable, i.e., there is no printed character that corresponds to the internal computer representation of any control character. When it is desired to indicate in print (as, for example, in books on operating systems) the occurrence of a control character, the character is shown preceded by an upward arrow, for example, ↑D: alternatively, one writes "control-D" or "ctrl-D." The most commonly used control characters are probably control-D, which generally denotes an end-of-file mark and therefore also serves for logging out; control-S, which allows terminal display to be halted temporarily; and control-Q, which allows terminal display to continue after being halted by control-S.

Running the System

All actions of which the Unix operating system is capable are requested by the user through the Unix command language, which is both rich and flexible. The Unix system provides the user an unusually wide variety of utilities—text editors, language translators, file management tools, and much else. These tools, like actions by the system itself, are also controlled by keyboard commands.

Commands

When the shell prompt is displayed at the left edge of the screen, the Unix command decoder is awaiting instructions. Nearly all Unix commands are actually requests to run particular programs. For example, the command

```
$ who
```

causes the system to find the program named **who**, and to execute it. (This particular program looks in the system tables to find out which users are logged in at which terminals and displays their particulars on the terminal screen). When execution is complete, the shell prompt is displayed again to indicate that another command is expected.

There is nothing particularly magic about Unix commands, for the set of commands can be extended at any time simply by adding more programs capable of being executed. The standard system-provided set of commands totals well over 100, and more are added from time to time. The system-provided commands most likely to be of interest to beginning users are

bas	run the Basic language interpreter
cat	concatenate files and display on screen
cc	run the C compiler
cp	copy contents of one file to another
ed	run the standard **ed** text editor
f77	run the Fortran 77 compiler
lpr	queue files for sending to line printer
ls	list the contents of a directory
mkdir	make a directory
mv	move (rename) a file
nroff	run the **nroff** text formatter
passwd	change the login password
pr	display a file at the terminal
rm	remove (delete) a file
tty	display the terminal name
vi	run the full-screen editor
who	display who is logged in to the system

Many of the commands listed above have to be augmented by file specifications. For example, to move a file to another name with **mv** it is (reasonably enough) necessary to specify which file, and what its new name is to be. Other commands permit (or require) additional qualifiers to specify how and where the desired action is to be taken. That is to say, the commands above are really command verbs and may need to be augmented by other words in order to form coherent sentences. Some informal illustrations will be found in the examples below. More or less complete details on the above commands and many others will be found in a later chapter. Full details on each command may be found in the *Unix Programmer's Manual*.

A user can add commands of his own easily, since no distinction is made between a command and an executable program. The name of every executable program is automatically a command, simply by virtue of being there. In fact, the only way of executing a program under the Unix system is to type its name, as a command, when the shell prompt shows. There is just one significant distinction between user-added commands and those supplied by the system: the programs added by a user are ordinarily accessible to him and him only and are thus not available to other users unless special arrangements are made. System commands, on the other hand, are always equally available to everybody.

What happens if the user, not knowing any better, introduces a new program with the same name as an existing system command? No serious interference results, for the system always searches for the command first in the user's own directory of programs. Only if the command is not found in the user's directory does the system search elsewhere. Thus the duplication of a name already in use as a system command causes only one inconvenience: the system command becomes unavailable. It might be expected, however, that users who unwittingly use names of system commands are unlikely to want or need those commands in any case.

Execution of any program may be stopped by pressing the DELETE key (sometimes labeled RUBOUT) on the terminal. This key is one of a select few whose effect is immediate, i.e., it is not necessary to send a carriage-return for it to take effect. In contrast to some other operating systems, Unix software does not respond to the BREAK key on the terminal.

Because new commands are easily added and existing commands can be modified just as easily, there are probably no two Unix installations with precisely the same set of available commands and precisely the same usage of the existing commands. This great flexibility allows tailoring every computer system to serve its user community to best advantage. Yet flexibility can also confuse users, because every Unix system seems forever fluid, forever very nearly as the manual describes it, but never quite exactly like that. There is no known cure for this ailment; all one can do is watch for unexpected behavior, and to enquire whether it arises from a recent local system modification.

Files and File Names

The Unix operating system is designed to process files, and regards practically every assemblage of information, no matter what its physical form or storage medium, as a file. The formal definition of a file is simple: a *file* is a string of characters terminated by an *end-of-file mark*. In some cases, it is desirable to organize a Unix file as a set of "lines." This form of file subdivision is assumed to be normal, and a file may alternatively be regarded as a set of lines. Every line terminates in a *newline* character, which is generated at the keyboard by pressing the RETURN key.

Files are identified by file names, and the system keeps track of files by recording their names in file directories. Every user is allocated a file directory of his own when his login name and password are authorized. Although there may be many files belonging to many users on the system, the allocation of a separate directory to each user means that he can ordinarily work in a universe of files which include (1) those he created himself, and (2) those supplied by the system, as system commands. No user need ever be aware of the names, or even of the existence, of any other users' files. Only very rarely will there be any interference between files listed in directories belonging to different users. When a user logs in, he gains full access automatically to all the files listed in his own directory, and only to those files, unless some special arrangements are made. A listing of all files in this directory is always available, by means of the `ls` command.

File names may contain up to 14 characters. The characters may include almost any the user desires except the blank character. In fact, no exception is made even for the erase and kill characters. For example, it is perfectly proper to use `file#27` as a file name. However, if a printing terminal is used, the # character may be understood to denote an erasure. Thus it is usually wise to name files using only the lowercase alphabetics and the numerals, because several of the special characters and punctuation marks have special uses which may cause grief.

The period (the . character) is usable and permissible within file names and causes no unexpected bad effects. It is used by many experienced programmers and by many system-provided programs to differentiate between related files. For example, the Unix Fortran compiler expects Fortran source file names to end in `.f`, as in `program.f`; it produces output files with the same names but substitutes `.o` for `.f` at the end. Thus `program.o` would be the compiled (object code) version of `program.f`. It must be emphasized, however, that characters preceding and following the period do not have any special significance to the Unix system, even though some programs (some provided with the system, as well as those created by the user) may attach particular meanings to them. In contrast to some other popular operating systems, file names are not divided into two parts separated by a period, with the two parts treated separately. The period is simply another character, as far as the Unix system itself is concerned, and several periods may well be included in a file name, for example, `file....a.y`.

File names very often occur in command sentences. For example, suppose it is desired to remove file `program.o`. ("Removal" means that the file name is removed from the directory, and the file space is released for reuse; in other words, the file is deleted.) To do so, the command

    $ rm program.o

is typed in response to the shell prompt. Most other Unix command sentences are constructed in an analogous fashion. Some actions, of course, will require more than one file name to be specified. As an example of a command with two file references, consider the `mv` ("move") command, which moves a file from one name to another (i.e., it renames the file). The command

    $ mv   a.out program.o

"moves" the file around in a directory, by reassigning its name from `a.out` to `program.o`.

Wild-Card File Names

File name references may be unique, or they may use *wild card characters*, i.e., characters which are understood to stand for several others. Wild cards are convenient and useful when several files with similar names must be referred to. For example, suppose it is desired to remove a whole set of files, all of whose names are of the form `problemfile....`. One may issue a string of commands

    $ rm problemfile01
    $ rm problemfile02
    $ rm problemfile03

etc., but it is easier to type

    $ rm problemfile*

The `*` character in file references is understood to mean "any and every string of characters." In other words, each and every file whose name begins `problemfile` and terminates in any characters whatever (or indeed none) will be removed by the above command. Similarly, the command line

    $ rm *fil*

will remove all files whose names contain the character string `fil` anywhere —with anything at all, or even nothing, preceding and following. In effect, the `*` character in a file reference means "any, or no, characters." In a similar way, the `?` character can be used as a wild card standing for a single character. The difference between `*` and `?` is that the latter signifies one, and exactly one, character. For example, `?fil?` denotes any file name containing exactly five characters, the middle three of which are `fil`.

Writing and Running Programs

One of the most common activities of computer users is the development of applications programs. Program development generally begins with the design and initial writing of a program, followed by testing and gradual elimination of errors. Typically, this kind of work requires repeated program compilation and trial execution, followed by editing of the source file to eliminate whatever errors turned up.

Program development requires at a minimum two kinds of facilities: a language compiler and loader to run the program, and a text editor to permit preparation of source programs. The Unix family of operating systems provides compilers for several computer languages, at least one text editor, and a host of advanced debugging aids for serious programmers.

Running Fortran Programs

The full Fortran 77 language and several other programming languages are supported by Unix systems. To illustrate how Fortran programs are tested and run, suppose the file `mainprogram.f` contains a source program in the usual form. The command

    $ f77 mainprogram.f

causes the Fortran 77 compiler to be run. The compiler translates the source program into the corresponding object program, which is left in file `mainprogram.o`. Because users very often wish to link the compiled object program with library modules and to execute it, the Fortran 77 compiler is automatically followed up by the linking loader, unless instructed otherwise. The loader assigns memory locations to the program, and performs other housekeeping tasks that permit the program to be actually run. Its output is always placed in a file named **a.out**. Any previous contents of **a.out** will be destroyed, so that if it is desired to save the executable object module for the long run, it should be moved to another name:

```
$ mv a.out mainprogram.x
```

Next, it is desired to execute the program. In Unix systems there is no distinction between commands and programs, so that to execute the program, it suffices to issue its own name as a command:

```
$ mainprogram.x
```

The Fortran program should now run and produce whatever output it might. When the program has terminated execution, the shell prompt will again appear to signify readiness for further commands. To check what files have been generated in the process the **ls** command may be issued; it produces on the terminal screen a listing of the files currently listed in the user directory.

If compilation had been wanted without linking—as often happens if subroutines are developed and compiled individually—the additional argument **-c** would be included in the request to compile, signifying "compile only":

```
$ f77 -c mainprogram.f
```

Other program modules, such as subroutines developed separately, may then be combined with the compiled program by asking for the linking loader explicitly:

```
$ ld mainprogram.o subprogram.o
```

The system will respond by running the linkage editor (linking loader), again producing an output file called **a.out**. All files named in the command will be linked, together with any system library components that may be necessary. Execution, possible moving of the file, and examination of output then follow as above.

The **ed** Text Editor

Preparation of text, such as source programs, is generally done using the text editor **ed**. This editor manipulates text stored in a text buffer (an area of computer memory). It understands about two dozen different commands for text manipulation, for reading files into the buffer, and for writing the buffer contents into a file. The buffer content is regarded as being composed of lines, each of which is made up of characters. Because it is oriented to material organized into lines, **ed** is very well suited to preparing computer programs. Of course, **ed** knows nothing of programs, it only handles lines composed of characters. It is therefore not restricted to program preparation, and may be used for any other textual matter as well.

The editor is invoked by a simple command. One types (and follows with a carriage return)

> **$ ed** *filename*

in response to the shell prompt; *filename* is the name of the file to be edited. The editor responds by reading the file and displaying the number of characters in it. If the file is being newly created, there are of course no characters in it; in that case **ed** shows a question mark and the file name. **ed** then awaits commands.

All operations of the **ed** editor are controlled by keyboard commands, which generally consist of a single letter, possibly augmented by some additional information. These commands are expected and understood by **ed**, not by the shell, so that their form is totally different from commands accepted by the shell. When ready to accept commands, some versions of **ed** display a prompting character (different from the shell prompt) at the left margin; other versions do not prompt the user, but simply wait. If there is serious question about whether **ed** is listening, or something bad has happened, one possible action is to type an equal sign,

> **=**

followed by the usual carriage return. This equal sign is understood by **ed** as a command, which asks **ed** to display the total number of lines in the text buffer. **ed** should respond by displaying a number under all circumstances, even when the correct answer is zero.

If alterations to a file are desired, the file is requested and read as indicated above. When alterations have been completed, the changed text must again be written to a file, either the same one or another. Writing the buffer content into a file is straightforward enough. One uses the **w** command,

> **w** *filename*

to copy the entire buffer content into the specified file, replacing whatever the file might have contained previously. After copying is completed, **ed** displays on the screen the number of characters written. If desired, the file name may be omitted from the **w** command. In that case, the **w** command writes the text buffer into the same file as was named in the original **ed** command, so that the newly edited version of the file replaces the original one. It should be noted very carefully that **ed** does not write out automatically. Before quitting an editing session, which is done with the **q** command, it is essential to save the results by using the **w** command. Thus an error in `mainprogram.f` might be corrected by the command sequence

```
$ ed mainprogram.f
562
..... commands to correct the error ....
w mainprogram.f
587
q
$
```

When the editing session is finished with a **q** command, **ed** stops running, and the shell prompt appears again to signify that the Unix system itself (not **ed**) is awaiting further instructions.

Creating and Modifying Text

There exist various ways for **ed** to modify the text contained in the editing buffer, but curiously, there is no explicit facility for creating text in the first place. When a new file is started, **ed** immediately considers it to be a perfectly normal and proper text file, which just happens to contain zero characters of text. These zero characters are placed in the text buffer, whose content, though not large, is now formally valid enough and may be modified. Of course, the only modification that makes any real sense at this point is to insert additional characters to the buffer content.

Text can be entered into the buffer by using the **a** (append) command. The **a** command causes insertion, after the last character in the buffer, of all text that follows it, up to the line containing nothing but a dot (the period, or . character). For example, the command sequence

```
$ ed mainprogram.f
?mainprogram.f
a
        write (6,100)
  100 format (" Hello")
        stop
        end
.
w mainprogram.f
65
q
$
```

begins with the text buffer empty, appends a simple Fortran program, writes it to a file, and quits (exits from the editor). Note that the character count following the **w** command includes four line endings i.e., four *newline* characters.

At all times, **ed** regards one line in the text buffer as being privileged. An imaginary pointer is thought to identify this line, called the *current line*. Most commands accepted by **ed** work with reference to the current line; for example, the **a** command appends text immediately after the current line. When a file is first opened for editing in the manner shown above, the last line in the file is made the current line.

Lines can be displayed at the terminal, and the current line pointer may be positioned using the **p** command. This command may be used with beginning and ending line numbers, a single line number, or none at all. Thus

   1,3p

causes display of the first three lines in the file and makes line 3 the current line. The command

   7p

moves the pointer so as to make line 7 the current line and displays this line. An interesting variation is *relative positioning*: whereas **7p** repositions the pointer to line 7, signed line numbers such as **+7p** or **−7p** will reposition it seven lines after (or before, respectively) the current line. Omitting the line numbers with **p** causes the current line to be displayed.

There exists a command **d** to delete lines, which works in a somewhat similar fashion. The command

   1,3d

deletes the first three lines; the first (previously fourth) line becomes the current line.

Since the user does not always know the number of the current line or of the last line, **ed** provides a symbolic notation for these rather important special lines. The current line may be referred to as "." so that

   1,.p

means "display all lines from the beginning of the file to the current line". The dollar sign **$** is also assigned a special meaning; it is taken to mean the last line in the buffer, so that the command

   .,$p

means "display from the current line to the end of the buffer."

The **a, d, p, w, q** commands suffice to prepare and edit simple programs. However, **ed** can use much more sophisticated command forms, and some familiarity with it should be acquired at an early stage if any substantial program preparation is contemplated. A much more detailed description of **ed** will be found in the chapter of this book on text processing.

Sample Terminal Session

It may be useful for the beginner to examine a sample terminal session and perhaps even to try duplicating it on his own Unix system to acquire some feel for what the system will or will not permit. The following may serve the purpose. In this terminal session, the actual terminal conversation is printed at the left-hand margin; the right-hand column contains explanatory commentary. The ellipsis (...) in the left column denotes a more or less lengthy conversation, pointless to report in detail since the user is prompted for precisely what is required.

```
                                        Type control-D to reset.
login:bftsplk                           Login using name bftsplk
...                                     ... password verification ...
$ ls                                    "list" working directory:
                                        there are no entries in it!
$ ed test.f                             Create a Fortran program:
$ test.f                                ed declares test.f new.
a                                       Start: a ("append") command
        write (6,100)
  100 format (" Hello")                 Fortran program
        stop                            Fortran program
        end
.                                       End text input.
w                                       write out the text into file.
65                                      ed responds with character count.
q                                       Quit editor.
$ ls                                    "list" working directory:
test.f                                  there is now one file.
$ f77 test.f                            Fortran compiler yields a.out.
$ mv a.out test.x                       Move (rename) file a.out.
$ test.x                                Execute the test program:
Hello                                   program produces output.
$ ls                                    User lists working directory,
test.f                                  which contains his two (source
test.x                                  and executable) files.
$ rm test.x                             User removes the executable copy,
$                                       and logs out, typing control-D.
```

Some of the actions in this session are a little unrealistic—for example, it takes a true optimist to run a Fortran compilation without even troubling to read a listing of the program first. The object, however, is to show how the Unix commands are used. Those not very familiar with Fortran should probably substitute a simple program in their own favorite language.

Chapter 3

Files in the Unix System

One of the most important functions of any operating system is to save, retrieve, and manage various files. To be useful, files must be easy to store and easy to find again. To be practical, files must fit conveniently onto the available physical media. These requirements imply that the file system must have a good logical structure, i.e., one which makes sense to users in terms of their needs; and that it must have a good physical structure, well suited to the devices used for file storage.

Logical Structure of Files

The Unix system allows quite complex structures of files to be managed fairly easily. Its flexibility and ease of use result mainly from separating the physical organization of files (their form of storage) from their logical organization, which deals with their content and purpose and therefore concerns the user directly.

There are three kinds of Unix files: ordinary files, special files, and directory files.

Ordinary Disk Files

A magnetic disk drive is considered to be the normal storage medium for Unix files. The files which make up the Unix operating system itself reside on a disk also. Files can be written on the disk and read back with equal ease. An *ordinary file* is simply a string of bytes, stored on disk or on some other convenient physical medium such as magnetic tape, the last byte in the string containing an end-of-file mark (the control-D character). The bytes in the file may represent printable characters; in that case, the file is termed a *text file*. Characters stored in a text file do not have any special significance to the system itself, though they presumably mean something to the user or to particular programs.

No special form of internal organization is prescribed for an ordinary file. However, when files are transmitted, the control-D character is employed as an end-of-file mark. To avoid confusion, text files should therefore not contain end-of-file characters. It is often convenient to subdivide text files into *lines*, separated from each other with the newline character (ASCII 012 octal). The lines need not be of any particular length so that a text file may quite properly consist of a single "line." Of course, individual programs may be quite demanding as to the structure of any particular file; for example, Fortran programs that read data usually expect specific data items to be located in predefined positions in the input line. But in such cases the structural requirements are imposed by the Fortran program, not by the Unix operating system.

While no particular logical structure is imposed on files, the physical structure of a file must be precisely defined—otherwise, the operating system could not find files and would not know how to read them. Fortunately, most system users are never concerned with exactly how the reading and writing of files is actually carried out. They need only be aware of the internal logical structure of files and the rules for naming files.

Special Files

Under the Unix operating system, all input-output devices are made to look like files. Programs that transfer data to and from files can with equal ease transfer data to input-output devices; in fact, the programs themselves cannot tell whether their sources and sinks of data are true files or peripheral devices. For example, to print a file, the system may be instructed to copy its contents into another file, called **/dev / lp**. The latter is a *special file*—special in the sense that the instruction to copy into it does not overwrite the original file content but causes the line printer to be activated. The special file itself contains the rules according to which characters are treated by the peripheral device. In other words, an attempt to copy into file **/dev / lp** does not result in **/dev / lp** being overwritten by a new character string, as would be the case if **/dev / lp** were an ordinary file. Instead, the Unix system identifies **/dev / lp** as being a special file and uses its contents as a rule book for determining what should be done with the characters copied (in this case, they are simply passed on to the line printer). Of course, the physical file /dev / lp must never actually be written into; otherwise, the rule book will be destroyed.

Every input-output device on the system is associated with at least one special file. It could be associated with several, however. If a line printer is also to be used for graphic plotting, for instance, the plotting routines may conveniently be placed in a special file, say /dev / grphplot. Copying to this special file will then cause character strings to be interpreted in such a way as to produce graphic output; copying to /dev / lp will print out the characters themselves. Thus the two special files appear to the programmer like two distinct output files, although only one physical device is actually in use.

Directories

Once a file has been written on the magnetic disk, a way must exist to find it again when required. Files are stored on disk in some convenient fashion, not necessarily in the order of their creation. They are made easy to find by name by creating an additional file called a *directory*, which shows where to find the individual files. A directory is simply a file which contains the file names and their physical addresses on the device. Directories have a strictly prescribed internal structure, for they must be accessible to quite a few internal system routines; but there is no physical difference at all between a directory and any ordinary file. Every directory is itself a file and is stored on disk like any other file.

To furnish a simple example, suppose that a disk has room for 960 blocks of 512 characters and that it contains, at a particular moment, the following layout of files.

Blocks	Contents
001–028	*unused*
029–112	*file, index number* 003
113–219	*file, index number* 002
220–227	*unused*
228–473	*file, index number* 001
474–478	*unused*
479–480	*file, index number* 004
481–960	....*other files*...

The index numbers assigned to the files are not related to the file contents in any way and are assigned as needed. They can be made visible to users, if desired, but they rarely are, for few users consider them to have any value. Users always access files by their names. In fact the main purpose of a directory is precisely to keep track of which name corresponds to which index number, so that users may be spared the bother of knowing about index numbers. If file 004 in the present example is a directory, it might contain (among others) the entries

datafile	001
matrixprogram	002
matrixoutput	003
.	004
..	265

showing the correspondence between file names and index numbers. In the normal course of events, the user only refers to `matrixprogram`; the system itself will take care of looking in the directory, determining the index number, and finding out just where on the disk this program file is located. In addition, it will also determine whether the file is an ordinary file, whether the user has the right to access it, and a host of other administrative details.

The directory itself is listed as a directory entry, with the curious special name . (the dot, or period, character) assigned to it. It might seem pointless to list it, for the location of the directory itself must be known in order to consult the directory! However, the entry is conventionally included because it simplifies quite a few system operations, such as calculating how much unused space is left on the disk. When users list the directory contents, which they normally do by means of the `ls` command, this special entry is suppressed to avoid clutter and confusion, unless the user specifically requests that it be made visible.

Directory Hierarchies

Since a directory is a file, it is readily possible to construct directories of directories. In fact, most Unix systems assign a personal directory to each user and list that directory as an entry in a directory of user directories, which is in turn an entry in a system directory. (It really isn't quite so complicated as it first sounds.) In other words, each user's directory appears as a file entered in various other directories. In turn, the user can create subdirectories, which appear as entries in his own directory. The tip of this hierarchical pyramid is found in the *root directory*, which is maintained by the system. This directory structure is a great strength of Unix systems, for it implies that large numbers of users may create large numbers of files while still making it easy to find particular files. Each user need only be concerned with his own files and need not even know that any other user exists.

The Unix file directory structure always has the form of a tree, with the root directory at its root. That is to say, every directory must be listed in exactly one, and only one, predecessor directory. Such a relationship might be as illustrated in the following diagram:

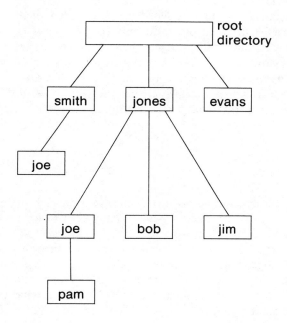

Here **smith, jones, evans,** as well as **joe, bob, jim, joe,** and **pam** are directories. Note that, by the tree structure rule, none of the directories **joe, bob, jim** (which are listed as subdirectories under **jones**) can appear as a subdirectory under **smith**, for they are subdirectories under **jones** and a given directory may be listed in only one predecessor directory. However, there may exist *another* directory called **joe**, entered as a subdirectory under **smith**. The analogy with people's names is apt: the Jones family may have only one son named Joe, but there is nothing wrong with the Smith family also having a son named Joe. However, the two Joes are two entirely distinct individuals who have nothing to do with each other. Correspondingly, the two directories named **joe** are entirely distinct and entirely unrelated. The rule that directories must have a tree structure permits creating one subdirectory named **joe** under every single directory, if users so desire.

A special entry appears in every directory as .. (two dots). This entry identifies the predecessor directory in the tree structure, i.e., the directory of which the present one is a subdirectory. The **ls** directory listing command normally suppresses display of this entry. However, if the user wishes, an option exists to call for it to be shown.

The tree structure rule—every directory must be listed in exactly one predecessor directory—prevents circular listings. Were it not for this rule, it would be possible to have directory A be a subdirectory of B and B a subdirectory of A.

The tree rule applies only to directories, not to ordinary files. In other words, an ordinary file may be listed in any number of directories, but a directory must be listed in one, and only one, predecessor directory. The ability to list an ordinary file in many directories means that it can be made available to many users. It can be exploited to allow many users to read a communal data file or to make use of a single copy of a program file. On the other hand, it can sometimes also create confusion if several users wish to write into the file at the same time.

File Names and Paths

Any file may be accessed by giving the *path* to it through the directory tree. When a user logs in, his directory is normally opened for his use. Any file names he may use then refer to files within his directory, including any subdirectories in it. Suppose that **jones** is the user directory assigned to the user currently logged in. He can refer to the subdirectory file **joe** by name, and Unix will interpret the reference as meaning that particular **joe** which appears as a subdirectory under **jones**. If an ordinary file, say **pam**, appeared as an entry in directory **joe**, it could be referred to as **joe / pam**. If user **jones** also possesses a subdirectory **bob**, he could also create a file **bob / pam**, without any interference.

Files are generally referred to by giving the hierarchical path through the directories in the form

   direc1 / direc2 / direc3 / ... / name

where *name* must be the ordinary file actually desired and *direc1* must be a directory file currently accessible to the user. Most often *direc1* will be a subdirectory listed within the user's current directory. If some other user's files are wanted, or if system files must be accessed, *direc1* must be the proper starting point for a downward path through the tree structure, which will lead to the desired file. Files not listed in some subdirectory of the current user directory can be sought out by beginning the path at the root directory. The root directory is the only directory not to have a name, so that the path

   / jones / joe / pam

will be interpreted as beginning at the root node: no name, followed by the **/** delimiter, is taken as specifying the unnamed, i.e., root, directory as the start. In contrast,

   jones / joe / pam

causes a search to start at the current user directory. If jones is not a subdirectory of the current user directory, the search will fail.

To state the matter in slightly different words, every Unix file is uniquely defined by specifying the path from the root directory to the file. But since the path is always downward through the structure, the rules permit the user to omit, as a matter of convenience, all those portions of the path which lie above the current directory. Thus

   / usr / jones / joe / pam

would be a full specification of a file, valid in all circumstances, but

   joe / pam

is its proper and complete specification only if the current directory happens to be /usr / jones.

Changing Directories

On many occasions it is useful to group various files containing logically related material into subdirectories. For example, Fortran programmers often find it convenient to store the source code for the subroutines of a large program in a directory structure which resembles the calling sequence of the subroutines themselves. Similarly, the author of a book may store individual subsections in separate files small enough to edit conveniently and then join them together through a hierarchy of directories. One such file might be called, for example, book / chapt3 / sect4 / subsec2.

Although it is in principle correct for the author of a program or a book to refer to his files by full pathnames, doing so often becomes inconvenient. To work on the subsections of a particular section, for example, it would be best to make that subdirectory which contains the desired material, for example, book / chapt3 / sect4, the current user directory. Changing directories is accomplished by the cd command, in the form

   $ cd book / chapt3 / sect4

which makes the named directory into the current directory. From this point on, all file references will be sought in the new current directory, so that file book / chapt3 / sect4 / subsec2 is referred to simply as subsec2.

Changing directories downward in the hierarchy is easy, since only the subdirectory names need to be specified. Changing upward requires knowing the full pathname of the desired directory. It can be determined by means of the pwd command, which produces the full pathname of the working directory. This command allows no parameters or arguments and returns the name of the current directory in the fullest form possible:

```
$ pwd
/ usr / bftsplk / book / chapt3 / sect4
```

The cd command may then be used to change to a different directory as the working directory:

```
$ cd  /usr / bftsplk / book / chapt2 / sect1
$ pwd
/ usr / bftsplk / book / chapt2 / sect1
```

If issued without any argument at all, cd returns the user to his home directory, the directory automatically assigned when he logs in. In most cases, the home directory of every user is a subdirectory of /usr:

```
$cd
$ pwd
/ usr / bftsplk
```

File hierarchies can become quite intricate. As a result, cd and pwd are among the most frequently used Unix commands.

File Access Permissions

Not all users need to have access to all Unix files, nor is it desirable that they should. There are quite a few occasions on which a user may wish to keep some files private, as often happens in commercial data processing. Others must therefore be denied access to those files. Even more important, there are ways in which a small mistake can result in disastrous damage. For example, destruction of the root directory of a file system can easily make the entire file system useless. To prevent such damage, users must be denied the ability to delete certain protected files, which surely must include the root directory. All Unix systems therefore include a formal scheme of file access permissions. Users generally have full access to their own files and restricted access to selected system files.

Under the Unix file access permission scheme, an ordinary file can be accorded three forms of permission: read, write, and execute. Any given user may be granted any desired combination of these; the three permissions are entirely independent, and none presupposes any other. Permission to write means permission to alter the file contents, including destruction of the file. Most often, users have writing permission to their own files, but at times they may wish even their own files to be denied writing permission, so as to guard against inadvertent alteration or removal of valuable material. Permission to read really means permission to copy. Since Unix systems do not differentiate between files and devices, listing a file at the terminal is regarded as copying it to the special file which represents the terminal.

Hence no distinction can be drawn between reading and copying; thus reading permission does have significance even for a binary file, which is quite unreadable in the ordinary sense. Execute permission means that the file may be used as a running process; execute permission does not presuppose permission to read, for the user does not need to make a copy of a file in order to execute it. Typically, users have execute permission for a large number of system facilities (the editor, Fortran compiler, linker, etc.), but they very likely do not have permission to read or write into those files.

It is worth noting that permission to write into a file, and permission to erase items from the file, are not distinguished. This arrangement is generally quite satisfactory for scientific computing, but it may complicate matters a little in some types of administrative or financial data processing. In an accounting department, for example, it may be convenient to allow many account clerks to write transactions into the same journal, but it is not at all desirable to allow any account clerk to delete transactions!

Directories are assigned the same three categories of permission as ordinary files: read, write, and execute. Directory files are stored in a binary format, not as text files, so that simple reading produces apparently random garbage on the terminal screen; they are displayed by means of the l s command, which processes the binary characters into legible form. Reading permission is therefore interpreted to mean listing permission, and writing permission constitutes permission to attach new files to the directory or to delete files. Having execute permission for a directory means that the files in the directory can be accessed (provided the appropriate permissions exist for the files themselves) or searched. For example, if a user has reading permission but not execute permission for file / u s r / s p o o l, he can list this directory and discover that it contains a subdirectory / u s r / s p o o l / a t. However, he cannot access / u s r / s p o o l / a t itself, because he lacks execute permission for / u s r / s p o o l.

Access permissions are granted to a user in three categories: personally, as a member of a group, or as a member of the general public. When first authorized by the system manager, every user is assigned a personal login name and membership of a group (though the group may well consist of the user alone). Classification of users by groups is a convenience, particularly in large installations. For example, a new experimental Fortran compiler might well be made executable by all members of the compiler development group, so as to permit testing by group members, but execute permission will probably be denied to members of the general public until the compiler has been certified to work properly.

When a file is newly created, it is assigned a set of access permissions by default. A common arrangement would be to grant full permissions to the file owner, read and execute permissions to the other members of the same user group, and execute permission only to the general public. But default settings differ from installation to installation, indeed from user to user. If the default settings used locally appear inconvenient, the system manager should be consulted, for it is a relatively simple matter to reset the default values.

Working with the File Structure

Although at first glance the Unix file system may seem to be complicated, familiarity makes it seem less so. Most Unix systems adhere to (roughly) similar structures of the root file system; so it is worthwhile to examine a typical file system at least briefly.

The System Directory Structure

A diagrammatic view of the directory tree for a typical Unix system is shown below. Only the portion near the root directory is given in detail; the farther from the root, the more individual implementations diverge from each other. It must be kept in mind that almost every installation involves not only a different hardware configuration but also a different user community, so that the system manager most often will have had to restructure the file directories to suit local needs. For example, in a user community with few Fortran programmers but a large amount of text processing to be done, the file system may well have been set up so as to have the **ed** editor quickly available, while the Fortran compiler may reside on a slower physical device. Nevertheless, the majority of installations resemble each other closely near the root directory and adhere to the same organizational principles elsewhere.

As may be seen in the diagram, the root directory has several subdirectories, with each containing more or less logically related matter. The first five directories shown—**/dev, /bin, /lib, /etc, /tmp**—are generally used by the system itself in carrying out user commands or by the system manager in maintaining administrative files and system software. The files are grouped within these directories primarily by the access permissions granted to users. For example, the general public is ordinarily given execute permission for files in **/bin** but not in /**etc.** It is usual to keep these five directories on a high-speed disk, so that users have rapid access to the files as they require them.

The sixth subdirectory **/usr** shown in the diagram is generally the largest. It is common for every user to have his root working directory attached to **/usr** as a subdirectory, which can easily account for hundreds of entries in **/usr** even in modest-sized systems. In addition, **/usr** is employed to house system utilities of the same kind as are found in **/bin,** **/lib**, and **/tmp**, but which are needed less frequently. **/usr** is physically housed on a large, but possibly slower, disk drive in many installations. There is considerable incentive to keep the most commonly used items (which usually amount to a small percentage of the whole) in a small but rapidly accessible place, while the less often used major part of the system files resides on a slower but larger device.

Keeping Track of Directories

At any one time, every user has some directory serving as his working directory. The operations that the user must be able to carry out, so as not to get lost in the system, include

(1) changing to another directory as the working directory,
(2) determining just which directory is the working directory,
(3) listing the contents of a directory,
(4) creating new subdirectories,
(5) removing an existing directory.

These operations are carried out through the use of five commands: cd, pwd, ls, mkdir, and rmdir. The cd and pwd commands have been dealt with above; the remainder will be briefly described in the following.

Making new directories and removing old ones is almost as easy as changing them. A new directory is made by the mkdir command. For example, the command conversation

```
$ pwd
/ usr / johnson
$ mkdir book
```

creates a new directory /usr / johnson / book. The new directory is automatically made to be a subdirectory of the current directory, unless a full pathname is given in the mkdir command so as to create it somewhere else. Naturally, a new directory can only be created in an existing directory where the user has write permission. It should be noted that the working directory is not changed by mkdir.

Removal of a directory, if desired, is accomplished by the rmdir command, which is analogous to (but not the same as) the rm command:

```
$ rmdir manuscr
```

Removal of a directory should not be attempted unless the directory is empty, i.e., unless it contains no subdirectories and no ordinary files. Otherwise, disaster may befall the files listed in the directory to be removed! Whether the directory is empty or contains any entries can be verified by listing the directory contents using the ls command. This command simply

A TYPICAL DIRECTORY STRUCTURE

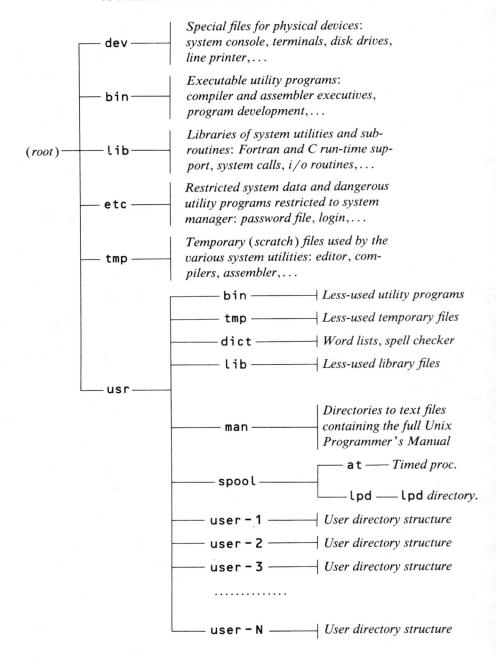

Special files for physical devices: system console, terminals, disk drives, line printer,...

Executable utility programs: compiler and assembler executives, program development,...

Libraries of system utilities and subroutines: Fortran and C run-time support, system calls, i/o routines,...

Restricted system data and dangerous utility programs restricted to system manager: password file, login,...

Temporary (scratch) files used by the various system utilities: editor, compilers, assembler,...

Less-used utility programs

Less-used temporary files

Word lists, spell checker

Less-used library files

Directories to text files containing the full Unix Programmer's Manual

Timed proc.

lpd directory.

User directory structure

User directory structure

User directory structure

User directory structure

lists the file names at the terminal, in alphabetical order:

```
$ ls /usr / johnson
book
grub
progrms
```

The listing may produce one name per line, or it may string out the names across the screen (a better idea), depending on the version of the Unix operating system. In any case, it is not absolutely necessary to give the directory name in the ls command. If none is shown, the current directory is assumed. The ls command is necessary; simple printout of a directory file will not do, because directories are stored in a special, compacted, binary format. Attempts to display directories in the same way as ordinary text files (e.g., using cat) will produce what appears to be gibberish.

Altering Access Permissions

A file can be attached to a directory in various ways. It may be attached to that directory only at its creation, or it may be linked to it at some later date. Further, it may be attached with various user access permissions.

The access permissions, indeed almost every conceivable form of information about a file, may be determined by using the ls command, which allows a very wide range of options. In its simplest form, ls merely lists the names of all files in a directory. However, there are options for asking ls to sort the listing by the time of last file access, time of last modification, time of last permission alteration, or alphabetically—or any of these in reverse order. There are also options to list not only the file names but to give much more extensive information (file sizes, internal indexing numbers, etc.), as well as to include the directory itself and its parent directory. Some of the more commonly employed options include -l (long form), -a (all entries), -t (sort by time of last modification), and -r (reversed order). For example:

```
$ ls -al
total 24
drwxrwxr - x  6  johnson  678   Feb 28 17:32  .
drwxrwxr - x  9  johnson  212   Jan 12 10:02  ..
drwxrwxr - x  1  johnson  143   Mar 11 15:50  book
- rwxr - x - --  2  johnson  8822  Feb 14 12:09  grub
drwx - -----  1  johnson  657   Feb 22 19:33  progrms
```

In this listing, the first line indicates the total number of 512-character blocks occupied by the listed files. The remaining lines give the actual directory entries, beginning with the directory itself (.), then continuing with its parent directory (..), and finally giving the files listed in the directory (grub, book, progrms).

In the line given for each file, the first character indicates whether the file is a directory (d), special file (b or c), or ordinary file (-). The next nine characters are three groups of three and describe the access permissions granted to the owner of the file (first three characters), other members of the group (next three), and the general public (last three). The letters r, w, x are used to denote read, write, and execute permissions and are always listed in that order. If the relevant letter appears, permission exists; if it has been replaced by a minus sign, the indicated permission is denied. For example, grub is identified as an ordinary file by the absence of a leading d. The file owner *johnson* has full access privileges to grub. Members of his user group may read the file or execute it, but they may not write into it. The general public is denied all access to grub.

The long-form listing above also shows, following the permissions, the number of directories in which the file appears (the number of links, in Unix jargon), the owner's name, the number of characters in the file, and the time the file was last modified.

A subtle point about ls is that the file name given in the command line could be the name either of a directory or of a non-directory file. If it is the latter, and if such a file is resident in the current directory, information will be given about that file only. This feature is quite useful if there are many files listed in a directory and full information is only required about one file.

To alter the permissions on a file, the chmod (change mode) command is used. In this command, it is necessary to specify (1) whose permissions are to be set, (2) what the settings are to be, and (3) which file. Thus the command has the form

   $ chmod { *who* } *settings filename*

The characters u (user = login owner), g (group), o (others), or a (all) may be used to indicate whose permissions are to be set. The settings are given in the form of a sign (+, −, or =) followed by one of the characters r, w, x. For example,

   $ chmod u − w precious

says that the user wishes to deny (minus sign) himself (u) write permission (w) on file precious, presumably to guard against accidents. The minus sign (−) removes permission, the plus sign (+) grants it, and the equal sign (=) assigns permissions absolutely (without reference to what they may have been previously). The command

   $ chmod a = rx precious

sets the permissions to r − xr − xr − x, i.e., for everybody to have read and execute permission and nobody to have write permission.

chmod can be used equally well for ordinary files or for directories, with exactly the same results. It should be noted that, unlike most commands, **chmod** insists that no blanks may be placed between the who-identifier, the signs, and the **r, w, x** characters. Blanks placed there will usually result in error messages, because the next character following a blank will be assumed to be a file name.

Moving and Removing Files

Files attached to a particular directory may be moved to another quite easily. The command **mv**, issued in the form

$ mv *filename directoryname*

moves a file to another directory. The moving is accomplished by rewriting the links (directory entries) that form the directory tree, not by actually copying the file. Thus the moving really is just a matter of moving the file name; the name is removed from one directory and inserted in another. Nothing is left behind in the old directory.

Variations on **mv** are obtained by moving a file to another file or a directory to another directory. These operations amount to simple renamings, since once again the moves are accomplished by rewriting names and links (indexing pointers), not by actually copying the files. An exception arises when a request is made to move a file from one physical device to another, say from disk file to magnetic tape. To remain consistent in usage, **mv** in this case does actually copy the file; the old copy is destroyed, and all directory links are rewritten to the new copy.

Removing a file by the **rm** command amounts to deletion. The removal is effected by destroying the specified link in the tree structure, then checking whether the file has any links left to any other. If no links are left, the file has become inaccessible and has ceased to exist so far as any user is concerned. The physical storage space occupied by the file is therefore cleared and released for other use.

It is possible for an ordinary file to be listed in two or more different directories, just as a single physical telephone may be listed in several telephone books. Any number of listings is permitted, all with different names if desired. A new directory entry may be created for an existing file by the **ln** (link) command, which has the form

$ ln *oldname newname*

The names *oldname* and *newname* are given in the usual form of file names —either as full pathnames or as partial pathnames from the working directory downward. Creation of multiple links is particularly convenient if, for example, several users need to have access to a common data file. However, it should be noted that under the general system rules, directory structures must always be strictly hierarchical. Therefore it is possible to create a duplicate listing for an ordinary file but not for a directory.

It should be emphasized that creating a new link with the `ln` command does not create a new copy of any file—it merely lists the same physical file in another directory. Any alteration made to the file will be made in the file as seen by every user, a point to keep in mind if several users have permission to write into the file.

File Location and Identification

The hierarchical directory layout used by Unix systems is powerful and flexible. But it does make it easy for users to lose themselves in the intricate nooks and crannies of the directory structure. There is probably no experienced user who did not at some time remember with absolute certainty that a particular file was called `trig` but could not recall the precise directory and subdirectory path. In such circumstances, the `find` command is invaluable. It permits searching an entire tree structure, from a specified directory on downward, to find all files that answer a particular description. `find` is in general used in the form

$ `find` *pathname conditions*

where *pathname* identifies the root directory for the search (all its subdirectories, sub-subdirectories, etc., will be searched) and *conditions* is a set of qualifiers which tells what characteristics are to be sought. Conventionally, the pathname of the current working directory may be given as . and the pathname of its parent directory as .. if it is not desired to specify full pathnames.

A simple application of `find` occurs when the name of a file is known, but its full pathname is not. The command

$ `find . −name'trig' −print`

will begin searching at the current working directory (signified by .) and continue through all subdirectories for all files named `trig`. Whenever one is located, its full pathname will be displayed at the terminal, as a result of the `−print` qualifier. In a more or less similar fashion, one can search for files whose names contain specified character strings, files of a particular size, files belonging to particular owners, etc., indeed almost all specifiable characteristics of a file. These descriptions can be joined in logical combinations using logical union, intersection, and negation operators. The complexity of combinations is only limited by the imagination of the user. For example, it is possible to issue a command (despite its appearance, it is not gibberish!) such as

```
$ find /usr / joe -name´trig*´ -o ( -mtime-3 -atime
  -6) -print
```

which will find (and display full path names for) all files whose names begin with the letter string ´trig´ and continue to any length, and which were either modified less than three days ago or accessed less than six days ago. The search will start at directory /usr / joe.

The find command can locate files, but it does not examine their contents. Although ls does indicate the general type of a file (ordinary, special, or directory), it does not identify what kind of material the file might contain. Thus there is need for some command which will permit identifying file contents without necessarily printing them out. The file command attempts to do so by examining the identification bits attached to each file, and also by looking at the file content itself. It has a form as simple as one might hope for,

$ file *filename*

which contrasts pleasantly with the complexities of find. Several file names, or file names with wild cards, may be specified. file then responds by producing an informed guess of the contents of each file named. Frequently encountered guesses include the following possible file characteristics and contents:

cannot open	*empty*
directory	*executable*
c program	*data*
nroff, troff, *or* eqn *input*	*English text*
ascii text	*commands*

file does not always guess right. To see why, a somewhat contrived little example might suffice. The set of lines

```
call johnny
stop
end
```

constitutes a correct and valid Fortran program. It is also a syntactically correct shell command file. It might well be intended as input for the nroff text formatter, and it would be valid as such. It might even be thought to constitute English text. The correct answer can never be known by examining the file itself, only by asking its owner what was intended!

Removable File Volumes

One great convenience that results from setting up directories hierarchically is that it is easy to attach whole new file volumes to the system. Such volumes may take the physical form of magnetic tapes, disk cartridges, or floppy disks. Particularly the latter are assuming increasing significance, as the computer user community comes to recognize the inherent merits of a cheap machine-readable medium which will conveniently fit into a standard filing folder. However, having removable media means that the operating system has to be informed, whenever appropriate, that the disk or tape on a given storage device has been changed. Appropriate commands for this purpose are provided; they are described in this section.

The **mount** and **umount** Commands

To use a removable (demountable) volume, it must first be mounted (i.e., attached to the Unix system). The physical act of mounting, for example by placing a disk cartridge in a disk drive and turning on the power, is necessary but not sufficient. In addition to making the new volume physically available, the system must be told of its existence and its place in the file hierarchy by means of an appropriate command. To be compatible with directory management rules, every physical file volume must contain a directory structure of its own. The directory structure of a volume is hierarchical, as always, and begins at a root directory which has no name. All files on the volume can be made available to the user by making the volume directory a subdirectory of the user's own directory. To do so, the user requests the system to substitute the new volume directory for an existing (but empty) directory in all file references, until further notice.

The user with a volume to attach generally performs the physical mounting first, then tells the system about it by using the **mount** command. Unfortunately, Version 7 does not permit the general user public to employ this command but reserves it for use by the system manager. The reasons for this seemingly curious omission are probably historical. The Unix system was developed largely before the era of the floppy disk, so that removable volumes by and large meant big magnetic tapes, mounted by the system operator. In large systems this arrangement is not only appropriate, but it is the only one possible that will safeguard all files absolutely. System versions serving only one or a few concurrent users and employing floppy disk drives are becoming increasingly common. Variations on the **mount** command are therefore becoming necessary. As yet, there is no generally accepted standard for mounting by users, since Version 7 makes no provision for it. The newer installations mostly employ some variation on the general **mount** command. These are often set up so as to allow users to mount volumes on only a restricted set of physical devices, e.g., one or two floppy disk drives.

Under the Version 7 Unix system, a volume is mounted with the **mount** command in the form

$ **/etc / mount   /dev /** *xxx   filename*

where **/dev /** *xxx* is the name of the special file that handles the physical device in question and *filename* is the name of the directory file for which the volume root directory will be substituted. Both the device special file and the directory which will be taken over by the root directory must exist when the **mount** command is issued. The directory to be taken over must be empty at the time when it is taken over. It should be noted that the **mount** command itself resides in **/etc**, a directory normally reserved to the system manager.

If the physical volume (disk or tape) mounted by the **mount** command does not contain a Unix file structure, i.e., if there is no directory on it, the system will attempt to read and to mount it all the same. The most usual result is a system crash. This disaster potential is probably one reason why the Version 7 Unix system reserves the **mount** command to the system manager. It might be presumed that the system manager, of all people, should know better!

When the time has come to unmount the removable volume, the same steps are retraced in reverse. The command in this case is **umount** (not *unmount*):

$ **/etc / umount   /dev /** *xxx*

This command has only one argument, the name of the special file **/dev /** *xxx* associated with the physical device on which the volume resides. The directory file to which the volume root directory was attached is released after the **umount** and appears as a healthy, normal, but empty directory. The **umount** command, like **mount**, resides in directory **/etc**.

Mounting and unmounting a volume is possible also by way of system calls, which may be accessed from C, Fortran, assembler, or other programs. This possibility allows mounting and unmounting data sets while a program is actually executing. However, only advanced users will be interested in this possibility.

Making New File Structures

When a removable volume is mounted on some physical device, the logical task of mounting is performed by substituting the root directory of the demountable volume in place of an existing directory. As indicated above, the procedure is to substitute the volume root directory for one of the leaves of the Unix directory tree. (The substituted directory must be empty initially, precisely in order to guarantee that it really is a leaf of the tree.) Such a substitution is clearly impossible unless a directory structure exists on the removable volume prior to any attempt to mount it. A brand new magnetic tape, for example, cannot be mounted because it does not contain any directory.

To create a directory structure on a new magnetic medium, the mkfs command is used. This command first cleans the volume, irretrievably destroying all records on it. It next creates a single brand new (empty) directory on it. The volume can then be mounted in the usual fashion. The mkfs command is used in the form

$ /etc / mkfs   *specialfile filesize*

where *specialfile* is the name of the special file which serves to access the physical device in question and *filesize* is the size of the file structure in blocks, a decimal number. The file size will usually be equal to the full size of the volume, though in some applications less space is allocated to the file structure.

It will be noted that the mkfs command resides in directory /etc, as do the mount and umount commands. In standard Version 7 Unix systems, it is therefore only available to the system manager. This arrangement is not altogether unreasonable, since unrestricted access to mkfs makes it is possible for any user to destroy an entire diskful of files simply by mistyping the name of a special file!

Restrictions on Removable Volumes

Once a removable volume has been mounted, the directory structure does not show, indeed it makes it difficult to find out, on what physical device the files reside. However, there are a few subtle difficulties which may arise in the use of removable media. These are resolved by placing some restrictions, fortunately fairly gentle ones, on the directory structure.

Suppose a magnetic tape contains a root directory, with a single subdirectory math which in turn contains ordinary files algb and trig. Suppose user *joe* mounts the tape on a tape drive and attaches its root directory to a previously empty directory file whose pathname is /usr / joe / tape. To the user, it then becomes invisible whether the ordinary files reside on tape or elsewhere, since reference to /usr / joe / tape / math / trig serves to access the ordinary file trig, just as if it had resided on the system disk files. The resulting user directory structure is shown in the diagram below.

The file naming rules in general insist that directories must be related to each other in tree structures. On the other hand, ordinary files may be listed in any number of directories. In other words, the insistence on hierarchical structuring applies to directories only, not to ordinary files. In fact the ln command exists precisely to allow ordinary files to be listed in two or more directories.

A problem may arise when ordinary files on removable volumes are cross-listed in several directories. For example, file /usr / joe / tape / math / trig may also be of interest to user *bob*, who may therefore wish to attach it to his directory. Within the rules, incorporating the file as /usr / bob / trig would be acceptable in principle. But the directory /usr / bob is resident on a physical device (typically, the system disk) different from the device where file /usr / joe / tape / math / trig is located (the magnetic tape unit). If the tape is unmounted in due course, user *bob* will no longer be able to access this file!

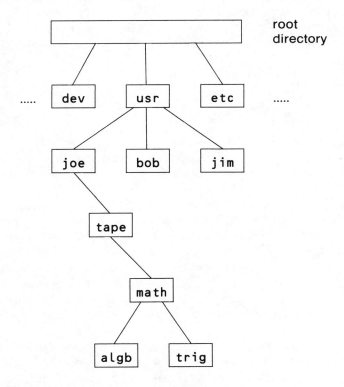

To avoid problems of the sort described, ordinary files on removable-medium devices may not be cross-listed to directories on other devices. Linking file trig to directory /usr / bob as above is therefore forbidden. This rule is imposed to keep system management relatively simple; if the rule did not exist, the procedure of dismounting any volume would have to include a large number of cross-checks to determine whether any files were being made inaccessible. This prohibition does not actually prevent any user from having access to files, merely from listing them in directories in a particular way. If user *bob* really wishes to have a copy of `math / trig`, he must request it by means of the `mv` command, which will actually copy the file across devices. Alternatively, he may make a copy of it by means of `cp`.

Internal Structure of Files

All ordinary files contain strings of 8-bit bytes, which may represent characters or numeric values. Files may contain byte strings of arbitrary length, or they may be subdivided into smaller units (usually called *records*) which contain logically related material. Their physical structure is dependent on the recording medium employed; their logical structure is always the same.

Logical and Physical Structure

The logical structure of a file may be compared to the logical structure of a book. Books are typically subdivided into chapters, with each chapter in turn composed of sections or paragraphs. Paragraphs consist of sentences, which are made up of words.

It is vital to keep in mind that there is no particular relationship between the physical structure of a file and its logical structure. To pursue the analogy, a book is logically organized into chapters, paragraphs, and sentences; it is physically organized into pages and lines. The physical and logical structures are quite independent. Two different editions of *David Copperfield* must surely contain the same sentences, joined together into logically identical paragraphs. Yet the manner in which the sentences are stored in pages and lines (the physical structure) will generally be quite different.

In the Unix system, files are not subdivided into smaller logical units. They are simply regarded as byte strings of arbitrary length, which may contain anything at all. However, it would be wrong to assume that all files in a Unix system are unstructured. Many files are used as inputs to programs which do require specific logical structures.

Unix files are physically divided into 512-byte blocks on all random access media (see below). There is of course no particular correlation between the 512-byte physical file blocks and the logical record size, if indeed the latter exists at all.

Sequential and Random Access

The Unix system treats all devices and media alike, as containing files composed of strings of characters. However, various physical file media inherently differ in their access characteristics, so that some distinction must be made in practice between different kinds of file access. For example, a magnetic disk is an inherently random access device; it is substantially as much work and takes nearly as long (on average) to retrieve information from one place on the disk as another, and all characters on the disk are equally accessible. Hence it is practicable to read a file in essentially random order, e.g., to skip about in a dictionary file to find words here and there. Writing or reading can take place in various sequences, including in one place several times. It is then necessary to keep track of where the next character is to be transmitted to (or from). A very simple mechanism is employed for doing so: a pointer which is initially set to the beginning or end of a file and which is moved along as reading and writing are done. Random access to all parts of a file is achieved by repositioning the file pointer.

Certain other media (for example, input keyboards and line printers) are strictly sequential. Characters once sent to a printer cannot be read back, and characters cannot be printed over characters already printed some time ago. Thus it is not a matter of concern where the next unit of information is to be transmitted to or from; there is only one place. To maintain uniformity, these devices are also regarded as equipped with a pointer, although of course it is not actually possible to move the pointer backward.

Media of an intermediate character, such as magnetic tapes, are viewed as logically indistinguishable from disk files. The only differences arise in their physical response, for operation of magnetic tapes as random access devices can require frequent rewinding and thus result in excruciatingly slow operation.

In addition to being strictly sequential, keyboards and line printers are also read-only and write-only devices, respectively. This rather important physical fact presents no structural problem, since Unix software works with a system of read-write-execute permissions. A physical device which cannot be read is logically indistinguishable from a file without read permission. Thus the existence of read-only and write-only devices fits very naturally into the general system structure.

The Unix operating system provides random access to files through user programs written in high-level languages such as Fortran and C, so that the average user never needs to be concerned with how the internal operation is carried out. Explicit pointer positioning, if required, can be achieved by using the system call lseek. Actually, lseek only recomputes the pointer position. It does not perform any physical reading or writing operations; those are taken care of by the Unix file buffering system.

Input–Output Buffering

So far as the ordinary user can tell, Unix file reading and writing operations appear to be synchronized to programs. In other words, all Fortran **read** or **write** statements, or equivalent commands of other languages, appear to be executed exactly when and where they appear in a program. They appear to be unbuffered; every **read** or **write** operation appears to fetch or send exactly the required number of characters, without reference to the file block size.

Since the files are physically organized in blocks, and since the blocks do not necessarily occupy adjacent locations on the physical medium, such a synchronous and unbuffered appearance can be achieved only by actually reading and writing files in a buffered fashion. Although the details of the buffering are complicated, the principle is simple. A **read** instruction, for example, causes an entire block to be read from disk into a buffer area in memory, but only the required number of characters is transferred from the buffer to the program area. Similarly, writing is actually done by moving characters from the program area into a writing buffer; only when the buffer is full does physical transfer to disk take place. For example, suppose that a user program reads successive 64-character records via Fortran **read** statements. An actual disk transfer of data is required only once after every eight **read** requests, provided they ask for sequentially arranged data. On the other hand, reading randomly arranged 64-character records may require one disk access per **read** if a different file block has to be fetched for each one.

Because most user programs tend to read or write to sequential locations, a relatively complicated buffering scheme is used, in which the *next* file block is preread ahead of time. As a result, most input requests find the necessary file block already resident in buffers and do not need to wait for physical movement of disk heads or magnetic tapes. This speedup of operation is particularly valuable with large files, where multiple levels of indirect indexing may be needed to locate and retrieve the next sequential file block.

Data are always stored in 512-byte file blocks so programs which do a great deal of input–output will usually run a little faster if reading and writing are done in units of 512 bytes or submultiples of 512 bytes. However, the Unix input/output buffering scheme removes a substantial part of the speed advantage, and most users do not find it worthwhile to concern themselves with this level of detail except where large numbers of truly random file accesses are involved.

Buffering of output to and from special files is carried out in different ways for block and character files. Block files, i.e., special files that correspond to block-structured devices, are handled in much the same way as ordinary files. Character-structured special files naturally must carry out their input–output operations on a single-character basis. Their buffering scheme is quite simple and straightforward by comparison, without the many clever ideas incorporated in block buffering.

Archives and Libraries

A special form of object file called a *library* or *archive* is available under all Unix systems. Such files differ from other object files in having internal directories which the ld (loader) program can scan. Typically, libraries are used to keep stocks of frequently used items. Most operating systems provide ready-made libraries of mathematical functions, commonly used input–output routines, and much else.

The distinction between a library file and any other object file lies in the possibility of extracting and loading library programs selectively. If the loader is instructed to use a particular library containing trigonometric functions in conjunction with some Fortran program, for example, it will load into memory only those routines actually required by the program. On the other hand, an ordinary object module has no internal directory, so the loader will load all of it, whether or not all parts are needed.

Any user can create and maintain archives or libraries using the ar archive maintainer program. Users with many small subprograms of frequent application are wise to do so.

In using and creating libraries, it should be borne in mind that searches performed through libraries are done strictly in one direction. Thus it is very important that, when loading programs, users always specify file names in a sequence which will make searches successful. If program A calls B as a subprogram, which in turn calls C, loading will be successful if the files are organized so as to present the program modules to ld in the order A, B, C, but loading will be unsuccessful in the order C, A, B because (searching one way only) C cannot be found when it is required by B. The ar program permits the user to arrange the order of modules in a library, so that at least within each archive such problems can be avoided.

Chapter 4

The Command Shell

The Unix operating system proper consists of many software components. Two hold particularly privileged positions: the *kernel* and the *shell*. The kernel is the system supervisor, which schedules all processes and executes them in the proper manner and at the right time. Although it is a vital central part, the kernel is quite small compared to the overall size of the system. By far the major proportion of the total executable code is in various programs (utilities), including the different language compilers, the editors, text formatters, and a great deal besides. Which programs to execute, how to run them, what to do with the output, and many similar matters are for the user to determine, and the user's desires must be communicated to the kernel. The shell program is the only channel provided for such communications. In this chapter the external appearance of the shell is described in sufficient detail to allow reasonably complete use of its main facilities. However, the shell is a complex program, and many of its more esoteric features can only be hinted at here.

Issuing Commands

The shell program requests commands from the user, decodes them, and communicates the user's wishes to the kernel. Practically all communication between the kernel and the user is handled by way of the shell. Its name was chosen to imply that the command decoder program surrounds the kernel, isolating it from the outside world. While the shell facilitates user access to the kernel, it also serves to separate the two, so the user can never readily tell just exactly what the kernel actually does.

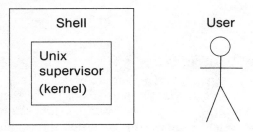

The Shell Prompt

When a user logs in, the Unix shell is automatically invoked and started running. The shell then immediately displays the **$** prompt on the screen, thereby infroming the user that it is ready to accept a command. When the user issues a command, the shell institutes a search for a program with the same name as the command. If such a program is found, the shell instructs the kernel to execute it. Once execution is complete, the shell tells the user, and requests another command, by displaying the **$** prompt again. In other words, the shell alternately requests commands and executes them, in the following cycle:

issue **$** prompt
wait for keyboard reply
decode command line (i.e., search for program)
instruct kernel to execute program, and wait
accept kernel reply, and go back to issue a prompt

This cycle continues until the shell encounters a control-D character in the keyboard input. This character is used consistently everywhere in the system to denote the end of a file. From the shell's point of view, the string of keyboard characters coming from the user is very much like a file, so the shell interprets control-D to mean "end of keyboard transmission", i.e., to signify that the user does not intend to send any further commands. The shell therefore instructs the kernel to log out the user.

Almost all command verbs available in the Unix system are in fact program names, so that execution of a command really means execution of the program with the same name. Indeed every user can define more commands for his own convenience, simply by creating programs and using their names as command verbs.

Form of Shell Commands

All commands understood by the shell, and therefore all commands that can be acted upon by the kernel, have the same general form. This fact should not be surprising since they are all processed by the same decoder! The form is

> *command-verb* { *argument* } { *argument* } ... { *argument* }

The *command-verb* is always required but *arguments* are optional; they may or may not be needed. The command verb is understood by the shell to denote the name of a program to be run. The shell will therefore cause the system file directories to be searched for a name to match the command verb, ordinarily in the following sequence:

1. user's current directory; *if not found there,*
2. directory /bin;   *if not found there,*
3. directory /usr / bin;   *if not found there,*
4. *message issued, search terminated.*

The command must appear in one of these directories as the name of an ordinary file. Because this prescribed searching sequence is defined in advance, the shell does not expect full path names for files which can be located unambiguously by the above order of searching. For example, the Fortran compiler is invoked by the command

> $ f77 *arguments*

There is no need to specify it by its full pathname as

> $ /bin / f77 *arguments*

An exceptional case occurs if the name of a system-provided command is duplicated by a file name in the user's own directory. If, for example, the user has created a file with the name f77, it will be found in the very first step of the search, but it will not be the Fortran compiler. To override the default search sequence, the full pathname will be required in such cases.

Most of the system-provided general utilities reside in directory /bin, some in /usr / bin. The user's own contributions of course may reside anywhere he cares (or is able) to put them.

Arguments in the system-provided commands are of two principal forms: file names and adverbs (modal arguments). Adverbs are usually called *options* in the *Unix Programmer's Manual* as well as in other descriptive literature. For example, to compare two files file1 and file2, one may use the command

> $ cmp -s file1 file2

The argument -s is an option; in this particular case, it indicates that printout is to be suppressed (cmp otherwise prints whatever differences it finds between the two files). The option must be preceded by a hyphen (a minus sign) in this command, and indeed in practically all the system-provided commands, to show the shell that -s is not a file name. Command options are usually single alphabetic characters.

The options which may be attached to any particular command differ from command to command. Nevertheless, the standard commands provided by the Unix system tend to use the same letters to signify the same action (though exceptions do exist). For example, $-l$ usually denotes "long form", whatever that may mean in the context of a particular command. Some of the standard commands allow few or no options; some admit more than ten, which may be specified in almost any sensible combination. Multiple single-character options can usually be preceded by a single hyphen, provided they are concatenated without any spaces left between; e.g., $-sl$ requests that both the s and l options should be included. (If a blank is inserted, the shell will ordinarily assume that the next character belongs to a file name and will not interpret it as being an option.) Any user-added or locally provided commands, on the other hand, will use whatever options or other qualifiers their creators saw fit to endow them with. One can only hope that their tastes parallel those of the original Unix design team.

When file names are specified as command arguments, the standard conventions for file naming are used. In other words, the name by itself is taken to imply that the file is to be found in the user's current directory. Pathnames beginning with / denote paths starting at the root directory, and pathnames beginning without the / character at the current directory.

Standard Files

At login time, every user is automatically assigned a *standard input device* and a *standard output device*. In most ordinary cases, these will be the terminal keyboard and screen. Most commands that produce output produce it on the standard device; correspondingly, they expect input from the standard input device. Under this scheme the user often does not need to bother specifying where output should be directed. For example, to list directory contents, it is sufficient to give the command

```
$ ls
```

without any indication that the listing should be presented on the terminal screen. That is precisely where the listing will appear, unless the standard output assigned by default was altered.

If the user prefers to have input and output directed to devices other than the predefined standard, such data movements can always be redirected elsewhere. In the normal course of events, the redirection is desired only for the duration of one particular command. Such temporary reassignment is achieved by the characters > or >> as in

```
$ ls -l > file1
```

or

```
$ ls -l >> file1
```

which cause a listing of the current directory to be created (in long form, as specified by -l). The single right-arrow character > causes the contents of file1 to be replaced by the listing, without presenting the listing on the terminal screen. The double right-arrow >> causes the listing to be appended to the existing contents of file1, without affecting previous file contents. If there was no file1 in the first place, one is created. In a similar fashion, the left-arrow character < may be used to reassign input temporarily.

The standard devices are sometimes referred to in Unix jargon by their *file descriptors*, which are integer numbers: 0 for standard input, 1 for standard output. However, the ordinary user rarely needs to worry about these designations—he will only need to understand them occasionally when reading the manuals.

Multitasking and Waiting

In the ordinary course of events, the shell initiates execution of a command, and does nothing until the appropriate process has entirely run its course. For most tasks, this arrangement is good and sensible: the user requests a process to be run, the output is displayed on the terminal screen, and the shell comes back with the $ prompt when ready for the next command. For example, a user desiring to know who is currently logged on the system may use the **who** command in response to the $ prompt:

```
$ who
tom        tty3        Feb 27 12:08
dick       dz5         Feb 27 12:02
harry      dz6         Feb 27 13:14
$
```

who checks the system tables to see which user is logged on at what terminal and since what time. The answers are presented on the terminal screen, while the shell simply waits for **who** to finish. On completion of **who**, the $ prompt reappears, indicating that the shell has regained control.

There are occasions on which it is desirable to set a program running but to go on doing something at the terminal while the job runs. For instance, computing the weekly payroll of a company may be a quite time-consuming job, but one that requires no user intervention. The user may therefore simply wish to set it going and to get on with editing some other data with the **ed** editor while the payroll program runs. Unix is fortunately a *multitasking* operating system, i.e., one which permits a user to have multiple tasks running concurrently. To make the user program **payroll** and the system utility **ed** run at the same time, the user instructs the shell to run **payroll** but not to wait for its completion. Such an instruction is implied by the **&** (ampersand) character when used as a suffix:

```
$ payroll hours employee payment &
21
$ ed
```

Here the program **payroll** is told to use the input files **hours** and **employee** to produce an output file **payment** but not to wait for completion. In response to the command, the shell requests the kernel to set the payroll task running and returns to the user a *process identification number*, 21 in the above example. Because the ampersand sign **&** was included in the command line, the shell does not wait for the kernel to signal that the payroll job is complete; instead, it immediately issues the **$** prompt, showing that it is prepared to accept another command. The user replies that he wishes to run **ed**, and from that moment on, two tasks are running for the same user, **payroll** and **ed**. The latter is interactive and will eventually be terminated by the user; the former will keep going until its job is complete. Noninteractive tasks set running in this fashion are sometimes known as *background tasks*, because they run invisibly while the user is engaged in something else.

Background tasks are identified only by their process identification numbers. When a process is set running in the background, it is wise to note down its process identification number so as to be able to give the system further instructions about it later on. It may happen, as it sometimes does, that the user realizes, just a moment after pressing RETURN, that he set the wrong process running or specified the wrong input file. In that case, the process can be stopped by the **kill** command. The instruction

```
$ kill 21
```

will stop the payroll program, provided of course it has not yet terminated its run.

A user is naturally not restricted to just one background process. In principle at least, he may launch any number of them; in some implementations there may be a limit, usually fairly high. It is possible to enquire after the status of background processes by means of the **ps** (process status) command. This command produces a screen display to show, depending on the options selected with it, from which terminal the job was started, by what command, and how long it has been running; whether it is still running; for which user it is running; and a host of other (for the most part rather less interesting) things.

Pipes and Pipelines

The Unix shell permits establishing interprocess *pipes*. Pipes are data channels which funnel output from one program directly to another without creating any intermediate files. A pipe appears like an output file to one program and an input file to another. In fact, a pipe can be created by rerouting the output and input of programs so that the output file buffer of one program feeds directly into the input file buffer of the other. The vertical rule character | is used to denote a pipe in shell commands. The command line

```
$ who | lpr
```

requests execution of who concurrently with the line printer spooler lpr in such a way that the output of who is piped directly to lpr as its input. The lpr command copies its input file to the line printer, so that this command pair should list who is currently logged on the system, but on the line printer instead of at the terminal. The apparent effect is precisely the same as would be achieved by the command sequence

```
$ who > temporaryfile
$ lpr < temporaryfile
$ rm temporaryfile
```

However, no file space is needed for temporaryfile, because no such file is ever actually created.

What actually happens when a pipe is specified is that the kernel starts both processes running, just as if they were background tasks. In the above example, who can start immediately, but lpr can only start running once there is some input for it to read, that is to say, after who has actually produced some output. In the pipeline the output of who is handed over to lpr immediately it is produced, without waiting for who to terminate. By way of contrast, in the sequence of three commands the lpr program is only launched after completion of who. In the pipeline, who and lpr will run concurrently, with the output of who fed directly to lpr as input. No intermediate files will be produced. The two processes will thus execute synchronously, forced into synchronism by their interlocking needs for input and output. In fact, for all practical purposes the two may be regarded as a single compound process.

A sequence of two or more processes connected by pipes is called a *pipeline*. Pipelines may be made to contain as many processes as desired. The individial processes in a pipeline are always executed from left to right, with the output of one process chained to the next as input. To illustrate, the example above may be extended to include alphabetic sorting, using the sort utility. The names of all currently active users may be printed out on the line printer in alphabetical order (important if there are many!), using the pipeline

```
$ who | sort | lpr
```

This pipeline works as follows. The who program will produce as its output the identifiers for all users currently logged in. Next, sort will place them in alphabetical order. Finally, lpr will send the output to the line printer, which will eventually produce

```
dick        dz5        Feb 27 12:02
harry       dz6        Feb 27 13:14
tom         tty3       Feb 27 12:08
```

All processes in a long pipeline are set running simultaneously, and their running is synchronized by the need of each to wait until it receives input from the process preceding it. The effect is that of a bucket brigade moving information from hand to hand as soon as it becomes available, never waiting for more information to accumulate than is actually required for the next step.

The Shell Programming Language

In the above description of shell commands, it has been assumed throughout that commands are issued by the user at the keyboard and are executed immediately. In other words, the shell command language has been regarded as a control language which enables the user to specify each action as and when he wishes it to be carried out. But there is an alternative possibility: shell commands can be used as a programming language. Sequences of shell commands actually constitute programs, for they prescribe sequences of actions. Such sequences, called *shell procedures* in Unix jargon, may be stored away in files in the same manner as a Fortran or Pascal program, to be executed when required.

Shell Procedures

The key to understanding how shell procedures are written and used lies in recognizing that the shell itself is just another utility program. It differs from all the other system utilities in only one way: the shell is automatically set running when the user logs in. However, being just another program, a copy of the shell can be started up at any time by means of the **sh** command. When this command is given, the **sh** procedure is invoked; it reads input from a specified file. For example,

```
$ sh file1
```

reads all the lines in **file1** in turn and uses them as shell commands. Because the default input file is generally the keyboard, simply issuing the command

```
$ sh
```

causes the shell to run, taking its input from the keyboard. This way of running is precisely the normal manner in which the Unix system and its many cousins operate! Confusing as it may seem at first glance, two copies of the shell will now be running for the same user. The most recently launched copy is awaiting input; the earlier copy is waiting to be signaled that the more recent one has finished running. There is generally not much point in launching several copies of the shell, all taking input from the keyboard, even though that is perfectly legitimate. However, there may well be profit in getting several copies of the shell going, each taking input from a different source.

Shell procedures are sets of commands intended for execution in a their natural sequence. For example, suppose a file, called whoprint, is created and that it contains the text

```
who > temporaryfile
lpr < temporaryfile
rm temporaryfile
```

To execute the commands in this file, the user instructs the shell to run, but with this file instead of the keyboard as the source of input:

```
$ sh whoprint
```

The commands in file whoprint will be read one by one and executed. Two copies of the shell will be active at this time: one which was invoked automatically when logging in, and a second one which the user requested explicitly. The first takes its input from the keyboard; the second one from the file whoprint. When no more unused input lines remain in whoprint, the shell encounters an end-of-file mark when trying to read the next line. The second copy of sh is therefore terminated. The first (automatically system initiated) copy, which was forced to wait for completion of the second, now resumes work and asks for input with the $ prompt. As previously described, waiting could have been avoided by

```
$ sh whoprint &
```

with the result that the first shell could request commands immediately when it had started the second one running. The user could thus be allowed to get on with other jobs. The noteworthy point here is that the second copy of the shell is started up as if it were just another program (in fact, it *is* just another program), with its input file specified in the usual fashion.

Because the shell can accept input from shell procedure files, users can create processes not ordinarily provided in the Unix system simply by putting together a string of existing processes in an appropriate fashion. To illustrate, suppose it is desired to know which users are logged in on terminals of type *tty*, ignoring users logged in at any other type of terminal. The who command gives a full listing of users, which contains the desired information as well as many superfluous items. Weeding a file can be accomplished by the `grep` command, which extracts from a file those lines containing a predetermined character pattern (almost unbelievably, `grep` stands for *global regular expression print*), in this case *tty*. The two can be pipelined to form a file called `whotty`, containing just a single command line:

```
who | grep tty
```

Whenever it is desired to determine what users are logged in on terminals of the *tty* type, one issues the command

```
$ sh whotty
```

and the above short pipeline is executed. In the illustrative case shown above in connection with the `who` command, the result was the screen display

```
$ who
tom        tty3      Feb 27 12:08
dick       dz5       Feb 27 12:02
harry      dz6       Feb 27 13:14
$
```

but in the present situation, there will only result

```
$ sh whotty
tom        tty3      Feb 27 12:08
$
```

Two users (*dick* and *harry*) are shown in the output of `who`, because they are logged in; but they are filtered out by `grep`, because their corresponding output lines from `who` do not contain the string *tty*.

Parameter Passing

Shell procedures may contain symbolic parameters, for which real values are substituted at the time the commands are actually interpreted and executed. Symbolic parameters are handed to shell procedures in an extremely simple manner. Up to nine special symbols `$1, $2, . . . , $9`, each consisting of a dollar sign and a numeral, may be used in place of character strings in the procedure definition. When the procedure is invoked, the corresponding number of file names, procedure names, numeric values, or other actual arguments must be provided as strings of characters. These are then substituted in place of the symbolic parameters by the shell, the first one in place of `$1`, the second in place of `$2`, and so on.

To illustrate, suppose once again that a listing of all users logged in at a particular type of terminal is desired. Procedure `whotty` as described above works for one particular terminal type but not for any arbitrary type, because the character string **tty** is permanently embedded in it. One might generalize the **whotty** procedure above by creating a procedure file **whoterm** which contains just the one command line

>   who | grep $1

This procedure contains one symbolic parameter; so when it is invoked, exactly one actual parameter value must be supplied. Since **grep** expects a character string to use in pattern matching, the actual parameter must be a character string also. Thus

```
$ sh whoterm tty
tom        tty3       Feb 27 12:08
$
```

produces exactly the same result as **whotty**, because the command string has the character string **tty** substituted for **$1** prior to execution. The flexibility afforded by parameter passing is evident if one considers

```
$ sh whoterm dz
dick       dz5        Feb 27 12:02
harry      dz6        Feb 27 13:14
$
```

Here the same procedure **whoterm** was used unchanged, but with a different parameter substituted for **$1**.

Conditional Execution

The command language understood by the shell has an interesting and somewhat unusual feature: when executed, every command has an attribute called *exit status*. The exit status is merely a logical flag which indicates success (or failure) in executing the command. For example, suppose the **rm** command is issued to remove a file. If the specified file cannot be found, it cannot be removed, and the attempt to execute **rm** is regarded as unsuccessful. The exit status is therefore returned as *false*. Internally, the exit status is stored as a logical variable buried deep within the shell, it is not directly accessible by the user. However, its value can be tested so as to determine the outcome of the last command. The shell can then use the exit status to decide whether to take some other action. Using this decision mechanism, it is possible to give the shell conditional commands such as "remove file **qtty.c**, and if successful, remove file **qtty.f** as well". The mechanisms by which such commands are made to run are called *conditional execution constructs*.

Two basic conditional execution constructs are provided by the shell, so that the user can make the execution of one command dependent on the success of another. These are the **if** and **while** constructions. The **if** construction resembles the **if** of the Pascal language and exists in two forms: **if ... then** and **if ... then ... else ...** , as illustrated in the following two cases:

> **if** { *command list* }
> **then** { *command list* }
> **fi**

> **if** { *command list* }
> **then** { *command list* }
> **else** { *command list* }
> **fi**

The command lists may contain one single command (probably the most usual case), or there may be a set of several commands. However, the **if** always checks only the success of the last command to be executed. The shell keeps track of only a single exit status flag, and that one is set or reset after each simple command under the control of the shell. The terminator **fi** is used to identify the end of the command list for conditional execution. A terminator is essential; otherwise, the shell would not know how far the command list extends. However, it is not necessary to have a terminator before **then** and **else**, because these keywords themselves serve to delimit the preceding command lists; only the last list might be ambiguous unless a terminator is used to show where it ends.

The **while** construct permits repetition of a command string, as long as another command list continues to be executed successfully:

> **while** { *command list* }
> **do** { *command list* }
> **done**

This provision also has an obvious resemblance to the Pascal **while** except for the **done** terminator. Indeed the **done** terminator is curious even within the command conventions of the Unix system; it is inconsistent with the command string terminator **fi**, which is merely the initiator **if** spelled backward. By the same logic, one would have expected **do ... od**, not **do ... done**!

Input Handling by the Shell

All keyboard input to the shell is handled through a text buffer, an area of memory reserved for storage of characters received from the keyboard until such time as they are needed by the shell. Whatever is typed at the keyboard is not immediately processed by the shell; it is stored in the buffer until the shell is ready to accept input and at least one input line is complete. Only at that time is the input line actually decoded by the shell. This manner of receiving and treating input leads to some unexpected results and also provides some important convenience features.

Input Buffering

The manner in which the shell handles keyboard input typed by the user may be best understood in terms of a pipeline. The shell could be imagined to comprise two separate programs connected by a pipe: a keyboard monitor and the command decoder (the shell proper). The keyboard monitor has only one function: to collect characters from the keyboard and to store them in the buffer area, ready for collection by the command decoder whenever it develops a hunger for input. Under the general Unix pipeline rules no data may be transferred from keyboard monitor to command decoder unless (1) the decoder is ready to receive input and (2) the monitor has at least a complete input line ready for sending on. Thus the shell can never receive and decode less than a full command line. On the other hand, the keyboard monitor may accept from the keyboard, and store in the buffer, two or more lines. If the decoder is not ready to accept the extra lines, they are simply left to wait in the buffer.

The buffer area used for shell input is 256 characters in size. In normal use, the shell displays the $ prompt on the screen, and the user replies by typing a command, terminated by a RETURN keystroke. Since RETURN signifies completion of a line, both requirements of a pipe are now satisfied; the first program has output ready, and the second is waiting. The command line is therefore handed on to the decoder and processed. However, if the user continues to type at the keyboard without waiting for the command to be executed and for the shell prompt to reappear, no harm is done. The keyboard monitor simply stores the characters as they are typed, they will be transmitted from the keyboard buffer to the decoder program once the latter is ready for more input. A difficulty only arises if the user attempts to type more than 256 characters, thereby overflowing the buffer. In that case, the extra characters are simply discarded without any prior warning to the user. However, such a situation does not arise very often in practice, since 256 characters represent over a dozen average commands.

Experienced users turn the keyboard buffer capacity to good profit by typing ahead the commands they know they will wish to issue next, especially if the execution times of some are known to be long. The only truly curious and confusing part is the resulting screen display. The keyboard monitor echoes characters on the screen as they are typed, but the shell prompt and any program responses only come when the commands are actually executed. The screen display therefore will not reflect the actual sequence of operations, but it will show all the commands as they are typed and then a sequence of shell prompts and program outputs as they are produced.

Errors and Error Correction

Even the most expert computer user occasionally issues a wrong command, or strikes the wrong key. The manner in which the keyboard input is buffered means that no action is ever taken in response to keystrokes until RETURN has been typed at the terminal. Errors can therefore be remedied at least until that moment.

Incorrect characters typed at the keyboard may be corrected by erasing them. Erasure of a single character is achieved by the *erase character*, which is usually **#** for printing terminals, the BACKSPACE key for screen-type terminals. Backspacing is then followed by overwriting, which works just fine for display terminals capable of erasure. There is no way of making the terminal display "back up" several characters without erasure, so that if the error is not immediately discovered, erasing several characters may be necessary. For example, the input line

   $ paxxwd####sswd

will be understood to mean **passwd** despite its curious appearance. The corresponding keystrokes typed at a screen-display terminal (with true backspacing substituted for the erase character **#**) would in fact look perfectly normal because the corrections overwrite the erroneous input and therefore do not become visible on the screen.

If an error occurs near the beginning of a long command line, it may well happen that a great many characters have to be erased and retyped, so that it may be easier to start all over again. Starting the line over, without individually erasing every character, is accomplished by typing the *kill character*, which expunges all of the line typed so far. The kill character is usually **ə** and often control-X.

The erase and kill characters are both resettable. That is to say, they are not permanently fixed as **#** and **ə**, respectively; rather, a table of terminal characteristics is maintained to describe every terminal connected to the system, and these two characters are part of the terminal description. The user can reset the erase and kill characters, as well as a number of other things, through the **stty** command, which is described more fully below. The most common default settings are those described here. However, if there is some reason why the default settings should prove inconvenient, a user may indeed define some other characters, for example **%** and **<**, to be the erase and kill characters for his use.

The BACKSPACE key on a normal terminal generates the control-H character. If a terminal does not have a BACKSPACE key, control-H will always do precisely the same job.

Characters Given Special Treatment

The shell does not consider the erase and kill characters to have their literal meanings as characters but to denote special actions instead. There are several other characters to which the shell assigns special meanings. These will be considered briefly in the following.

The semicolon ; is treated as equivalent to RETURN, provided the keyboard buffer contains at least one full line terminated by RETURN. To restate this bit of gobbledygook in plain words: it is permissible to type several shell commands on a single line, with semicolons between commands, and to terminate that line in the usual fashion with RETURN. When the time comes for command decoding, semicolons will be replaced by RETURNS, so that the individual commands will be decoded as individual lines. The shell does not act any differently, but the screen display looks different. This feature is quite useful when long shell procedure files are built up. Since many shell commands are quite short, long shell procedures form narrow ribbons of typing along the left edge of the terminal screen. They can be made to occupy fewer but longer lines, thereby becoming easier to read, if semicolons are used judiciously.

In quite a few commands, it may be desirable to name a whole range of file names. As an example, a particular project may have involved creating a whole family of files `project.f`, `project.o`, `project.a`,..., and it may be desired to remove all the files at the completion of the project. Rather than requiring the user to type out the names individually, the shell decoder permits using so-called *wild card* characters, which are considered equivalent to any and all others. The asterisk * and question mark ? are used for this purpose; the asterisk stands for any string of characters (of any length, including no characters at all), and the question mark stands for any one character. Consequently

```
$ rm project*
```

will remove all files whose names begin with the character string `project` and continue with any (or no) characters. On the other hand,

```
$ rm project.?
```

will remove all files whose names begin with the eight-character string `project.` and contain one additional character.

Sometimes it is desired to identify groups of characters more finely, e.g., "any lowercase alphabetic from a to k" or "any one of the numerals 3, 5, 8". For such purposes, wild cards that match only within specified character sets may be defined. A range of characters, or a list of characters, encased in square brackets is taken as a match for exactly one character which belongs to the set. For example,

```
$ rm project.[a-k][3,5,8]
```

will cause removal of all files whose names begin with the eight-character string **project.**, contain a lowercase alphabetic in the range **a** to **k** next, and terminate in one of the numerals 3, 5, or 8 (for example, **project.b3**). As indicated in this example, the square brackets may contain either a range of characters which are naturally ordered (e.g., alphabetics or numerals) or a list of individually identified characters separated by commas.

It is not generally a good idea to use special characters in file names, because confusion may arise. For example, **star*wars** is a legitimate Unix file name, but one best avoided because the asterisk character may be understood as a wild card and cause problems thereby. If such difficulties are encountered, all is not yet lost. The backslash character **** can be used in shell commands to force one of the special characters to have its literal (rather than special) meaning. The commands

    $ rm star*wars

and

    $ rm star*wars

are not the same. The former removes all files whose names begin **star** and end **wars**, no matter what characters may occur between these two strings. The latter, however, treats the asterisk as an asterisk character, not as a symbol for any other character string; it removes the file named **star*wars** and no others. The backslash may be used in this way to suppress the special meanings of any of the characters

    < > * ? | & \

which otherwise have particular significance apart from their natural character meanings. Although the backslash treatment is always possible, it can lead to confusion; it is not easy to enter a file name such as **star*wars** without risk of misunderstanding!

Argument Echoing

Because the shell command decoder may understand wild cards or other special characters in a way not intended by the user, a utility command **echo** is provided for previewing the effect of any particular command line. The **echo** command actually does nothing except display on the terminal screen the arguments entered with the command, but it displays them in fully expanded explicit form. For example, a user may feel diffident about a file name such as **project.***, particularly in a destructive command like **rm**. To verify just what would be removed, he may first issue the command

    $ echo project.*

The response, which might be

    `project.c project.f project.o`

lists all the currently possible values of the `echo` argument, i.e., all the file names in the current directory which match the wild card construction given. Similarly, a user may feel uncertain about a construct such as `star\\\*wars` (how many and which backslashes are going to be taken literally?). He may check whether the shell's understanding of the character string is the same as intended, by entering

    `$ echo star\\\*wars`

The echo will again show exactly what the character string, as finally decoded by the shell, will look like. The `echo` program is of course not actually a part of the shell but merely one of the many system utilities.

Resetting Terminal Parameters

Experienced users at times find it desirable to alter the erase and kill characters associated with their terminals or to reset other terminal characteristics. To do so, the `stty` program may be used. Like `echo`, the `stty` program is not really a part of the shell at all, but it does affect the operation of the shell quite directly.

    Resetting the erase and kill characters is easily accomplished. The new characters are given in the command as arguments; for example,

    `$ stty erase % kill +`

will make **%** the erase character and **+** the kill character, until the system is otherwise instructed by another `stty` command.

    Terminals vary widely in their operating characteristics. The basic machine, on which nearly all subsequent computer terminals have been patterned, was designed and built by Teletype Corporation quite a long time before the computer era. Standard terminals are therefore widely termed "teletypes" in computer jargon, and the name is echoed in such abbreviations and mnemonics as `stty`. Modern terminals generally are equipped with either a cathode-ray-tube (television-type) display screen or a paper printing mechanism. The latter are generally slower because of the mechanical motions required to make them run. At line ends, they usually need extra slack time to allow the printing head or carriage to return to the start of a new line. They generally also require slower character transmission than display terminals. The speed settings, the tab settings, and in fact all the characteristics of the terminal can be reset through `stty`. Of course, resetting these merely tells the system what the terminal characteristics are, it does not alter the terminal itself; a slow mechanical printer will still run at its natural speed regardless of what the system might expect. Most of the facilities of **stty** are therefore used when changing the actual terminal characteristics, such as the transmission speed or character parity. To find out the current settings of a terminal (as the system terminal communication software imagines them to be, not necessarily as they really are), the **stty** command is issued without any arguments. For a fairly ordinary printing terminal, the result might be

```
* stty
speed 300 baud
erase = '#'; kill = 'a'
 odd -nl echo
```

meaning that the speed is 300 baud (30 characters per second), the erase and kill characters are the usual ones, character transmission is checked for odd parity, lines are considered to be terminated by RETURN keystrokes, and characters are to be echoed to the screen as typed. The character pair nl denotes the *newline* character, and the negative sign before it indicates that the line terminator is RETURN, not *newline*.

Chapter 5

The System Kernel

The kernel is that part of a Unix operating system which actually controls the allocation of machine time, memory space, and communication channels to the various tasks that system users may have running at any particular moment. It consists of a central supervisory program and a number of low-level service routines, which take care of such essential activities as fetching characters from a keyboard, writing to memory and looking at the system clock.

A great many data processing activities are relegated to separate, essentially autonomous programs under the Unix system and other similar operating systems. Many, though not all, of these programs are directly visible to the user; they are stored in separate files, and the shell is able to interpret the file names as commands. The user normally issues instructions to the shell, and the shell arranges to have the desired programs executed under the supervision of the kernel. Since most users communicate only with the shell, not with the kernel, a knowledge of what the kernel contains and how it operates is not really necessary for most people. This chapter is directed primarily to those users who wish to know a little more about the inner structure of the system, as well as to others who may occasionally need to access some of its internals and need a brief guide to the much more complete information provided by the system manuals.

Nature of the Kernel

By its external appearance, the Unix operating system seems to be made up of two parts: a large set of programs, each one corresponding to a command; and the shell, which manages user commands and coordinates the running of programs. In an analogous fashion, operating systems of this type may be divided into two parts on the inside: a large set of service routines, which perform functions actually related to hardware and software tasks; and the kernel, which takes care of their interplay with the commands which the shell wishes to have executed. The service routines are invoked as needed, while the supervisor resides permanently in memory. It provides the basic software environment for practically everything that happens. This part is designed to occupy only a small amount of computer memory, so as to leave as much as possible to the running programs.

Functions of the Kernel

Most computer users are not very interested in the detailed structure of the machine hardware they employ for solving their problems, nor in the details of the operating system software. The Unix system caters to this common user preference by wrapping the kernel software in the shell, so that all external communication is addressed to a virtual Unix machine whose appearance is entirely that of the shell. The user rarely perceives the physical machine hidden beneath it.

The Unix kernel has an analogous role, but one level below the shell: it hides the physical machine from those programs and also from those sophisticated users who may from time to time require access to the lower-level system services. The kernel does so by creating a virtual machine whose characteristics resemble quite closely those of a broad class of physical machines. Real computers are then made to look like the virtual machine by interposing a few hundred or a few thousand lines of system programs. This structure is the key to creating portable operating systems. Since most of the system addresses itself to the virtual machine, it can be mounted on a new computer by rewriting the machine-level programs that convert the real machine into the virtual machine.

The virtual machine created by the kernel has three primary functions: (1) it schedules, coordinates, and manages process execution, (2) it provides system services such as input, output, and file management, (3) it handles machine hardware dependent operations. All three functions are related to the details of machine hardware structure.

Kernel Structure

The overall size of the kernel is around 10000 lines of program code, which translates into a greater or lesser number of machine words or bytes on different types of computer. The corresponding proportion of total Unix program code (shell, utilities, kernel, and all) may range from under 5% to over 10%. This figure is highly variable, not only because the kernel varies in size from machine to machine, but also because every installation contains a set of utility programs different from any other.

A substantial part of the kernel deals with memory management, including user scheduling and process scheduling. This part also keeps track of stack contents, machine register contents, and the various other environmental details when processes are swapped into memory. Furthermore, it responds to processor traps which may, for example, arise from hardware memory faults. This major portion of the kernel, some 7000–8000 lines of source code, is written in the C language, deals almost entirely with the virtual machine, and is therefore portable to any machine for which a C compiler can be found. Around 90% or even more of the kernel code is consequently the same in systems and system versions intended for broadly similar kinds of computer. The percentage is even higher for implementations involving similar machines and lower when comparing widely different hardware configurations.

Scheduling, memory management, and control of process execution are matters requiring extremely fast response. They are therefore handled by the permanently resident part of the kernel, or at least the necessary actions are initiated by the permanently resident part. On the other hand, the service routines are numerous and in some cases quite extensive, so they are loaded into memory only as needed.

Device drivers, the programs which actually address the writable and readable control and data registers in peripheral devices, handle interrupts raised by peripheral devices and effect error recovery. They form another substantial part of the kernel. Device drivers are entirely hardware dependent; after all, the whole object of a device driver is to write specific configurations of bits into particular hardware device registers! Most Unix device drivers are also written in the C language. The extent of the total device driver code in small systems may be around 1000 source lines, but it may rise much higher in systems with large numbers of different and complex peripheral devices.

The third important part of the kernel, and the only one totally written in assembler language for the particular computer in question, is a set of machine primitives. These are the true creators of the virtual machine. They invoke basic input/output operations (e.g., check whether there is a character in the line printer data register), switch execution between processes, enable or disable machine interrupts, reset interrupt priorities, and so on. These may amount to 1000 lines or so of assembler-language code. This number too is highly variable, depending on the complexity of the real computer and on how close is its natural resemblance to the virtual machine.

Machine Primitives and System Calls

Most of the time, Unix system users communicate with the kernel through the shell. This form of communication suffices if access is not required to the various internal facilities provided by the kernel. But the assembler-language programmer certainly needs to have direct access, for input and output if nothing else. The programmer in high-level languages may also find that he wishes to address himself directly to the system, in order to access the system clock, to attach a file to a program, or to perform one of the many other things that the system is clearly capable of but for which the high-level languages provide no specific commands.

System Calls

Most of the machine-dependent actions required to make a computer system perform are intrinsically quite simple, and those of the virtual machine created by the kernel are particularly so. They comprise actions such as

Initiate a new process.
Open a file for reading.
Write on a file.
Get system clock time.
Terminate running a process.
Change read, write, or execute permissions.

The entire list of system primitives extends to several dozen.

Access to the system primitive actions is through *system calls*. System calls are commands issued to the kernel. Internally each is implemented as a (usually quite short) program which fetches the necessary information, writes the desired word into a machine register, consults a table of files, etc. These programs are accessible to programs written in C, in much the manner of ordinary C functions. They can be made available to the Fortran 77 programmer through subroutine calls because the conventional Unix language processor structure handles Fortran 77 through the second pass of the C compiler. System calls are of course always possible from assembler-language programs.

The relative portability of Unix systems derives largely from the ability of C programs to issue system calls. Both the applications programmer and the systems programmer can do their work almost entirely in high-level languages, allowing machine dependence to be localized in the C compiler and the system primitives. As indicated in the chapter on language compilers, C is a language quite well suited to writing operating systems, for it is able to deal with entities at the machine word level.

Some of the more commonly employed system calls are briefly described in this chapter. They represent only the smallest tip of a very large iceberg, but most of the iceberg is usually of interest only to the true cognoscenti. For more information on what is available and on how to use system calls, a fairly serious session with the full *Unix Programmer's Manual* is recommended. Volume 1 in particular defines the actions performed by each system call and gives details of how they are accessed from both assembler language and C.

Errors from System Calls

Every system call has the ability to set an error number if an error should occur. In programs written in C, the error number is placed in the external variable *errno*, which must of course exist in the program. In assembler-language programs, the error number is returned in a manner that depends on the computer type; in PDP-11 systems, it is placed in register 0. Error numbers are only set if errors have occurred, they are not reset if there was no error. In other words, it is not sufficient to look at the variable *errno*; it is necessary to ascertain first whether an error has occurred at all. From C functions, an otherwise impossible function value (usually −1) is returned if there was an error. In assembler-language programs, errors are made to affect certain condition codes (in PDP-11's, the carry bit is set).

Process Coordination and Management

Under a multi-user operating system, many user programs can run at the same time. Of course, there is only one central processing unit in the computer, and only one program can really be running at a given instant; the phrase "at the same time" means that the several programs are allowed to be executed in an interleaved fashion, with brief bursts of central processor time allocated to each one in turn. Although only one user program may be actually running, several could be resident in memory at the same time if none is large enough to require all the available memory. In other words, two major responsibilities of the kernel are *process scheduling* and *memory management*. Process scheduling is, in essence, the sharing of time slices between competing processes. Memory management comprises sharing out the available slices of memory between processes and deciding whether and when to swap a process from memory to disk or back again.

Process Initiation

The normal way for a process to be initiated under the Unix operating system is through the action of another process: processes initiate other processes. When a user first logs in, the kernel sets a copy of the shell running for him, and if the user issues some command, say **who**, the shell finds and initiates **who**. In fact, there is no way for the user to initiate a process, other than to have it done by some other process which is already active. The natural result is a hierarchical structure of processes. The hierarchy is created by means of a mechanism called a *fork*. To fork, the kernel replaces an existing process by two, as in the sketch below: itself and another, newly initiated, process. The original process is called the *parent* process, the newly added one is called its *child*. The child generally shares all files with the parent process. Once forked, both processes run as if they were independent, unless a specific request is made for the parent process to wait until completion of the child process. Forking is accomplished by means of the system call `fork`, and a request to wait is communicated by the system call `wait`.

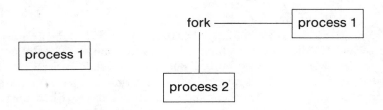

It is of course quite possible that the child process (process 2) may need to initiate yet another process. It can do so by forking again:

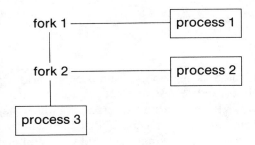

The new process (process 3) is regarded as a child of process 2. It will have access to files opened by the previous two processes, though they may not have access to files it has opened. The general rule is that files are always made accessible to processes lower down in the hierarchy.

When a user first logs in, the kernel initiates a copy of the shell to run as a process for him. To initiate process 1 above, the user must issue an appropriate command to the shell. The shell receives the user command, and responds by forking to initiate whatever process the user specified. As a result, process 3 would actually be executed in an overall structure such as sketched below:

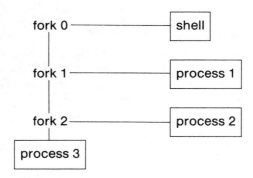

When new processes are initiated by the shell, the forking is normally arranged so that the shell waits for the process to complete. If it did not, the shell prompt would be issued immediately once the child process had been initiated, so that it would appear at the user terminal intermixed with the output of process 1. On the other hand, there are occasions when a job is to be run in the background without waiting. Such might be the case for a long program listing which can and should be printed without making the terminal user wait. The shell can then be instructed to spawn the new process and to continue without waiting (by appending an ampersand **&** to the shell command). More detail on forking and waiting will be found below.

Memory Allocation

Unix is both a multitasking and a multiprogramming operating system. That is to say, it not only keeps track of several concurrent tasks but also maintains control over several different programs which may reside in main memory at the same time, provided only that the memory is large enough. In normal operation, each program is loaded into a different area of main memory. Timesharing operation can then proceed without swapping the memory content onto disk. Each program can be made to run for its allocated slice of time in turn, remaining quiescent in memory when it is not running. Only the machine registers themselves are shared between programs, so that swapping programs really only amounts to swapping register contents. The system kernel is responsible for keeping track of which processes are considered active at any given time and which one is actually executing, deciding whether and when to swap, and determining where in memory to load newly initiated programs. When a process terminates, the kernel decides whether termination was normal (successful) and sets a success flag (the *exit status*) accordingly. This flag is a logical variable which can be examined and used by the shell.

Unix programs are generally set up in such a way as to have program instructions occupy a set of memory locations separate from any modifiable data and conversely, to have all writable data occupy locations separate from the program code. While running, processes are in fact allocated three distinct portions of machine memory: a *text segment*, a *data segment*, and a *stack segment*. The text segment contains pure code and is write-protected. The data segment contains all user-defined data, values of variables, etc. The stack segment contains all the system information that is required to keep the process intact when it is swapped in and out.

Making the program code and data separate achieves two useful goals. First, by swapping the text segment one way only, it reduces the quantity of information to be swapped. Since the text segment is open for reading only, it must always be an exact image of the user program initially available on disk; so there is no need to write it to disk when swapping the process out. Second, some programs such as the **ed** editor are used often, and in larger installations it often happens that several users need the same program at the same time. The shell, in fact, must exist in at least as many copies as there are users logged in, for a new shell is started for every user at login time. If two or more users need the same program text, there is no need to create duplicate copies of the text segment, for the text segment is guaranteed to be and remain identical in all copies. It suffices to create, and swap when needed, one writable data segment and one stack segment for each user. In the case of a complicated program like the shell, the writable segments are not at all large compared with the program code.

Time and Resource Sharing

In multitasking operating systems individual processes are not ordinarily allowed to run to completion, instead they are granted slices of processor time on a modified round-robin basis. It is not usual to grant them equal time slices in turn, because the needs of different processes may differ considerably.

The lengths of time slices granted to individual processes by the Unix system depend on a number of factors, among which task priority, availability of required input data, and availability of output devices are important. Some factors, e.g., task priority, can be decided and acted upon entirely by examining the process itself. Others are subject to modification by the needs of other processes (e.g., if input data are awaited from some other program) or the computer hardware (e.g., printer presently busy). Most operating systems therefore allocate time slices to individual tasks on some basis which seeks to maximize the use of hardware resources while respecting the priorities of critical tasks.

Time is allocated to competing processes under the Unix system in accordance with process priorities. Priorities assigned to processes are updated periodically, typically at intervals of a few seconds. At every updating interval, jobs with a high ratio of processor time to terminal time are downgraded in priority, while those requiring relatively less computing are upgraded. In this way, users with a great deal of interactive work (e.g., typing at the keyboard) have high priority and therefore should have nearly instant terminal response. Tasks with large amounts of actual computing, it is argued, are quite likely to keep someone waiting anyway, so there is no harm in making the wait a little longer. Following a similar argument, system-initiated tasks always have higher priority than user-initiated tasks. Because priorities are updated periodically, processes which change character will have the wrong priority for only a short time. For example, a computation-intensive task initially launched with high priority will quickly have its priority drop. Conversely, a user with initially low priority will tend to move into the foreground if his work requires little processing but a good deal of terminal input and output.

When the time allotted to a particular user has been used up and another's turn has come, the first user's program may need to be removed from main memory to make room for the second user's program. *Swapping out* is accomplished by writing into a disk file (the *swap file*) an image of the user process; when the user is swapped in again the swap file is read and the state of the computer is restored exactly as it was when the user was swapped out. In this way, the user program can resume precisely where it left off, having merely been delayed. The process image maintained in the swap file includes the contents of the user-writable parts of memory, the contents of the machine registers, the name of the directory currently in use, a list of open files, and a few other relevant items of information.

fork, execl, and wait

The fork system call permits a new process to be created, with both parent and child active. However, forking itself merely creates a new process, i.e., it enters a new process in the Unix system tables and lists it as active, but it does not actually set any program running. From C programs, fork is invoked in the simplest way imaginable,

    i = fork ();

The system call fork has no arguments and therefore knows neither whether a different program might be wanted nor what it might be. fork resolves this difficulty by merely making the second process an identical copy of the first. In other words, it creates a fork with two identical prongs. This procedure may seem a little curious, but it does have its own logic. Since the two processes are identical, there is no need to swap any program code in or out and no need to copy anything but writable data areas. Execution of another program is requested by another system call, which specifies what program is desired. There actually exists a range of half a dozen system calls for this purpose, which are essentially alike but differ a little in the way their arguments are presented. For example, execution of the program file *name* can be requested by C programs through

$$j = \text{execl } (name, arg1, arg2, ..., argn, 0)$$

where *name*, *arg1*, ..., *argn* are pointers to character strings which specify the program name and the names of its arguments. In response to **execl**, the kernel will cause the original program to be replaced (overwritten) by the new one. In other words, the sequence **fork–execl** first cheaply creates a copy of the parent process and then replaces the child with the program it is actually desired to run. Internally, the child process is regarded as not having been altered by the **execl** call, even though the instructions being executed and the data being worked on are no longer the same. For system management purposes, the process retains its process identification number, and has the same files open.

If it is desired to make the parent process wait until the child process has completed, the **wait** call may be issued, for example, in the form

$$k = \text{wait}(status)$$

where *status* is a pointer to an integer value. This call forces the parent process to hang, for returning to it is delayed until the child process terminates. On termination, the value of **k** is returned as the process identification number of the terminated child process.

A frequent application of **execl** is in program chaining. For example, a multipass assembler or compiler will ordinarily need to load the program and data areas of its first pass and to execute, then to proceed likewise with the second pass. Once the first pass has completed running, there is no longer any need to return to it. Overlaying the memory occupied by the first pass with the program and data areas of the second pass therefore makes good sense.

Many practical applications programs are large compared to the available real memory. Chaining, however, is not always practical, for the sequence in which parts of a program are required may be data-dependent. In such circumstances, the parent process can **fork** a child process with a request to **wait** until the child process is completed. The child process will exist as a swappable process, and therefore it has access to as much memory as the parent. The child process can **execl** the next program, causing itself to be overlaid. However, since the child process is considered to be still the same process for administrative purposes, control will return to the parent when the (modified and overlaid) child process has completed. Since the number of permissible concurrent processes is practically unlimited, this scheme allows execution of immensely large programs in relatively limited memory, provided that it is possible to subdivide the program text and data in such a way that each and every executable program fits within the memory limitations of the machine.

Input and Output Operations

So far as the shell is concerned, all input-output operations look like file operations; the shell does not recognize the existence of any peripheral devices. Indeed this equivalence of files and devices is a key characteristic of the shell command structure. However, this viewpoint cannot be appropriate for work involving the kernel because the kernel's job is precisely to hide the real physical devices behind the facade of apparent files.

Device Independence

Most present-day operating systems permit programs to access files on different physical volumes in a similar fashion, so that applications programs which read files can read any files on any volume or device. Systems with this characteristic are said to exhibit a high degree of *device independence*. Device independence is achieved by creating a fictitious physical machine which has the general appearance of a disk drive with numerous files and then writing all system programs as well as applications programs to communicate with files stored in this virtual device. Every real physical device naturally does not have all the assumed characteristics of the virtual device. Each physical device is therefore endowed with a special program, called a *device driver*, which translates the required actions of the virtual device into those of the real one. User programs can then communicate with any new device added to the system without any modification, provided that a device driver exists for it. The Unix system carries device independence to its logical conclusion, by making each and every physical device available on the system look to the user's programs as if it were simply a file. Because such files are somewhat different from user files, they are referred to as *special files*. Reasonably enough, special files have read and write permissions attached to them, as indeed they must; after all, the line printer is a write-only device, and all users must therefore be denied reading access.

First Level Interrupt Handling

Many events that occur in a multi-user computing system occur in real time and must be dealt with on the spot. Such events include, for example, a user pressing a key at the terminal keyboard. A keystroke may quite possibly be followed by another within a few milliseconds, and whatever action is to be taken in response to it must be taken within that length of time.

Events requiring immediate attention are signaled to the kernel through hardware. The appearance of such an event causes an *interrupt condition* to exist. Whatever program is currently running is halted at the end of the current machine instruction cycle, and control is transferred to another, usually very small, program called an *interrupt service routine*. The interrupt service routine determines the cause of the interrupt, does whatever is necessary in response, and thereafter returns control to the program that was executing previously. Servicing an interrupt is thus an action somewhat similar to executing a subroutine—the principal program is left waiting while some other calculation is carried out. Unlike a subroutine, an interrupt service routine is initiated by hardware and executed asynchronously, in response to some external event.

Since a multi-user installation may contain a substantial number of terminals and each terminal might send out characters separated by only a few milliseconds, the time available for dealing with interrupts is small. Keyboard input is therefore handled in a two-level fashion by almost all operating systems. The first-level interrupt handler merely collects the newly arrived keyboard character, examines it so see whether it is one of the special characters to which immediate response is required (e.g., DELETE), places it in a keyboard buffer area for later attention, and echoes it to the terminal. The time taken for these actions might amount to a few dozen or a few hundred microseconds, depending on the type of computer. The user can easily gain the impression that the characters are merely stored at the terminal, so fast is the echo sent by the interrupt handler. Even several users typing along furiously will leave quite enough machine time for other processes to run.

If the first-level interrupt handler finds that the character typed at the keyboard requires action, a second level of activity is called into play: the action required is identified and carried out. For example, if an end-of-line character is received from a terminal, the input line is examined for *kill* and *erase* characters, and any necessary editing is done. The processed text is then placed in another queue from which it is sent on to the program expecting input. This process is likely to take much longer than a simple storage of commands.

Special Files: Block and Character

Special files are of two generic varieties: block and character. Prototypes of these are disk files and terminals, respectively. In other words, two kinds of peripheral devices are recognized: disk-like and terminal-like. Devices which are neither are made to look like one or the other to the system, and the system in turn strives to make all devices look like files to the user.

Block input–output is arranged through a pool of data buffers. Typically a dozen or more buffers may be in use. In normal operation, none are permanently dedicated to any particular user; rather they are allocated as required. When a process requests input, the kernel searches the buffers for the desired data. If the text requested is resident in a buffer, it is communicated to the process without any data transfers between memory and disk having to take place. Correspondingly, a request to write is understood to mean writing into the buffer. The buffer content is actually transferred only at a later time when the buffer is needed for some other purpose or when an explicit request is made to flush buffers. Since the buffers are not earmarked for any particular user, output buffer contents are not transferred as soon as each buffer is full but rather when all buffers are full and more buffer space is requested by some process. The input buffers are generally kept filled by doing a good deal of reading ahead, and output operations can involve delayed writing. Input–output operations are thus generally performed asynchronously with the program, so that programs do not very often need to wait for data transfers.

Character oriented input–output operations by Unix device drivers are of the classical mold: the driver deals with individual characters which it either passes on or else recognizes as having particular meanings. As a simple example, a *newline* character, which denotes the end of a line in a Unix file, must be recognized and transmitted to a terminal as a sequence of two characters, *carriage-return* followed by a *line-feed*. Similarly, terminals unable to tab to a particular column must be sent an appropriate number of blank spaces, and terminals unable to skip pages must be sent the right number of blank lines in place of a *form-feed* character. These substitutions all take place in the device driver.

Block input–output devices require only simple device driver programs, for all operations are directed to buffers which have a highly standard form. By contrast, character devices need fairly complex drivers but can make do with less sophistication in the buffer management software.

Unix input–output arrangements are generally transparent to the user and appear to be program synchronous, i.e., input is read and output is produced in exactly the sequence one would expect from reading a listing of the program. In case of system malfunction, however, the complexities of the relatively complicated buffering scheme can sometimes be annoying. For example, output may sometimes be delayed or lost because it is still resident in buffers and hence not printed, although completely terminated as far as the program is concerned.

Physical Structure of Files

Generally, the user need not be at all concerned about the physical structure of files because the Unix system makes every file appear to the user as a simple contiguous byte (or character) string. However, there are some occasions when even a rudimentary knowledge of the physical file structure allows better applications programs to be written. Besides, some users are interested as a matter of simple curiosity.

Disk files under the Unix system are physically organized into packets or *blocks* of 512 bytes. Every file is allocated an integral number of blocks, and every block begins at a multiple of 512 bytes from the beginning of the file. However, successive blocks of a file are not necessarily contiguous on the disk; they may reside anywhere at all. This file organization contrasts with many other small computer operating systems, which allocate space in one single area of disk or in a very few contiguous disk areas. The advantage gained is that no file compaction or "garbage collection" is ever needed. In fact, the speed advantages of contiguous space allocation remain largely valid for Unix files, since contiguous space is used when it is available. Fragmentation of disk space, with every file spreading all over the disk in little pieces, occurs only when the disk is very full. But it is hardly necessary to point out that the management of files scattered about in penny packets is trickier than constructing simple tables of contents for contiguous files.

Ordinary files and directory files may be classified into four different size classes, occupying at most 10, 138, 16522, and 2113674 blocks of file space. The reason for this curious classification is that space is provided for 13 actual block numbers, which are used to access data. The method of access is described below.

Storage of small files is straightforward enough. If a file occupies ten blocks or fewer, the spaces provided in the system tables are used simply to house the actual block numbers. For example, a file that requires three blocks might have the 13 block numbers given as 07526, 16201, 01004, 00000, 00000, 00000, ... , 00000. The first three denote actual block addresses of the file blocks as they exist on the disk; zeros show unused space. Up to ten blocks are addressed in this way, the last three words being reserved. This scheme is beautifully simple but only allows small files. Ten file blocks are only 5120 bytes, about two or three typewritten pages.

Larger files are stored by means of an indirect addressing scheme. The first 10 of the 13 block address words are used to point to file blocks which contain data, exactly as if a small file were being stored. The eleventh address points not to data but to a block containing the addresses of up to 128 further file blocks. The desired data are stored in those further blocks. Since there can be up to 128 further blocks, files up to $10 + 128 = 138$ blocks, or 70,656 bytes, can be stored in this way. In other words, the first 10 blocks are addressed directly, the next 128 are addressed indirectly via the thirteenth block. This chapter is approximately 50,000 bytes long.

To store still larger files, a second level of indirect addressing is employed. The first eleven addressing words are used exactly as described above, but the twelfth is used to point to a block which contains the addresses of up to 128 blocks, which in turn contain the addresses of up to

128 data blocks each. The number of additional data blocks made accessible this way is clearly 16,384 (128^2), so that the total accessible data space is $10 + 128 + 16,384 = 16,522$ blocks, or roughly eight megabytes (about 12 copies of this book).

The largest files are arranged in a similar fashion, but the thirteenth addressing word is used in a triple-indirect addressing scheme. The amount of additional space made available in this way is 2,097,152 (128^3) blocks, so that the largest possible file is approximately one gigabyte in size.

Directories are treated in the same way as ordinary files, though it is unusual to find directories growing quite so large; most users tend to structure their files hierarchically, with successive subdirectories perhaps one or two dozen entries in size. It is usual to keep directories to a size convenient to display on the teminal screen at one time.

In the case of special files, the first of the 13 block addresses has a different significance. The first byte of this word is viewed as the identification of a physical *device type* (e.g., magnetic tape drive), the second is regarded as the identification of a *subdevice number* (e.g., tape drive number 7). In any case, special files are very unlikely to grow to megabyte size!

System Calls for File Access

Before a program can read or write to a file, the file must be opened or, if it did not previously exist, created. Similarly, a file should be closed before exiting a program which opened it; in a number of circumstances, harm to the file could otherwise result. These actions are achieved at kernel level by the system calls **open**, **close**, and **creat**.

File opening is done by means of the **open** and/or **creat** system calls. In C programs, these calls can appear as function invocations, e.g.,

    i = open (*name*, *mode*)

or

    i = creat (*name*, *mode*)

where *name* is a pointer to a character string which contains the file name and *mode* is an integer which indicates whether the file is to be opened for reading only (*mode* = 0), writing only (*mode* = 1), or both (*mode* = 2). The function value returned by **open** is a nonnegative integer called the *file descriptor*, i.e., the file number in the internal system table that keeps track of open files. All further system calls dealing with the file must refer to it by this file descriptor. For example, closing the file is achieved by

    j = close (*i*)

i being the file descriptor of the file to be closed.

Two basic system calls are provided for file reading and writing: **read** and **write**. These transfer a specified number of characters from a file (which could be a special file, such as a peripheral device driver) to a specified memory area. The file to be accessed must be opened beforehand, and the file is referred to by its file descriptor. These calls take the form

> i = `read` (*fildes*, *buffer*, *nchar*)

or

> j = `write` (*fildes*, *buffer*, *nchar*)

where *fildes* is the file descriptor, *buffer* is a pointer which points to the start of the character buffer area in memory, and *nchar* is the number of characters to be read or written. The function value returned by either call is the number of characters actually transferred; it might well be smaller than *nchar* if, for example, the file contained fewer characters than were requested by a `read`.

A Unix file is simply a string of bytes, terminated by an end-of-file mark (control-D). An `open` call opens a file and sets a pointer to point at the very first byte; a `read` call reads bytes, and moves the pointer the number of bytes read. Any subsequent `read` begins reading wherever the pointer last came to rest and moves it on by the number of bytes read. Writing operations move the pointer in a similar fashion. Files thus generally have the logical appearance of being sequential. If some part of a file needs to be accessed in a nonsequential fashion, it suffices to reposition the pointer in the appropriate place, for any subsequent reading or writing operations will then proceed from the new pointer position. Repositioning is done by means of the `lseek` system call, issued in the form

> i = `lseek` (*fildes*, *bytes*, *where*)

Here *fildes* is the file descriptor, and *bytes* is a long integer which indicates the desired pointer placement in the file. The manner of placement depends on the value of the integer *where*. The pointer may be placed at the actual location specified by *bytes* (*where* = 0), or *bytes* may be added to the present pointer location (*where* = 1); or the pointer may be set to a place *bytes* past the end of the file (*where* = 2), thereby increasing the size of the file. The value i returned by the `lseek` call is the pointer location after the execution of whichever movement was requested.

Few programmers in high-level languages have frequent cause to write or read through system calls. The assembler-language programmer has no choice: there is no other practical way to access files or other input–output devices.

Standard File Assignments

Certain file descriptors are allocated by default under the Unix operating system. File 0 refers to the standard input file, which is the terminal keyboard by default. File 1 is the standard output file, usually the terminal screen by default. File 2 is normally attached to the terminal input screen also. It serves for handling error messages and diagnostic information issued by the system. Having this file separate from the standard output permits system messages to appear on the terminal screen even if the standard output has been diverted to a disk file or printer.

The default file assignments are actually set up by the shell. Since the shell is merely another process, the normal rules on forking apply to the shell. In particular, any files opened by the shell are accessible to any process spawned by the shell and therefore also to all its children, their children, etc. The standard file assignments of the parent process are therefore carried through to all of its descendants.

File Identification

Directory entries in Unix directories only identify files by giving an index number (called the *i-number* in Unix system programming jargon) for each file. The index numbers for any given physical volume (disk, tape, etc.) are actually pointers to another table, called the *i-list*, which resides on the same device.

The i-list of a given device contains a set of entries called *i-nodes*; for this reason, the i-list is sometimes referred to as the *inode table*. An i-node is a set of data, which contains the following information regarding each file:

1) the identifying number of the user who created the file,
2) the protection status of the file (read-only, open, etc.),
3) thirteen words showing device blocks occupied by the file,
4) the size of the file,
5) the time the file was last modified,
6) the number of times the file is referred to in directories,
7) bits to identify directories, special files, and large files.

Keeping track of the number of times the file is listed in directories is important, because a nondirectory file may appear in the directories of several users. If one of them wishes to remove the file from his directory, only the directory entry should be removed if there are any other directories in which the file still appears. On the other hand, the actual file itself should be purged (the file space should be released for other use) if the last user of the file removes it.

There are some occasions on which users may wish to inspect the actual i-numbers associated with files, usually because information regarding disk space is needed. The i-numbers are available through the usual ls command, invoked with the −i option. This option provides the listing that would normally be expected from ls, augmented by the i-number corresponding to each file name. These name-to-number correspondences are called *links* and serve as the main file identification and management tool. In principle, the mv command moves a link, rm removes one, and ln creates a new one. This fact may explain the curious command names employed for file deletion, renaming, and synonym creation.

Chapter 6

Facilities and Utilities

The Unix operating system provides a large number of utility routines for performing computations, communicating with other users, and handling files. Many of these utilities are so important as to merit a chapter of their own (as in the case of the shell program) or to deserve at least a large part of a chapter (as in the case of **ed**). Others appear in context with the shell, language compilers, or files. However, there are still others of very considerable use which do not naturally belong in another chapter of this book. They have been collected together here, as a miscellany of handy items.

Communications

Under the Unix system and other similar operating systems, facilities are provided for the system manager to communicate with users and for users to communicate with each other. Two forms of communication are provided: mail and immediate messages. In principle, these message-passing channels are analogous to the post office and the telephone company. One leaves messages in a mailbox for later collection, while the other sends messages directly, but risks that no one will answer the phone.

Mail Services

Every user is assigned a file called his *mailbox*, which is not part of his directory structure (it actually resides in file **/usr / spool / mail** in most systems) but which he can read using the **mail** command. The same command makes it possible to write into another user's mailbox, thereby leaving messages there for later collection.

Most Unix systems are set up so as to tell every user when logging in whether there is any new mail waiting. If desired, the system can also be set up to delete old mail when the intended recipient has read it—it is then up to the user to save it if he prefers. Such automatic deletion is considered desirable in systems with large numbers of users relative to the available disk space; it tends to economize on space by leaving little unused trash on disk. Whenever a message is added to the mailbox file, the system notes that an unread message exists. It then informs the user at login time, by means of a message preceding the first appearance of the shell prompt:

```
you have mail
$
```

When the user reads the message in his mailbox, the system notes that he has read it, so there no longer exists any unread mail. The *you have mail* message will then not appear at the next login, unless of course another new message has actually been placed in the mailbox in the meantime.

The message regarding mail is sent out at the conclusion of the login procedure, and before the shell is started running. Thus the message will only appear once, preceding the first appearance of the shell prompt. Any further **$** prompts will appear without the mail message, as usual.

To read mail, the user enters the command **mail**. In response, **mail** fetches messages from his mailbox and displays them one at a time, the most recent one first. For example,

```
$ mail
From bftsplk Thu Feb 29 11:29:44 1984
check your files, I may have wrecked some by
   accident
```

Every piece of mail is stamped with its time and date of transmission, exactly like ordinary post office mail. The name of the sender is also affixed to each message.

When the addressee looks at his mail, only one message is displayed at a time; it is followed by an enquiry as to how the message is to be disposed of. Its recipient may simply make a mental note of the message. He may have it deleted, or ask for it to be saved. In fact, quite a wide range of choices is open to the user: the message may be saved with or without the header (postmark), mailed on to someone else, repeated (useful for long messages), or retained in the mailbox. The most usual response is for the user to send a blank line (by simply striking the RETURN key) to signify that he wishes to go on to the next message.

The **mail** command permits a few options, of which the most useful are **-r** (reverse order) and **-q** (exit any time, without changing mailbox contents, by sending a DELETE or RUBOUT).

Sending Mail

Any user may send mail to another, again by means of the `mail` command. To do so, the addressee's name is appended to the command, as in the following message sent to user *bftsplk*:

```
$ mail bftsplk
Which files do you suspect?
All my directories look OK.
```

The `mail` command line is followed by the message to be sent. It is perfectly all right to send more than one line; the message is considered terminated whenever either a control-D character is sent or whenever a period (the . character) occurs on a line by itself. However, it is usually wise to keep messages reasonably short. The entire message is displayed on the terminal screen at once when the recipient looks at his mail, so that long messages (more than a screenful) can be difficult to read.

Mail may be sent to more than one recipient at a time by listing the names of all the recipients in the command line. It should be noted that all mail handling is done by the user login name; obviously, it is impossible to send anybody a message if his login name is not known. The login name thus plays the same role here as do name and address at the post office. If a nonexistent login name is given in the command, `mail` may reply with an error message or (in some systems) simply ignore the command. If a message is addressed to the wrong login name, it is delivered as addressed.

A user is permitted to address mail to himself. The procedure for doing so is precisely the same as for sending to any other system user. Many users like sending messages to themselves, as reminder notes to remove unneeded files or to take action in some other matter. However, there is a basic danger here: when greeted by the *you have mail* message, it is tempting to assume the mail consists of the reminder note and not to bother reading it. Real mail from other users may thus become lost or at any rate ignored.

Immediate Messages

In addition to mail, which is deposited in a mailbox for later collection, system users may send messages directly to other users by means of the `write` command. Such messages are not placed in the intended recipient's mailbox, instead they are immediately transmitted to his terminal. Naturally, such direct transmission is only possible if the addressee is actually logged in at the time. The `who` command may be used to determine whether the addressee is logged in and at which terminal (or terminals). Attempts to write to nonexistent users or to users not logged in generally result in an error message and no communication.

To send a message to another user, one employs the **write** command, which works somewhat like sending **mail**:

```
$ write abner
Please check your files.
I may have corrupted some by mistake.
```

In contrast to the **mail** command, **write** transmits every message line immediately when the RETURN key is pressed. The **write** command line itself causes display of a line which identifies the sender, e.g.,

```
message from bftsplk tty6
Please check your files.
I may have corrupted some by mistake.
```

Transmission initiated by **write** overrides whatever else the addressee may have been doing, and each transmitted line is displayed at his terminal even if that puts it in the middle, say, of a directory listing he may have been trying to read.

Once the **write** program has been set running, any lines typed at the keyboard will be transmitted to the addressee. Transmission is turned off by sending a control-D and thereby exiting from **write**. This control-D will not cause logout, merely exit from **write**. Once the **write** program is running, it takes two successive control-D's to log out: one to exit from **write**, and one more to exit from **sh**.

If a user is logged in at more than one terminal at the same time, it is possible to indicate in the command line which terminal the messages are to be sent to. For example,

```
$ write bftsplk tty6
```

will display the transmitted lines at terminal *tty*6, but not at any other terminals where user *bftsplk* may also be logged in.

Two-Way Communication

When a message is received from another user logged in on the system, it is natural to reply immediately. But doing so is a little tricky, because only one user can be transmitting at a time. Two-way communication thus resembles radio rather more than the telephone, for it is important to let the recipient know when the other fellow is prepared to listen for an answer and when he intends to keep on talking. One widely used method is to employ the word *over*, usually abbreviated to **-o -**, to signify "I will now listen for a reply", the words *over and out* (**-oo -** for short) to mean "I have finished and will neither transmit nor listen". A conversation may then look (from one end) like

```
$ write abner
Please check your files.
I may have corrupted some by mistake. -o-
message from abner tty3
Which files do you suspect?
All my directories look OK. -o-
Glad all is well, thanks for checking! -oo-
```

The words **message from ...** signify that the other user has also started up a copy of **write**. They will only occur once at the startup of that program, not between every pair of messages.

Avoiding Messages

There are times when a critical job is running and no messages are wanted from anyone. Some sensitive processes (for example, the **nroff** text for-matter) disable the message facilities automatically whenever they are initiated. However, users may block the message-passing channel at any time by means of the **mesg** command. Blocking is achieved by

```
$ mesg n
```

where the **n** indicates "no". To turn messages on again, the same command is issued, but this time with a **y** (for "yes") argument replacing **n**. Blocked messages are not saved for later presentation to the intended recipient, they are discarded. If **mail** may be considered analogous to the postal service, then **write** and **mesg** represent a sort of telephone. If nobody answers, the message is simply not communicated.

File Management

The Unix family of operating systems provides a rich selection of file management tools applicable to text files. In fact most of the common operations users may wish to perform on files require no programming; they are already provided as system programs, and the user need only ask for them. Where more complicated operations are needed, the programmability of the shell and the provision of pipes may be brought into play to combine various operations available from the individual programs, so as to create new and unexpected combinations—all without any programming effort other than that expended on constructing a shell command file.

File management programs may be classified into three very broad categories: those which copy and print files, those which combine or separate files, and those which measure the characteristics of files.

Copying and Printing Files

Making copies of files, one or several at a time, in disk file form or as printed copy, is one of the most elementary operations of file management. There are various ways of doing so. The most useful commands for this simple kind of file management are

cat   which concatenates files,
cp   which copies a file, or several files,
lpr   which sends a file to the line printer spooler,
pr   which prints and paginates files.

cp is very straightforward: if one issues the command

   $ cp *file1 file2*

file1 is copied, the copy being named *file2*. Full pathnames may of course be given, so that the two files need not be within the same directory. When making copies, it will pay to remember that cp will quite happily replace an old file named *file2* by overwriting. In fact cp always destroys first and writes afterward; care should be taken not to make mistakes in file names!

To copy files from one directory to another, a variant form of the cp command is available, which avoids the necessity of typing full pathnames both times. In the variant form, it is sufficient to name the files to be copied, and the directory to which they are to be copied. Copies in both directories will then have the same file name, though of course the full pathnames will differ.

It is important not to confuse cp with mv or ln. cp makes an actual copy, so that after the operation there are two real copies of the file occupying physical space on the disk. mv, on the other hand, merely renames the existing copy; no data transfer takes place. ln establishes two or more synonymous names but retains only the original physical copy of the file. After an ln operation, there will be two or more directory entries for the file, though only a single file will actually exist. Directory entries (links) are allowed only if both the directory and the file reside on the same physical device (e.g., the same magnetic tape) or if the device is permanently attached to the Unix system (e.g., the permanent system disk drives). But cp, which makes physical copies, can be used to copy across devices.

To avoid the irreparable loss of precious files that might occur in a power failure or other computer malfunction, it is a good idea to make backup copies of files from time to time. These should preferably reside on a removable medium such as floppy disk or magnetic tape, which can be physically removed from the computer. After all, the building might burn one day!

The **cat** command sends a copy of one or more files to the standard output device. Thus a file is easily inspected by the simple command

    $ cat *file1*

Naming several files in the **cat** command merely produces a concatenation of the files in the standard output. The files will be concatenated in the order that they are named in the command. **cat** may be made to perform much of the work of **cp** by suitably redirecting input and output. In fact, **cat** may be used to turn the whole Unix system into a rather large electric typewriter by taking its input from the keyboard and directing its output to the printer.

When files are displayed at the terminal, lines are ordinarily scrolled up from the bottom to the top of the screen, and the top line is discarded. When large files are displayed, the inconvenience of losing the top line may be avoided by stopping the display scrolling. A control-S character sent from the keyboard at any time will halt transmission of more lines to the terminal, thereby stopping scrolling; a control-Q will restart transmission.

To print a file, **cat** may be used by redirecting the standard output to the line printer. However, **cat** merely echoes the exact file content; to obtain tidy file listings, it is usually more convenient to use **pr**, which breaks up large files neatly into numbered and dated pages. The output of **pr** is sent to the standard output device, so that the word *print* should really be understood to mean *display*; no printed output will be obtained unless a printing terminal is in use. The **lpr** command should normally be used to obtain listings of programs or of long files, for it is both fast and convenient. **lpr** directs the output to the line printer. However, it does not wait for the printing to proceed. Instead, it deposits the text to be printed into a special printer queue, from which the line printer is fed as it finishes jobs. Thus the user may send a file to be printed, using **lpr**, even though the line printer is busy with a very large job and will not actually be available to do the printing for an hour or more. The **lpr** command will send an image of the desired printout to the queue, from which it will be taken and printed automatically when its turn comes—even if the user has long since logged out and gone home.

File Sorting

One major sorting program, called **sort**, which is very comprehensive and flexible, is standard equipment in all Unix systems. **sort** expects input organized as lines and sorts the lines into sequential order. There are no particular requirements as to what the lines should contain, so **sort** can be applied to text files, numeric data, or even to nonprintable files containing anything at all. In its simplest usage, one invokes it by

> **$ sort** *filename*

and *filename* ends up sorted. Order is determined by the standard ASCII code for characters, so that alphabetic characters are sorted into alphabetic order while numerics are sorted into ascending order. (A table of the ASCII character codes is given at the end of this chapter.) The ASCII character set includes not only the alphabetics and numerals but punctuation marks and special characters, so these will be sorted too.

It is important to note that **sort** replaces the original file with a file containing the sorted lines. No copy of the original file is kept; if one is needed, it is up to the user to make a copy before requesting a **sort**.

Sorting can be carried out according to a fabulous variety of criteria. First, characters may be sorted in different ways. It is possible to force "dictionary" sorting, i.e., to ignore all characters except alphabetics, numerals, and blanks. It is possible also to ignore the distinction between upper and lower case. White space (blanks and tab characters) can be ignored if desired. Duplicated lines can be eliminated, and lines can be sorted into reversed as well as natural order. These possibilities are exercised through options specified in the **sort** command. For example,

> **$ sort -ubdfr** *filename*

will dictionary sort (**d** option) *filename* in reverse (**r**) order, ignoring blanks and tabs (**b**) while eliminating other than unique lines (**u**); upper and lower case will be considered equivalent (**f** option).

Sorting can be carried out using only parts of a line. In general, **sort** considers a line to be made up of a set of *fields*. A field is a string of characters, with a minimum width of one character. Fields are considered to be demarcated by a *separator character*, which is normally the blank character but can be set to be any other character by means of the −t⟨*character*⟩ option, which makes ⟨*character*⟩ into the field separator. **sort** can be instructed to skip one or more fields at the start of a line and to ignore all fields following some subsequent one. For example,

> **$ sort -t∗ +2 -4** *filename*

will begin sorting (+) after field 2 (i.e., with the third field) and will ignore (−) everything in the fourth field and thereafter; in other words, only the third field will be considered. Fields will be taken as defined by the ∗ (asterisk) character.

Even within a field, initial characters can be ignored so as to refine sorting still further. For example,

> **$ sort -t∗ +2.1 -4** *filename*

performs exactly as above, except that the sorting only starts at the second character of the third field, one character having been ignored. In other words, the specifier **+2.1** is interpreted as meaning "skip two full fields and then skip another character position." Such a specification can make it possible, for example, to sort a price list while ignoring the dollar sign that precedes each price.

Sorting can be carried out on a set of key fields, not merely a single one. Furthermore, each key field can have a string of options attached. Very complicated sorting procedures can be designed in this way, e.g., ignoring blanks in one field but not another or sorting by item type first and price subsequently.

The **sort** command can be employed to merge files if the **-m** option is specified. Together with the **-u** ("unique", i.e., eliminate duplications) option, it can be used for tasks such as merging mailing lists, indeed for updating them, since the entry retained is always the one first encountered.

Comparing Files

Two distinct commands are available for comparing two files: **diff** and **cmp**. Most users probably find **diff** to be the more useful, since its output is richer and primarily intended to be human readable; the output of **cmp** is numeric and may be better suited to some machine processing operations.

diff compares two files on a line-by-line basis, looking forward and backward in an attempt to spot where the common ground lies. It keeps two line counters, one for each file, and tells the user how the lines correspond. The correspondence is expressed in algorithmic terms, i.e., **diff** tells the user what should be done to turn one file into the other. The command

   $ diff *file1 file2*

will produce instructions on how to modify *file1* so as to make it identical to *file2*. The modifications are typically in the form of two line counter readings and a single-character instruction, followed by a line. For example,

   $ diff *file1 file2*
   9d8
   < this ninth line of the file
   . . . .

indicates that the first difference between the two files occurs at line 9 of *file1*; it is necessary to delete (**d**) line 9 of *file1* so as to make the files identical at line 8 of *file2*. The actual line to be deleted is then shown. In other words, **diff** produces a set of editing instructions which will allow one file to be recreated from the other. It is possible to ask **diff** to produce an editing script in either direction, i.e., to list the changes required to produce either file from the other.

A very interesting feature of di f f is that there exist two formats of output. One, illustrated above, is readily comprehensible for people. The other is possible, but not quite so easy, to read; it is in the form of a set of instructions to the ed editor. It may be used to recreate *file2* (by means of ed itself) from *file1*:

> $ **diff** *file1 file2* **>** *differnc*
> $ **rm** *file2*

If *file1* is large, the space required for saving *file1* and the editing script *differnc* will amount to only a little more than *file1* itself. A great deal of economy can thus be effected in use of disk space—for example, in program debugging where quite a few editing operations may be needed but each involves only a few lines. In effect, it becomes possible to save a whole lot of intermediate versions of the program source code in little more disk space than is required by the original version itself.

The **cmp** command also compares two files, but it does not yield an editing script. Instead, it lists (in numeric form) the precise places where differences were found.

Filtering Files

As used by the *Unix Programmer's Manual*, the term *filtering* refers to the extraction of specific lines from a file or the copying of a file with certain types of lines removed. There are three principal filtering mechanisms provided: **comm**, **uniq**, and **grep**.

comm compares two files, both supposed to have been sorted into sequence with **sort** or some equivalent process, and looks for differences. It could be regarded as a highly specialized version of **di f f**, which does not produce an editing script. Instead, it filters its input lines into three columns of output: those unique to file 1, those unique to file 2, and those contained in both files. In other words, if the files are regarded as sets of lines, **comm** locates the intersection of both (column 3) and the exclusions both ways (columns 1 and 2). When output is produced, any one or two columns may be suppressed. Suppressing all three columns is also possible, but then there will be no output at all.

In contrast, **uniq** works on a single file. It compares successive pairs of lines and spots repeated lines. The output consists of the input file, but with repetitions eliminated, or it can be made to contain only the lines repeated two or more times. In order to work fast, **uniq** only compares adjacent lines, so that any files to be processed should be sorted with **sort** first. In a certain sense, **uniq** may be regarded as highly specialized version of **sort**, for the comparison operations it must carry out are somewhat similar. Like sort, it can be made to ignore leading blanks, to compare part of the line only, and to ignore segments of input lines. However, its searching arrangements are not quite so sophisticated as those of sort.

The grep command works on a single input stream, which may consist of a single file or a sequence of several files. It finds the lines that contain a particular character string, and it takes some action when such are found. Its basic action is simply to display the line, but variations are possible. One may count the line toward a total but not display it; one may also display or count all lines which do not contain the required string. As in sort, distinctions between upper and lower case can be suppressed, in which case "grep", "Grep", and "GREP" are considered to match.

Because the input to grep may consist of a whole sequence of files—keeping in mind that wild-card file names can cover very large numbers of files—it can be very useful for identifying all documents containing a particular string. Such could include, for example, all those Fortran programs containing a given variable or all letters signed by a particular person.

Determining File Size

File size is generally of interest and may be measured in two distinct ways. In the case of a text file, the number of lines, words, or characters may be of value as indices of its overall length. On the other hand, lines and words do not make much sense for a file containing data or executable programs. In such cases, the most important index of size is probably the amount of disk space occupied by the file. Commands exist for both forms of size assessment.

For readable files, the wc command may be used to produce a word count. wc also counts lines and characters and outputs the number of lines, words, and characters (in that order). Like most other Unix system utilities, it is able to accept input streams consisting of numerous files or indeed file specifications containing wild cards. Line and word counts can therefore be produced for numerous files by a single command. For example,

```
$ wc chapt*
850 6227 32261 chapt1
662 4591 20834 chapt2
```

yields the word count for all files in the current working directory beginning with the character string chapt.

When nroff files are processed by wc, some confusion may arise between word counts that include nroff commands and the true net word count. If the difference is likely to be significant, the net word count may be found by piping nroff output directly into wc. Although the processor time will be increased thereby (since nroff itself must process the text), no intermediate disk files are created by the pipeline.

For files of any kind at all, readable or otherwise, the du command may be employed to determine the amount of disk space used. The space used is reported by du in terms of 512-byte blocks. Block counts may be requested either for files or for directories. If the block count is requested for a directory, the result is returned for that directory and for all its subdirectories as well. There does exist an option (-a) which also gives the block sizes for every file listed in the directory and its subdirectories.

The complementary question, How much disk space is there left?—is of particular significance with removable file volumes, such as floppy disks. The df command permits enquiring after the space remaining on a particular device; again, the answer is reported in terms of 512-byte blocks.

Other General Utilities

In addition to the file-handling utilities listed above, Unix systems incorporate a large number of other very convenient items. It is never easy to determine which will please most users by satisfying a real need and which might be regarded as luxuries. The following list therefore includes only a relatively small number of commands, all likely to be thought nearer to the necessary than to the frivolous.

Timed Requests

Because it is a timesharing multitasking operating system, it is quite inconceivable that any Unix system could be run without a time clock. The user may access this clock in two ways: by examining the clock and by asking the system to keep an eye on the clock for him.

The usual way of looking at the clock is through the date command, which causes the current day, date, and time to be displayed in the standard output. Time is given to the nearest second. In addition to serving a useful purpose for people who do not wear watches, date is often employed in shell scripts for date-stamping processes. By redirecting the output of date into a file along with other program outputs, the time and date of file creation can be recorded automatically.

One reason users are interested in clock times is to find out the execution speed of individual programs. It is not really convenient to determine execution times by asking for the clock time before and after; in fact the answers are quite likely to be wrong because date reports the clock time, not the processor time devoted to that particular program. With many users on the system, the difference could be extremely large. A tidier and more accurate procedure is to ask the system to do the timings, by means of the `time` command. On requesting

$ `time` *command*

command will be executed, and its execution time will be monitored. Unavoidably, the result may still be a bit inaccurate if there are many other users on the system and the process has to be swapped in and out several times.

The accuracy of the time given by the system clock depends on the type of computer hardware used. Many small systems simply use the power line to generate clock pulses, so that the time accuracy is exactly that of an electric wall clock. A more critical point is that the system manager may well have just set the clock by a wristwatch when bringing up the system; the clock time is then as reliable as the system manager's watch.

Users can ask the kernel to keep an eye on the clock and to do some operation at a specified future time. Since "clock" in this context includes "calendar," the delay times requested can in some cases be quite long. Examples might range from writing a message at the user terminal after a half-hour, as a reminder of the time, to the automatic removal of unused files at the end of the month. The `at` command is used to this purpose. Its general form is

$ `at` *time file*

file will be used as input to the shell at *time*. In other words, *file* contains the sequence of shell commands to be executed at the time *time* specified in the command. The commands might include almost anything, even another `at` command to set up another timed process.

Execution of `at` commands does not actually take place at exactly the time specified. The kernel periodically looks for pending `at` commands and executes them if their time is due or overdue and if they have not been executed yet. In other words, `at` processes are picked up on a specified schedule, each time taking those processes which are currently waiting, much as a bus picks up waiting passengers. The time specified in the `at` command is not the exact time of execution but rather the time at which the process is set waiting for the next scheduled time (the time of joining the bus queue, as it were, not the time the bus is scheduled to come). An `at` process may therefore execute at the set time or a bit later, depending on the frequency with which the local system handles such processes. Delays of minutes, even of a quarter or half an hour, may occur in some installations. If there is any reason for concern, the system manager should be consulted to find out how often waiting `at` processes are disposed of.

System Documentation

Substantial sections of the *Unix Programmer's Manual*, the defining document for the Version 7 system release, are furnished in machine-readable form, as an `nroff` text file. These sections may be consulted by users by invoking the `man` command. For example,

    $ man date

will produce at the terminal the manual description of the `date` command. If required, this description can of course be redirected to the line printer, so as to yield a readable paper document. However, few users are likely to wish extensive printouts of command descriptions, because the same machine-readable documentation will still be there the next day.

By default, the `man` command searches that section of the manual which gives descriptions of the shell commands. Other sections of the manual also exist; the classification is

1   shell commands,
2   system calls (kernel access points),
3   subroutine libraries,
4   input–output device driver descriptions,
5   include files and formats,
6   computer games,
7   special files,
8   system procedures.

Sections 1 and 3 are further subdivided. Section 1 covers one unsuffixed and three alphabetically suffixed subsections:

1   general-purpose commands,
1c   communications-related commands,
1g   graphics-related commands,
1m   system maintenance commands.

Section 3 includes

3   standard subroutine library,
3f   f77 support subroutines,
3f4p   f4p introduction and subroutines,
3m   mathematical subroutines,
3s   input–output subroutines,
3x   various specialized subroutines.

If material located elsewhere than in section 1 is desired, it is usually wise to save time by giving the section number and the title of the material desired. If the section number is not given, searching may cover a rather large part of the manual and waste a good deal of time. Thus, to produce the ASCII character table which appears in section 7, one should enter

```
$ man 7 ascii
```

Naturally, restricting the search to a particular section is only useful if it is known what section to look in.

Not every installation provides online access to all the manuals; and those manuals which it does provide may not have precisely the sequence and form of standard Version 7. Indeed a major purpose of providing manuals in machine-readable form is to allow system managers of individual installations to adapt the manuals to their own user requirements and to include any locally relevant implementation differences. Furthermore, the manuals amount to quite a bit of text, so that in some small systems they may be abbreviated to save space.

The ASCII Character Set

Most of the sorting, text processing, and character handling operations for which utilities are available are carried out relative to the ASCII character set. An ASCII (American Standard for Computer Information Interchange) character is defined as 7 bits (binary digits). The ASCII characters represent both printable and nonprintable characters. For example, 1 101 010 represents the character j, whereas 0 001 010 represents the *newline* character. For ease in reading, the binary digits are often written in groups of three, and even more frequently each group of three is given its natural numerical interpretation, i.e., an octal representation is often used. Thus 1 101 010 is normally written as 152, the groups 101 and 010 having been interpreted as the octal numbers 5 and 2, respectively.

Since a character is exactly seven bits long, 128 characters can be formed. These are given in the table below. The left column (octal 000 to 032) and the last entry in the table (octal 177) are nonprinting characters; all the rest are printable. It is conventional to refer to the nonprinting characters in the left column as *control* characters, since they are formed by pressing a key while the CONTROL key is held down; for example, the *newline* character (octal 012) is often referred to as *control-J*.

Perhaps surprisingly, there are some installation-dependent differences between the printed symbols that correspond to certain bit configurations. For example, 043 (0 100 011) is rendered as the crosshatched "pounds" sign in American practice and as the "pounds sterling" symbol on many printers in Britain. There is no ambiguity, however, about the alphabetic and numeric characters or about the mathematical operators and common punctuation signs.

The ASCII Character Set

000 *nul*	040	100 @	140
001 *soh*	041 !	101 A	141 a
002 *stx*	042 "	102 B	142 b
003 *etx*	043 #	103 C	143 c
004 *eot*	044 $	104 D	144 d
005 *enq*	045 %	105 E	145 e
006 *ack*	046 &	106 F	146 f
007 *bel*	047 ´	107 G	147 g
010 *bs*	050 (	110 H	150 h
011 *ht*	051)	111 I	151 i
012 *nl*	052 *	112 J	152 j
013 *vt*	053 +	113 K	153 k
014 *np*	054 ,	114 L	154 l
015 *cr*	055 –	115 M	155 m
016 *so*	056 .	116 N	156 n
017 *si*	057 /	117 O	157 o
020 *dle*	060 0	120 P	160 p
021 *dc1*	061 1	121 Q	161 q
022 *dc2*	062 2	122 R	162 r
023 *dc3*	063 3	123 S	163 s
024 *dc4*	064 4	124 T	164 t
025 *nak*	065 5	125 U	165 u
026 *syn*	066 6	126 V	166 v
027 *etb*	067 7	127 W	167 w
030 *can*	070 8	130 X	170 x
031 *em*	071 9	131 Y	171 y
032 *sub*	072 :	132 Z	172 z
033 *esc*	073 ;	133 [	173 {
034 *fs*	074 <	134 \	174 |
035 *gs*	075 =	135]	175 }
036 *rs*	076 >	136 ↑	176 –
037 *us*	077 ?	137 _	177 *del*

Chapter 7

Text Preparation and Processing

Everybody who computes needs to do some text processing from time to time. Even scientific programmers must be able to prepare source files and to write program documentation. Other users may be more directly concerned with text as an end product—manuscripts, letters, and other documents all have to be prepared somehow. The Unix operating system caters to these needs rather better than most. Its principal text handling facilities are described in this chapter.

Tools and Facilities

The Unix system includes an unusually good set of software tools for text preparation, editing, and formatting. In fact a large number—perhaps even the majority—of its users at Bell Laboratories during the 1970s used Unix software tools not to compute numbers but to set up and format text. The Unix programming team responded to the needs of this substantial user community by creating many sophisticated utility programs, which are now part of the standard Version 7 system. The techniques developed there have quite profoundly influenced text processing software ever since. Users acquainted with word processing machines will be interested to discover here the roots of many methods now considered conventional.

Text Editors

Any operating system must provide, at the very least, an editor program for its users, so as to permit text to be typed into disk files. Editors are needed for a variety of purposes ranging from program preparation to the writing of books, tasks which cannot all be best fulfilled by the same editor. Hence various different editors have been written to run under the Unix system. The most common ones, which are described in this chapter, are **ed** and **vi**.

The truly basic editing tool included in the Version 7 software is a text editor called **ed**, which this chapter will deal with in some detail. **ed** is the fundamental working tool in many Unix systems. It is an editor simple to learn and simple to use, with a small enough command set for casual users to remember from one session to the next. It is strongly line oriented, i.e., it deals with material organized as individual lines, an aspect which makes it particularly attractive for the preparation of computer programs. In addition, **ed** is very tolerant of terminal characteristics; almost any terminal can be used with **ed**, whether of the printing or screen type, slow or fast, intelligent or dumb. Even terminals unable to handle lowercase characters can be pressed into service, though they are hardly to be recommended!

There exists a host of other editor programs, of which **vi** is probably the most widely known. This editor is much more powerful than **ed**, having a large and flexible set of commands. It is better suited to book writing and document preparation than **ed**, yet no less convenient for programming. **vi** is a screen editor, with the text to be edited displayed on the terminal screen along with the changes to be made. It is easy to see just what is happening to the text being edited, certainly easier than with **ed**. Of course, **vi** can only be used with screen-type terminals, not printers. On the debit side, **vi** derives much of its power from a repertoire of about 100 commands and a fairly complex set of syntax rules; it is therefore not considered easy to master. Having been developed by the Berkeley Unix team, **vi** is not part of Version 7. However, it is locally available at many installations, and it is distributed with several commercially available systems based on Version 7.

Text Processing Programs

While text editors are essential to have, most users need facilities far beyond that minimum to prepare properly formatted and attractive documents. The main formatting program available under the Unix system is **nroff**. The structure and style of **nroff** derive from an earlier precursor program **roff**, which is still in use at some Unix installations. The command syntax of **roff** and **nroff** has been widely accepted by the text processing community. Indeed numerous commercial word processors unrelated to **nroff** now routinely use similar command structures. **nroff** will justify margins, place footnotes at the bottom of the page, number pages, center titles, indent paragraphs, and perform a thousand and one other things normally expected of a professional typesetter. The full command language of **nroff** is extensive and not easy to master. However, a small subset, one or two dozen commands, suffices to do practically everything required in

routine report writing. This chapter describes it sufficiently to enable users
to cope with simple documents.

In addition to **nroff**, which produces output suitably formatted for a
printing terminal or lineprinter, there is **troff**, a program which is similar
in principle but produces book-quality output from a phototypesetting
machine. For mathematical typesetting (equations and the like) there exists
a program called **neqn**; for setting up tables, there is **tbl**, a table editor.
The **troff**, **neqn**, and **tbl** programs are able to drive an ordinary printing
terminal, but obviously they cannot do things which the terminal cannot do.
For their full potential to be realized, they require a phototypesetting
machine. Because such machines are much more rare than terminals, these
programs are of interest to a much smaller community than **nroff** and are
only described briefly here.

For checking documents for spelling errors, Unix software includes a
program called (not surprisingly) **spell**.

There exist also many other utility programs able to perform file comparison, sorting, and testing, which may be of use in text processing
applications. However, they are more broadly useful than that; they are
therefore described in the chapter entitled *Facilities and Utilities*.

Using the **ed** Text Editor

The basic text editor in the Unix system is **ed**. It is line oriented, i.e., it
regards a segment of text as being composed of individual lines. This feature
makes it very convenient for preparation of computer programs.

In normal use, **ed** is asked to read a file, which may then be modified,
and to write out the modified text to another (or the same) file. The reading,
writing, and intervening modification are all controlled by a simple set of
keyboard commands.

The Editing Buffer

The general operation of **ed** resembles that of many other editing programs.
To edit a file, **ed** makes a copy of it in an area of computer memory called
the *editing buffer* or *text buffer*. The user can examine the text in the buffer,
correct it, rearrange it, and modify it in various ways. When alterations to
the text are complete, the content of the editing buffer is normally written to
another file. If the file being edited is small, the editing buffer is entirely
contained in the immediate-access memory of the computer. If the file is too
large to be kept in memory and therefore requires a buffer larger than
memory, space is allocated for the buffer partly in memory and partly in a

temporary disk file. Any text movement between memory and temporary
file is handled automatically by **ed**, so that the user normally does not
know, indeed cannot find out, whether the buffer is entirely housed in
immediate-access memory or swapped into and out of it. So far as the user
can tell, the buffer is extremely large, large enough to handle any file
without having to segment it into parts.

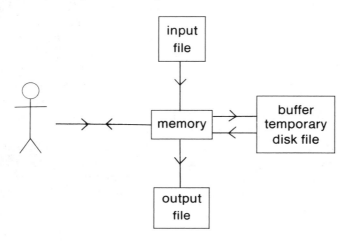

While text is automatically moved between memory and disk, so as to make
the buffer size appear essentially infinite, no automatic movement is provided from input file to editing buffer or from the buffer to the output file.
The user must instruct **ed** explicitly when and where to read and write files.
When **ed** ceases operation, the content of the editing buffer is simply
discarded, and it is the user's own responsibility to ensure that the content is
first saved in the appropriate file. Exiting from **ed** without having previously
written the text buffer content to a file means that any work done on the
text in the buffer will be irrecoverably lost!

Line Numbers

The text buffer content is regarded by **ed** as being subdivided into lines, a
line being simply a string of any printable characters including blanks. At
all times during the editing process, **ed** maintains a *line pointer*, which
identifies one particular line in the file as being the *current line*. Thus a small
text file might contain the character sequence `This is a small` $\backslash n$
`text file to` $\backslash n$ `demonstrate editing.` $\uparrow D$. Here $\backslash n$ represents
the *newline* character (ASCII 012 octal) which signals the beginning of a
new line, while $\uparrow D$ is the control-D character (ASCII 004 octal) which
identifies the end of file. If this file is copied into the text buffer for editing,
ed will regard it as containing three lines, with a pointer pointing at one of

them:

```
            1     This is a small
     ==>     2     text file to
            3     demonstrate editing.
```

ed permits reference to lines by number. The line numbers, be it noted, refer to the editing buffer and not to any file. That is to say, when the buffer content is written out to a file, line numbers are not included in the file.

At all times, **ed** assigns the number 1 to the first line in the file and numbers the rest sequentially. If any new lines are inserted in the buffer, or if any lines are deleted, **ed** automatically renumbers all lines then and there. Line numbers are never displayed on the terminal screen, however, so that the user does not see the renumbering taking place.

The user can easily move the line pointer around, with appropriate editor commands. Because the first line in the buffer is always numbered 1, there is never any difficulty in locating it. However, the number of the last line is not usually known. For convenience, the symbol **$** is used to denote the line number of the last line in the buffer, whatever the actual number may be. Similarly, the user does not usually wish to keep track of the current line number as a number; the symbol . (pronounced "dot") is used to denote it. Both symbols may be employed in any **ed** command which refers to line numbers. Use of these symbols means that text normally appears to the user as

```
            1     This is a larger
            2     text file which
                  .....
     ==>     .     This is the current line
                  .....
            $     and this line is the last.
```

As will be seen in the more detailed descriptions below, the user rarely needs to be concerned with the actual numerical values of **.** and **$**; he ordinarily employs the symbols instead. Naturally, the actual numeric values may always be given instead, if desired.

The dollar sign **$** used to stand for the last buffer line number is of course completely unrelated to the dollar sign used as the shell prompt.

Editor Commands

Most of the text manipulation commands used by **ed** comprise a single command verb. The verb may refer to a particular segment of text, in which case it is augmented by a line number or a pair of line numbers to indicate the line or lines referred to. Of course, the symbols **.** and **$** may be used instead of line numbers where appropriate. A few of the **ed** command verbs may also be modified by an adverb or parameter to specify in more detail how the command is to be carried out. The usual form of an **ed** command is

[*linenumber*,[*linenumber*]] *verb*

All command verbs are made up of just a single character. For example, **p** is a verb which can be used to display lines on the screen. Thus the command

1,$ p

will cause the entire buffer content to be displayed on the screen (the range is from line 1 to line $, the last line in the buffer). Some other commands available in **ed** are

a	*append*	appends more lines at a specified place.
c	*change*	changes specified lines to new material.
d	*delete*	deletes specified lines.
e	*edit*	sets edit buffer to contain a given file.
f	*filename*	prints a remembered *filename*.
g	*global*	applies the following commands to whole buffer.
i	*insert*	inserts lines at the specified place.
j	*join*	joins two lines to make one.
m	*move*	moves lines to a new place (cut and paste).
n	*number*	displays lines and their numbers.
p	*pointer*	positions pointer and displays lines.
q	*quit*	exits from the editor, to the Unix shell.
r	*read*	reads a file into the editing buffer.
s	*substitute*	substitutes new character string for old.
t	*transfer*	copies, like **m** but without removing original.
w	*write*	writes buffer contents into a file.
W	*write*	appends buffer contents to a file.
=		show current numeric value of **.** or **$**.

Where a line number is required for a command to make sense (e.g., for the **p** command), but the user does not supply one, **ed** assumes that the current line number is meant. In other words, commands with line numbers omitted are executed as if the dot symbol . had been included in the command.

Line numbers and line number ranges must make sense; otherwise, **ed** will ignore them. Line numbers below 1 or above **$** are not acceptable, and line number ranges must always run in increasing order. For example, line 0 cannot be printed, nor can all lines from number 12 to number 8.

Because **ed** is normally operated in an interactive fashion, any errors in commands can be identified immediately as they occur. They are signaled by the single error message provided by **ed**, a question mark **?** displayed at the left-hand screen edge.

Pointer Manipulation and Text Examination

The content of the editing buffer may be examined by displaying lines with
the **p** ("pointer" or "print") command. Displaying causes the line pointer to
move, coming to rest at the last line displayed. Thus the **p** command may be
used not only to cause display but also to move the pointer about.

In general, the **p** command has the usual **ed** command form, in which
one or two line numbers precede the command letter **p**. If only one number
is supplied, it is understood to denote the line desired; if two line numbers
are given, they are taken to identify a range of line numbers, beginning at
the first and ending at the last. Display may be stopped, even before the last
line has been reached, by pressing the DELETE key. The **p** command is
specially privileged as compared to all other **ed** commands; if an **ed**
command is issued with the command verb omitted, **p** is understood by
default. Thus it is not necessary to type

    5 p

to position the pointer at the fifth line of text; it suffices to enter

    5

because **ed** automatically assumes that **p** is meant if the command letter is
omitted.

In addition to numeric values and the symbols . and **$**, the line number
identification may contain addition and subtraction operations. For example,

    .−1,$−10 p

will cause display to start at the buffer line preceding the current pointer
position and to continue until the tenth last line in the buffer. Because it is
permissible to omit **p**, the same effect will result from the abbreviated
command

    .−1,$−10

As stated above, **ed** always assumes that the dot (.) is meant if line number
information is omitted. Hence

    −1,$−10

would do equally well. Furthermore, whenever the arithmetic operators
minus (−) and plus (+) are not followed by a number, **ed** assumes that 1 was
meant. Therefore

    −,$−10

is also acceptable and produces the same result.

It is worth noting that the + sign is not optional in line numbers. An unsigned number such as **5** is understood to denote the fifth line in the buffer, counted from the beginning. On the other hand, a signed number such as **+5** is interpreted to mean **. + 5** and therefore denotes the fifth line counted from the current pointer position. No ambiguity can arise with negative signs, since the lowest line number in the buffer is always 1.

The syntax rules of **ed** are such that very few unacceptable command lines can be devised. Almost any information may be omitted from commands, yet **ed** will do something, because of its very extensive set of assumptions about how to fill in missing information. The limiting case arises when trying to abbreviate

    . p

which requests display of the current line. By the rules, the letter **p** may be omitted, since it will be supplied by default; the dot may be omitted, since it will also be inserted by default. Typing a blank line (just pressing RETURN) should therefore display the current line. In fact, this ultimate abbreviation forms an exception to the rules: a blank line is interpreted as equivalent to

    . + 1 p

i.e., the line next after the current line is displayed, and the pointer is left at that next line. While nobody likes exceptions to rules, this one is quite beneficial because it permits displaying a succession of lines, one at a time, simply by pressing the RETURN key.

Inserting, Appending, and Deleting Text

Text may be inserted ahead of the current line by means of the **i** command. When this command is typed, **ed** assumes that any following lines of text (as many as desired) constitute the text to be inserted. Obviously the inserted text must be terminated somehow; otherwise, any further **ed** commands would be treated as text to be inserted in the edit buffer, not as commands. Insertion is terminated by typing a dot as the first (and only) character of a new line. For example,

    i
    This is an inserted line
    and this is another.

    .

results in insertion of the two lines shown (but not of the i and the dot .) in the editing buffer. When an insertion is completed, the current line pointer remains at the last line inserted.

The **a** command is similar to the **i** command, with one key difference: the new text is placed *after* the current line, not before it. Having both available makes it easy to append after the last line in the buffer and to insert in front of line 1. In all cases, lines are automatically renumbered to take account of the new insertions.

Deletion of lines is accomplished by the **d** command. It operates with precisely the same syntax conventions as the **p** command. Thus

d   deletes the current line.
1,2 d   deletes the first and second lines in the buffer.
-1,+1 d deletes current line, plus one before and after.
1,$ d   deletes the entire buffer contents.

When a deletion is made, the current line pointer is set to the next line following the highest-numbered line deleted—unless that was the last line, in which case the pointer is set to **$**.

The need occasionally arises to delete a group of lines, and to replace them by some other text segment. This task can be carried out in two steps, first removing the unwanted material with the **d** command, then inserting new material with the **i** command. The two actions are combined in the **c** ("change") command. The current line and those immediately preceding and following it are removed and replaced by a single line by

> **.-1,.+1 c**
> **This line replaces three old ones.**
> **.**

The syntax rules of **c** are exactly those of **d** and **i** combined.

String Searching and Replacing

Line addressing in **ed** can be carried out through the use of line numbers, as in the examples above, or by reference to a character string in the line. Instead of using a line number, one may employ a character string delimited fore and aft by the solidus / , e.g., **/string/** . For example,

> **/use/,/string/ p**

causes display of the group of lines determined as follows. The first line to be displayed is the first line after the current line that contains the character string **use**; the last line is the first line thereafter to contain the string **string**. If the current line counter had been set to the title line of this section, for example, the first two lines of the first paragraph would be displayed in response to this command. In other words, **/use/** means "the next line to contain **use**." Of course, the rule still holds that **p** is assumed if no other command letter appears. Hence

> **/use/,/string/**

causes the same action as described above; and

> **/use/**

causes the next line to contain **use** to be found and displayed. Note that the character string **use** need not coincide with the word *use*; the search may turn up other strings such as *use*ful, am*use*ment, and per*use*. Searching always proceeds in the natural text sequence. However, if the search is not successful when the end of the buffer is reached, searching is continued on a "wrap-around" basis, as if line 1 followed line $. If the search is totally unsuccessful, **ed** will simply display a question mark.

When a particular character string has been found, another can be substituted for it by means of the **s** command. Thus

> **1,5 s /use / employment /**

will find all occurrences of the string **use** in the first five lines of the editing buffer and substitute **employment** for **use**. The substitute string could be a string of no characters at all. For example, if the string **use3** was typed instead of **use**, by a slip of the finger, correction could be achieved by either of

> **s /use3 / use /**
> **s /3 / /**

The latter merely substitutes "no characters" for **3**. Note that since no line number range was given, **ed** will assume that the current line was meant, as if **.,. s /3 / /** had been typed.

Substitution is occasionally required for all occurrences of a word or a character string. The **s** command can achieve global replacement if the **g** ("global") command is attached to it. For example,

> **s /use / employment / g p**

will replace all occurrences of **use** in the edit buffer by **employment** and will print on the display screen every line in which the replacement is made. The latter echoing is very useful for detecting unwanted changes, since global replacement of **use** will result in *am*use*ment* being replaced by the unintended *am*employment*ment*.

Cut-and-Paste Operations

It is often necessary to perform "cut and paste" operations, in which text is rearranged by moving entire paragraphs or sentences around. The **ed** rules permit moving groups of lines by means of the **m** ("move") command. This command removes a group of lines and inserts them elsewhere. For example,

> **- 5,. m +7**

moves six lines (**.- 5** to **.** inclusive) so as to follow line **.+ 7**. It should be noted that the **m** command requires a total of three line numbers: two (or one) preceding the **m**, to identify the range of lines to be moved, and one following the **m**, to specify where to move them to. Of course, the line specifications may be either numeric or contextual; the command

```
/ necessary / ,/ example./ m /.-5 / -1
```

could be used to move the first paragraph of this section to a position after the example command, but immediately before the following text.

File Handling by the Editor

Since all text is stored in files, **ed** must be able to get at files. There are two basic commands for doing so: **r** ("read") and **w** ("write").

The **r** command reads in (appends) a named file at the end of the editing buffer. Material already in the buffer is left unaltered. For example,

```
r firstfile
r secondfile
```

causes two files to be read into the buffer. The files are not identified in any way in the buffer; in fact, they have now become a single string of text. To let the user know the size of text in the buffer, the **r** and **w** commands (and the **e** command, see below) not only read and write but also display at the terminal screen the number of characters transferred.

The **w** command is used for writing out buffer contents to files. It is used much like the **r** command but with the difference that, if desired, only part of the buffer need be written. Thus the commands

```
w wholefile
1,10 w partfile
```

will copy the entire buffer content into **wholefile** and the first 10 lines of the buffer into another file **partfile**. The buffer content is not changed by writing.

The **e** ("edit") command is equivalent to clearing the buffer and reading in a new file. For example,

```
e wholefile
```

has almost the same effect as

```
1,$ d
r wholefile
```

In addition, the **e** command writes the file name **wholefile** into a special location. When terminating work, the buffer may be written out with the **w** command without any file name; the name of the file is fetched from the special location and used. If the user forgets what the original file name was, the f command can be used to fetch the saved name. Editing sessions begun with e and terminated with a w without file name thus replace the old file content with the edited version without any need for creating temporary file names.

Since the w command does not alter the content of the editing buffer, it is a good idea to write out the buffer contents every ten or fifteen minutes during long editing sessions. Files on disk are relatively secure against hardware failures, whereas even a minor power interruption can destroy editing buffer contents totally. If the session is started with the e command, and if writing is done with the w command without a file name, the effect is to keep replacing the file with successive edited versions.

There is no provision in ed for automatically saving any copies of the original (unedited) file. In program development it is often wise to secure a copy of it before beginning the editing session and to delete it only after ensuring that the alterations had the intended effect. Extra copies can be kept with only a very small cost in file space if the diff command is used to create editing scripts. These list only the differences between files and do so in a form which can later be employed to convert the old into new ones.

If the e command is invoked with a file name which does not as yet exist, such a file is created. In this case, the editing buffer is initially made to contain one line, composed of 0 characters. The current line pointer is set to that line; indeed, there is no other place it could point.

To terminate using the editor, the q ("quit") command is issued. This command has probably caused more grief to beginners than any other because *the q command quits the editor without writing out the buffer content.* In other words, issuing a q without a preceding w command will simply abandon whatever work may have been expended in editing. Writing out the edit buffer content is the responsibility of the user!

The vi Screen Editor

A product of the Berkeley Unix project, vi was designed to overcome the shortcomings of ed. Its most obvious shortcoming is that ed shows text on the screen but does not show the location of the line pointer. Nothing much can be done about that with printing terminals, but displaying a pointer in a screen display is a relatively easy matter. The resulting editor can be used only with screen terminals, but that might well be regarded as an advantage by some.

The second shortcoming of ed which vi was apparently intended to cure is the relatively low power of ed; it does not know how to do very much. The same cannot be said for vi; if there is fault in its design, vi knows too much! In fact **vi** understands a total of over a hundred commands. Some of these are context-sensitive, and some are synonymous with others. As a result, **vi** is an immensely powerful editor. It can also be immensely difficult to learn to use well. Use at a simple level fortunately is not very hard.

Window Display

The basic idea of editing with **vi** is similar to **ed**: the required text file is copied into an edit buffer and edited there. However, the display technique is rather different. The terminal screen is thought of as a "window" on the text buffer. A section of the buffer can be seen through this window in its natural form, one line of text per line of display. The window size is variable and can be reset by the user. By default, it is half the screen height for slow terminals and the full screen height for fast ones.

The display window can be moved so as to expose different parts of the buffer to view. It may be moved forward or backward along the buffer, either a full window height at a time, or a partial window height at a time. There are four commands for doing so, all communicated by control characters (formed by striking a key while holding down the CONTROL key):

control-F   forward a window,
control-B   backward a window,
control-D   forward part of a window ("down"),
control-U   backward part of a window (" up").

When **vi** is first started, the partial-window commands scroll up or down half the window size. The amount of scrolling can be reset by prefixing either command with a number. The number is taken to be the number of lines to be scrolled; not only is it used in the command executed immediately, but it is remembered for all future control-D and control-U commands. Similarly, the control-F and control-B commands may be preceded by a number, which will be taken as defining a new window size. Again, the new number remains in effect until reset.

Just precisely how the window movement is carried out depends on the terminal type. There are so-called intelligent terminals, with plenty of built-in memory used to buffer text. Such terminals can carry out nearly all the above operations by scrolling text already stored in the terminal. At the other end of the intelligence spectrum, there are terminals which can only scroll in the "down" direction, to simulate printing. Backward movements can then be accomplished only by erasing the screen and rewriting whatever should be there. With many users loading down the system and using a slow communication line, the result can be less than joyous.

The Editing Cursor

Practically all editing operations in vi are guided by the screen cursor. For example, insertion and deletion of characters are always done at the cursor position. The cursor takes different forms in different terminals. It may appear as a video inversion, blinking underscore, or some other distinguishing mark attached to a single character.

To perform any editing operations with vi, it is necessary to move the cursor to a desired location. Because cursor placement is so important, vi provides a number and variety of cursor commands verging on the ridiculous. Fortunately, most users are able to make do nicely with just a small number.

Many terminals have little arrows on the keys in the middle of the keyboard: the H, J, K, and L keys often carry arrows pointing left, down, up, and right, respectively. Whether or not there are any arrows painted on the keytops, these four lowercase characters move the cursor just exactly as the arrows imply.

While moving the cursor up and down one line at a time is convenient enough, moving all the way across a line one character at a time can be painfully slow. To alleviate the pain, vi allows movement in units of a word at a time. The command characters w and b take the cursor forward a word and backward a word, respectively. A word is considered to cease at a punctuation mark or a blank, so that a.out and 127.53 are taken to be two words each.

Large movements of the cursor around the screen are possible using the H, M, and L commands. (Note that these commands use uppercase rather than lowercase characters). H takes the cursor to the top line of the screen, L takes it to the last line. M places it at the middle line in the screen window. In each case, the cursor is positioned at the first nonblank character in the line. Still finer control of positioning can be achieved by prefixing the H and L commands with numbers; thus 5H means the fifth line from the top, and 3L signifies the third line from the bottom.

Editor Commands

The commands alluded to above are only a small part of the vi command repertoire; others will be discussed below. All commands are typed while vi is in a receptive mood (the vi manual uses the term "quiescent state"). Most commands are echoed on the bottom line of the screen as they are typed; some, however, appear elsewhere.

Most commands given to vi involve a single basic keystroke (i.e., the command verbs are generally single characters), but these are frequently augmented by numeric arguments or other qualifiers. Thus the typical command will comprise several characters. Any command can be abandoned before it is fully typed, by striking the ESCAPE key. In general, this key serves to terminate a command and cause it to be executed; however, if the command is incomplete, it cannot be executed and will therefore be abandoned. A corollary of this argument follows: if unsure whether **vi** is prepared to accept commands, the user may strike the ESCAPE key a few times. (If **vi** wasn't in a receptive mood before, it will be now!)

The DELETE key may be used to abandon whatever activity is currently in progress. It may be used to cancel wrong instructions once their execution has begun.

There is a command **u** ("undo") which can be employed to reverse the unfortunate effect of almost any incorrect command even after it has been executed. **vi** generally keeps a record of what has happened in the last command or two and will simply restore the text buffer to the previous status quo on receiving a **u** command. The **u** command can only be used to go back one step, however, since a second **u** will simply undo the first **u**.

Inserting and Appending Text

Insertion and appending in **vi** differ from the corresponding operations in **ed** in being character, rather than line, oriented. While an insertion in **ed** inserts new text just ahead of the current line, an insertion in **vi** places additional text just before the cursor character. In other words, text can be easily inserted into the middle of a line in **vi**. The insertion command is **i**, followed by the character string to be inserted, terminated by an ESCAPE character ⟨*esc*⟩. In other words, typing

>   **ileftward** ⟨*esc*⟩

inserts the character string "**leftward** " at the immediate left of the cursor character. In a similar way, the **a** ("append") command, as in

>   **arightward** ⟨*esc*⟩

places the string "**rightward** " immediately at the right of the cursor character.

While typing the text to be inserted, on many terminals the newly typed words overwrite existing text on the screen. At the time, it may look quite unnervingly as if the existing text had been ruined. However, there is no need to worry; it will be cleaned up when the insertion is terminated with an escape character. This phenomenon applies to several **vi** command and generally happens on dumb terminals. Intelligent terminals generally manage to rearrange text at the terminal even before it is transmitted to the computer, and thus they maintain a tidier display.

Insertions may consist of many lines, not necessarily just one. Whenever the RETURN key is struck, it generates a *newline* character, which is then inserted into the text like any other character. As a result, several lines can be inserted or appended by simply typing them in a natural fashion.

While typing text to be appended or inserted, mistakes do occur from time to time. They can be corrected by backspacing with the BACKSPACE key (or control-H, which is the same thing). It backspaces just as a typewriter would and allows the wrong characters to be overwritten. A whole word can be "backspaced" with the control-W command keystroke and overwritten. A note of caution is in order, however. The erase and kill characters established for all keyboard communication still hold valid even while vi is running, so that any attempt to insert either character into the text will have unexpected consequences. The usual erase characters are # and control-H, while @ and control-X are the normal kill characters; but they could have been set by the system manager to be something else, so local enquiry is advisable. If they are really needed in the file, their special meanings can be neutralized by an immediately preceding backslash character, as in \@.

Text Deletions and Changes

Deletion and text change are accomplished in vi in a manner analogous to ed except of course that the reference point for all changes is again the screen cursor position. The characters d and c again serve to identify the actions, but there the resemblance to ed ceases.

The d command (the vi manual calls it an "operator") deletes the entity named in the next keystroke after the d itself. Such an entity could, for example, be a whole word forward or backward. Furthermore, numeric multipliers are allowed in the command. Thus dw deletes the next word, d3w deletes the next three words, and d2b deletes two words backward. If a number is given in front of d, it implies a repeat count, so that 3dw means "delete one word, repeating three times", while d3w means "delete three words". The effect of both is of course the same. 5dj deletes the last five characters, and so on.

The c command deletes and substitutes the string that immediately follows; in other words, c is a combination of deletion and insertion. Thus cwnone⟨esc⟩ deletes the next word and substitutes the character string none.

The current line (on which the cursor is now) can be deleted with the dd command. The logic of this command may not be immediately obvious, but it makes good sense in hindsight. All the objects which might be deleted are really cursor positions. If strictly interpreted, the delete instruction always says "delete up to ... ". But so far, there has not appeared any cursor position identifier meaning "the current line"; indeed none has been necessary, since there is no need for an instruction to position the cursor where it already is. Hence there is no letter code for "the current line", and a special rule is required to make the delete instruction work for the current line. A similar argument applies to the **c** command, and the solution is similar: the command **cc** is understood to mean the current line.

A great variety of other objects may be specified in a **d** or **c** command. For example, **d3L** means "delete from here on down to the third-last line on the screen". **vi** includes in its vast command set not only identifiers for words but also lines, sentences, paragraphs, indeed sections of text, both forward and backward. Thus extremely powerful deletions and changes are feasible. In part, this great power explains also why command cancellation (DELETE key) and undoing (the **u** command) exist. With so great a destructive power in hand, users are almost certain to create unintended mayhem from time to time.

Starting and Stopping **vi**

Starting up and exiting from **vi** are roughly analogous to the procedures used with **ed**. Starting up is accomplished by the obvious means,

   $ vi *filename*

where *filename* is the file to be edited. This command starts **vi** running, reads the file into the buffer, and initiates window display.

Exiting from **vi** is similar to exiting from **ed** in one important respect: simply quitting does not save the changes made to the file but allows them to die in the text buffer. To write out the file, then exit, the command

   :wq⟨*esc*⟩

is used. It writes the buffer content into the original file. The colon preceding **w** is essential; without it, **w** would be understood as the "word" command.

The **nroff** Text Formatter

Line-oriented editors such as **ed** are highly satisfactory for developing and correcting computer programs in which the layout and formatting of the text are relatively fixed. On the other hand, reports, manuscripts, and other purely textual matter look better if certain essentially cosmetic operations are performed. For example, it is often considered desirable to move words across line ends and to insert blank spaces so as to give justified right-hand margins. Such operations are provided for by **nroff**, a text formatting program. **nroff** reads a file containing the "raw" text and writes an output file containing the same text, reformatted in accordance with appropriate commands. The commands are embedded in the text file itself.

The **nroff** Command Language

In essence, **nroff** may be regarded as a processor for a batch programming language, in which program commands operate on data (the raw text itself) in a prescribed fashion. Every command in this language begins at the left-hand margin, preceded by a **.** (dot) to identify it as a command. For example, the command

```
.pl 55
```

sets the page length to 55 lines. An automatic line counter in **nroff** then causes a new page to be started whenever 55 lines of output have been generated. To produce the above paragraph and heading, the following text might have been set up using **ed**:

```
.pl 55
.ll 65
The nroff Command Language
.sp 2
In essence, nroff may be regarded
as a processor for a batch programming
language, in which program commands operate on
data (the raw text itself) in
a prescribed fashion. Every command
in this language begins at the left-hand margin,
preceded by a . (dot) to identify it as a command.
For example, the command
.sp 2
```

The commands at the head of this text segment instruct **nroff** to make the page length 55 lines and the line length 65 characters, and to insert two blank lines after the heading. The text itself is in lines of random length. **nroff** removes the line breaks from the text and inserts new ones so as to fit the text into the specified line length.

Every **nroff** command begins with the dot (or the apostrophe) at the left margin and contains precisely two other characters. The characters may be followed by a space and a signed or unsigned number. Unsigned numbers mean just what they say; for example, the command **.pl 55** means "make the page length 55 lines". If the number is preceded by a + sign, it is taken to mean "add to the previous value"; so **.pl +55** means "make the page length 55 lines longer than it was up to now". Correspondingly, the − sign (as in **.pl −55**) means "shorten the the page length by 55 lines". In practically all cases, a missing numeric argument is taken as 1 (page length = 66 is an exception). The numeric values are subject to a host of restrictions, most of which are obvious: line and page lengths must not become negative, paragraph indentations must not exceed the line length, and so on.

All the numeric values **nroff** is obliged to keep track of (such as line spacing and line length) have initial values set when **nroff** is first started up. The average user happy to fill pages 66 lines long with 65-character lines (on most printers, the right numbers for 8.5- by 11-in paper) need not bother setting page and line lengths, for example. The same goes for nonnumeric option settings; **nroff** will produce single-spaced output with blanks inserted to make left and right margins straight, unless instructed otherwise.

The full **nroff** language includes over 70 commands, a formidable list. Fortunately, a very modest subset is enough to permit working with ordinary text. The informal overview given here actually deals with only 15 commands, but these probably suffice to cover the great majority of requirements.

Filling and Adjusting

Text is really a one-dimensional entity, a string of characters. The purpose of any text formatter is to map this one-dimensional continuum onto a two-dimensional page in accordance with some set of rules. The first rule is to cut up the text into "lines" by inserting line breaks; a second rule is to make lines of equal length so that the output document has straight left and right margins. **nroff** achieves this effect by a process called *filling*. Each new line is formed by taking enough words from the input file to almost fill the line and then making up any shortfall by inserting blanks next to existing blanks. The result is quite excellent if lines are long and words short; otherwise, "white rivers" can occur in the text. Filling may on occasion not be desirable (for example, if printing out a table). It can be turned off by the **.nf** (no fill) command and back on again with the **.fi** (fill) command. With filling turned off, input lines are simply copied to the output, without regard to the line length setting.

Centered lines, often used in titles, are never filled by **nroff**. The **.ce** (center) command causes the next line to be copied into the output exactly as it is, but with enough blanks inserted at the left edge to make the text appear at the center. The **.ce** command may specify that more than a single line is to be centered. For example, **.ce 3** causes each of the next three lines to be centered.

When filling, nroff removes all line breaks and inserts new ones, usually somewhere else, so as to arrive at justified margins. Where a line break is definitely wanted, for example, at the end of a paragraph, the .br (break) command may be employed. This command causes a line break to be placed in exactly the place where it occurs, no matter what the effect on filling.

In addition to the .br command, a host of other nroff commands introduce forced line breaks; for example, .fi and .nf both do. These implied breaks may be suppressed by using the apostrophe instead of the dot at the left margin; the .fi command thus introduces a break, the ′fi command does not.

Page Layout

A new page is started in the output file by including the command .bp in the input. This command causes a line break as well as a page break, i.e., it will not delay starting a new page until the current output line is complete. If it is desired to force a page break at the next natural line end, ′bp can be used.

To set left and right margins in nroff, the .ll N (line length N) and .po N (page offset N) commands are used. The former defines line length; the latter moves the entire line N spaces to the right. No margin-setting commands exist, so the user can never set the left margin beyond the right. Page length is controlled by the .pl N command, as discussed above. These commands may be issued at any time, to take effect at the next line end or page end. None of them causes a line break.

When started up, nroff is set for single-spaced output. If double line spacing is desired, the .ls 2 command may be used. Triple, quadruple, or wider line spacing may also be requested. If a single block of blank lines is desired, the command .sp N is employed. It causes the output printer to move on N lines. A break is caused by .sp but not by the .ls command. Both accept only absolute numeric arguments; it is not possible to increase or decrease spacing by .ls +1 and .ls −1. However, no number at all is understood to mean 1, so .sp and .sp 1 are equivalent.

Paragraph indentations are achieved by the .ti N (temporary indent) command, which causes a break. "Temporary" means that only a single line is indented. The .in N (indent) command is similar but indents all subsequent lines. These two may be used in combination to cause indented text to be preceded by item numbers or other identifiers.

Underlining is effected by the .ul N command, which causes all alphanumeric characters in the next N lines to be underlined. This command does not cause a break, so that a single word may be underlined:

```
.ti 5
The full
.ul
nroff
language includes over 70 commands, a quite
   formidable list.
Fortunately, a very modest subset is enough to
```

The above will cause the word **nroff** to appear underlined in an otherwise normal, justified, paragraph whose first line is indented 5 spaces.

Defining and Using Macros

The true power of **nroff** lies in the fact that the user is allowed to define new commands (macroinstructions, or *macros*) in terms of the commands inherent in the system. Experienced **nroff** users, in fact, employ only a few of the system commands directly and do almost everything with commands of their own. To define a new command, it is only necessary to write out the string of commands, then to identify it as a macro definition by the **.de** (define) command in front and the .. (end of definition) behind. When **nroff** is called upon to execute the new command, it simply copies the definition and executes it step by step.

To give a simple example, paragraph breaks can be inserted by defining the **.pa** command to mean exactly what the user desires: a blank line and an indentation of five spaces. The macro definition is entered as

```
.de pa
.sp
.ti 5
..
```

To cause paragraph breaks, the newly defined **.pa** command is now used in the input file. **nroff** will actually substitute and execute the pair of commands that form its definition; so one command entered by the user is able to do the job of two. The real point, however, is not merely to save a little typing; it arises when the user decides that more white space between paragraphs and a deeper indentation would produce a better looking document. It suffices to replace the macro definition by

```
.de pa
.sp 2
.ti 8
..
```

and a job is done which would probably never have been attempted otherwise!

Macros may include instructions, as in the example above, text lines, and arguments. Arguments may be almost any character strings, numeric or alphabetic. They are included in the macro definition as character strings of the form \$1, \$2, ..., up to \$9; when the macro definition is copied, these place holders are replaced by actual values. For example, the paragraph break command above could be set up as

```
.de pa
.sp \$1
.ti \$2
..
```

and then invoked by the command

```
.pa 2 8
```

A double blank line and an eight-space indentation will result, just as if the actual values had been written into the macro definition.

Arguments passed to macros can be alphabetic strings. For example, the macro

```
.de dw
.bp
.sp 4
.ce
Appointments for \$1
.sp 2
.ti 5
..
```

might be suitable for creating a personal appointment calendar. It may be used to start a new day, for example, by

```
.dw Monday
```

The result will be to start a new page with the centered title **Appointments for Monday**, with some blank space above and below. Whatever text may follow is indented in good paragraph form.

Traps, Headers, and Page Numbers

Traps may be planted in any nroff input file by the .wh (when) command. This command has the general form .wh *N mc*. It causes the macro *mc* to be invoked whenever the line counter (on the current page) reaches *N*, i.e, after the *N*th line of every page of the output. If *N* is zero or positive, lines are counted from the top of the page; if *N* is negative, lines are counted from the bottom.

Traps are commonly used to create page headers and page footers. To begin printing six line widths (usually, 1 in.) below the top edge of the paper, and to stop printing six line widths above the bottom edge, traps are set

```
.wh 0 hd
.wh -7 ft
```

so as to invoke the macro .hd at the very start of the page and the macro .ft when exactly six lines remain (the trap is placed *after* the seventh line from the end). The macros themselves can be very simple, amounting to no more than insertion of blank lines and beginning a new page:

```
.de hd
'sp 6
..
.de ft
'bp
..
```

The 'sp and 'bp commands are prefixed with an apostrophe rather than a dot in order to suppress the line break that would otherwise result. Much more complicated and personalized header and footer macros are often used, e.g., to insert running titles with formats reversed for even and odd numbered pages. For such purposes, the .tl (title) command is very convenient. Inclusion of

```
.tl 'Leftstuff' middlestuff' Rightstuff'
```

in the input file will cause the string *Leftstuff* to be set flush to the left margin, *Rightstuff* to be placed flush to the right margin, and *middlestuff* to be centered between them. Obviously, the line length must be sufficient to house the whole lot.

Page numbering can be effected with the .tl command, which has a peculiar property: whenever the % sign appears in any of the alphabetic strings in the .tl command, it is replaced by the current page number. Hence the header macro

```
.de hd
'sp 3
.tl 'Draft Manuscript''Page %'
.sp 2
..
```

will left-adjust the words **Draft Manuscript** and right-adjust the page number. Right adjustment will of course shift the word **Page** leftward so that **Page 3** and **Page 103** will not have the character **P** in the same location.

Traps are usually set at the beginning of a file and left on. However, it may be desirable to alter them if the printout format is changed. Trap removal and resetting is achieved with the **.wh** command. To be very precise, **.wh** *N mc* does not *invoke* the macro *mc* at line *N*; it *alters the name of the macro to be invoked* at line *N* to *mc*. Hence issuing the instruction **.wh** *N* (with no macro name given) resets the name from *mc* to blank; i.e., no action will be taken.

The **-ms** Macro Library

For users with more or less routine document preparation requirements, there exist libraries of prewritten **nroff** macros, so that even novice users can realize a substantial part of the benefits of using macros without actually having to write any. The **-ms** macro library is designed particularly for technical paper manuscripts, technical reports, and similar literature. It provides a set of macros for commonly encountered constructions, such as

Footnote start and end	**.FS** to **.FE**
Keep blocks of text together	**.KS** to **.KE**
Unindented (left flush) paragraphs	**.LP**
Numbered headings	**.NH**
Indented paragraphs	**.PP**
Simple (unnumbered) headings	**.SH**
Titling	**.TL**

Multicolumn formatting, as often used for technical papers, is available, with the column arrangement automatically set up. A full description of **-ms** may be found in the Unix system manuals.

Other Text Formatting Programs

In addition to **ed** and **nroff**, which are vital tools for almost every user, three other programs are provided: **troff**, **neqn**, and **tbl**. All three are text formatting tools in the same generic family as **nroff**. They are intended for driving a relatively inexpensive phototypesetting machine and can produce output of excellent quality. In fact, the popularity of Unix in its early years was based very largely on the ease with which large numbers of sophisticated technical reports, scientific papers, and even books could be produced by engineers, scientists, and secretaries, working to tight schedules without any of the usual tools of the printing trade.

The **troff** Text Formatter

The **troff** formatter is in principle similar to **nroff**, but there are striking changes in hardware performance. The phototypesetter (unlike a standard terminal) is capable of producing several different fonts, so that boldface, italic, and varying sizes of type can be intermixed with the font selected as standard. User-selectable parameters include not only the font to be used but also the character size and line spacing, plus of course the overall page format: line length, default indentation, tabs, page size, page numbering, etc. The phototypesetter is in principle capable of drawing almost anything; it is able to move both horizontally and vertically, creating inked area as it goes. Hence the selection of fonts is limited less by the hardware than the cleverness of the embedded software. Character and line sizes are variable. Thus there is no longer much sense in instructions like "page length 51 lines"; it is more sensible and useful to say "page length 8.5 inches".

Font changes can occur anywhere in a text, and although they could be handled by standard **nroff**-like command lines beginning with a dot at the left margin, setting single words in italic or bold face by this method becomes rather messy. Various **troff** functions are therefore introduced by means of an *escape character*, which is usually the backslash \ but which may be altered by the user. For example, the character sequence \fB changes to a boldface font when encountered anywhere in the text.

Command lines used in **troff** are similar in structure to those employed by **nroff**, but a much wider range of possibilities exists. In fact the **troff** and **nroff** commands are deliberately created so that the **nroff** command interpreter can understand **troff** commands and can make substitutions within the limited capabilities of its printing device. It is thus correct to say that **troff** files can be processed by **nroff**; but hardware functions which are not available obviously cannot be used. Since the **nroff** and **troff** command sets are both programming languages, any **troff** script must be debugged and corrected before it can be finally printed. Debugging cannot be undertaken with much hope of success if the hardware functions are not available. Users without phototypesetting equipment, and with little hope of obtaining access to any, are probably well advised to stick with **nroff**.

Equation Processing with **neqn**

A great deal of scientific text involves mathematical or chemical formulas and equations, whose typesetting requires special symbols and mixed fonts as well as critical placement in both the horizontal and vertical directions. In principle, all the necessary phototypesetter motions and the font selection can be handled by **troff**. In practice, the detailed work required to make **troff** do so is very intricate, error prone, and unattractively time-consuming. To lighten this load, Unix software includes **neqn**, a utility capable of writing **troff** command sequences for equations.

There is a great deal of accepted convention and standardization in mathematical usage. Scalar variables are set in lightface italic, vectors in bold Roman; names of trigonometric functions appear in lightface Roman, their arguments in italic. Superscripts and subscripts are reduced in size by a conventional amount and offset by a standard height difference. The **neqn** package accepts input instructions in an essentially verbal language which describes equations. It transcribes these verbal instructions into **troff** commands to initiate font changes, vertical or horizontal motions, and special symbols (e.g., integral signs). **neqn** input will typically contain text like

```
2 pi sum from k = 0 to 20 A sub k cos (k omega t +
   psi sub k)
```

to denote a 20-term approximate Fourier series. **neqn** will recognize **pi**, **omega**, and **psi** as Greek letters and **sum** as a summation sign. It will automatically reduce the size of the subscripts identified by **sub**, and it will choose italic or Roman fonts for the remaining characters as appropriate.

The **neqn** package works as a preprocessor to **troff**. To use **neqn**, the mathematical portions of text are marked off with special delimiters by the user, thereby indicating to **neqn** that translation is required. All unmarked text, which normally includes standard **troff** commands and text, will be read by **neqn** and passed through to the output unaltered. Thus the output of **neqn** is actually the **troff** text that could have been produced, albeit laboriously and with errors, by a human programmer. In normal usage, however, this intermediate text is never actually seen by a human eye because it is easier to pipe the **neqn** output directly to **troff**:

```
$ neqn textfile | troff
```

The output then appears as if **neqn** and **troff** constituted a single program.

Since **troff** commands are fully acceptable to **nroff**, it is in principle possible to use **neqn** to set up equations for **nroff** as well. However, the results are in most cases not very attractive; mathematical typesetting does benefit greatly from the availability of Greek characters and multiple fonts.

Table Manipulation with **tbl**

Tabular matter is often quite difficult to set up in an attractive fashion with normal editing programs. Columns in tables are justified in accordance with various criteria, as may be seen in the following simple example:

Average Increase Rates with Time

Industry	Class	Increase
Electronics	B	12.7
Construction	AA	1.25
Aircraft	K	103.

Here one column is left-justified, one is right-justified, and one is justified to keep the decimal points in line. Many other variations are encountered, for example, the inclusion of special symbols or the ruling of boxes around tables.

The **tbl** program is another **troff** preprocessor that allows tables to be set up using specialized commands. These commands and the tabular data are encased in delimiters that identify material to be processed by **tbl**; **.TS** (table start) and **.TE** (table end) at the left margin identify the limits of tabular matter. When **tbl** is run, this material is processed into a set of **troff** commands; the rest is passed through unmodified. As in the case of **neqn**, the result is the same as if a human operator had produced the same command string. The command structure of **tbl** is not complicated to understand, but there are many commands simply because there are many ways that a table can be set up. The **tbl** reference article in the *Unix Programmer's Manual* is 18 pages long, but it is easy to read and well repays the brief study it requires.

The **neqn** and **tbl** preprocessors may of course be combined by a pipeline,

```
$ neqn inputfile | tbl | troff
```

The cost of invoking the extra preprocessor is very small since any text not flagged for preprocessing is simply passed through by both preprocessors. **tbl** can be used with **nroff** as easily as with **troff**, provided that the limitations of **nroff** are respected; i.e., there must be no changes of type size, style, or other attributes that a plain printing terminal cannot manage.

Spelling and Typographic Errors

Despite the best intentions, spelling errors and typographic errors will creep in when text is prepared. Standard Unix software provides a certain measure of error-proofing by allowing text to be checked against a built-in spelling dictionary. The spelling check may of course also turn up typographic errors.

The Dictionary Check

The basic Unix system facility for checking spelling is a program called
spell. spell is invariably used with a spelling dictionary. It reads the text
file to be checked and identifies as words those character strings which are
encased by suitable combinations of terminator characters—blanks, line
ends, and punctuation marks. Each word is then checked against entries in a
spelling dictionary. In most Unix implementations, the dictionary resides in
file /usr / dict / words, but in some installations it may be located
elsewhere. spell produces as output a list of the words which were not
found in the dictionary and which therefore qualify as potential spelling
errors.

Devising ways of checking for correctness of spelling is a fascinating
problem in both lexicography and computer science. To spot misspellings, it
is helpful to know what to expect, so that a detailed analysis of each word is
indicated. People automatically recognize the word *recreation* as being
composed of the prefix *re-*, the stem *creat-*, and the suffix *-tion*, the
composition being done subject to rules which drop one of the two *t*'s that
would arise from agglutinating *re-creat-tion*. People, as a rule, will therefore
spot *recreattion* as being misspelled even if the word is not a familiar one.
For a computer program to do as well is not at all easy. The rules are
complicated, the stems many and confusing.

The spell program can be run in two ways: it may be asked to spot all
words not found in the dictionary in their exact forms, or it may accept as
correct those words which can be formed from words in the dictionary by
applying a limited set of word transformation rules. When asked to check
for literal accuracy, without applying any transformation rules, a relatively
large number of words may be flagged as possibly erroneous, because
project, *projective*, and *projectively* will be considered unrelated words; each
will be accepted only if it appears listed in the dictionary in precisely that
form. Under the word transformation rules, possessive endings, various
prefixes, such as *re-*, *in-*, and a variety of suffixes (*-tion*, *-ing*) are all sorted
out nicely. In a few cases they may be spotted incorrectly, for the English
language is simply not so consistent as to permit encoding all valid
transformation rules in a program of reasonable size. Nevertheless, it is
surprising and pleasing how few real mistakes spell actually does make
when operated this way.

There is a considerable amount of difference between English and
American spellings for many words and some suffixes. spell provides the
option of examining for either form of spelling, but it does so by providing
alternative valid dictionary entries. As a result, spell can proofread text
that conforms to either one standard or the other but not to mixtures. Some
inconvenience may well be felt by Canadians or Australians, who are quite
accustomed to employ both spellings and frequently choose American
spellings for some words, British for others. Under the rules as understood

by **spell**, he who favors *colour* and *odour* is not permitted the *z* in *recognize*—not even if used with absolute consistency—and is required to spell *tyre* with a *y*.

Typographical Errors

The easiest way of finding typographical errors in text is to employ **spell**; words such as *ditcionary* and *dicctionary* will be flagged as suspect and can then be picked out. If there are not very many distinct typographical errors, they can be corrected easily enough with the **ed** editor. If there are really a great many, one of the fancier batch-mode editors can be used instead.

There do also exist some typographic error spotting programs which simply scan words and report as suspect any character string that does not satisfy certain rules of character sequences (e.g., three consonants in a row are suspect). Such checkers are fast but often unreliable. None is provided as part of the standard Version 7 Unix system.

It should be kept in mind that any presently existing program designed to find misspellings or mistypings can only look for errors in individual words; it will not perform textual analysis. Hence typographic errors can never be spotted if they result in lexically acceptable words which combine to produce semantic nonsense; for example, *test* in place of *text* will pass all spelling checks. Similarly, errors in homonyms (similar-sounding but differently spelled words) such as *waist* and *waste*, cannot be located by spelling checkers.

Chapter 8

Languages and Compilers

While some users are interested in the Unix system purely in order to run ready-made programs—to produce invoices, compile statistics, or photo-typeset reports—many computer users will at one time or another wish to use the program development facilities available. Because the Unix operating system is relatively transportable, compiler writers have found it very much worthwhile to produce language compilers to run under it. This chapter provides an overview of the programming languages generally available and gives details on the most important and popular of these.

Programming Languages Available

The language support provided by standard Version 7 Unix software is relatively restricted, but other versions of the Unix system, particularly those destined for the newer computer hardware configurations, have added many others. The result is a rich haul indeed, including most of the programming languages commonly employed in scientific computing as well as several others whose primary orientation is to commercial data processing.

Structured Languages

The key language of the Unix system, in which most of the system itself is written, is a language called C. A C compiler is naturally included in the basic Unix software tool kit. C is a structured language which bears considerable resemblance to Pascal but remains closer to the actual machine architecture. C occupies a rather special role, because most other high-level languages are processed at least part way by the C compiler. One important result of this arrangement is that intermixing of procedures originating in different-high level languages is often possible.

Pascal is also supported under virtually all Unix systems; indeed several Unix-compatible Pascal compilers are now in existence. Unfortunately, Version 7 as released by Bell Laboratories does not include a Pascal compiler. The University of California, Berkeley, version of the Unix system includes a Pascal compiler that has gained wide acceptance, however. It is available in a large number of Unix installations and is therefore briefly described in this chapter.

The Ada language is not yet supported but it is sure to appear before long. Ada is a structured language specified by the United States Department of Defense as its preferred high-level language.

Fortran

The best known and most widely used high-level language for scientific computing is probably Fortran. Despite its many acknowledged shortcomings, engineers and physicists habitually use almost nothing else. Fortran was intended for scientific computing from the outset; indeed its name was coined as an acronym for FORmula TRANslator. It has been in use for over a quarter of a century, so there now exists a large amount of acquired programming expertise in the scientific community and also an immense pool of Fortran applications software. Thus the scientific computing community will probably continue to use Fortran for many years to come. No operating system can be considered a serious candidate for large-scale computing if it does not support at least one version of the Fortran language, so despite their apparent distaste for the language, the Bell Laboratories Unix software team did make Fortran available.

Like its forerunners, Version 7 of the Unix system also supports a Fortran dialect called Ratfor (RATional FORtran), which permits structured forms similar to those of Pascal or Ada. `ratfor` is the corresponding Fortran preprocessor; it translates Ratfor text to ordinary Fortran. A reverse translator, for turning Fortran into Ratfor, is also provided.

A Veritable Babel

Turning from the languages distributed in the Version 7 package and Pascal, which is so widespread as to qualify at least as "semiofficial", the Unix system user is faced with a veritable Babel. The languages include almost everything the computer user might imagine, from Basic to Lisp.

Snobol, APL, and Algol 68 are three high-level languages for which compilers are available under Unix. While these languages are not part of Version 7, various Unix systems do support them, and they are fairly widely used. Cobol appears to be running satisfactorily at some computing installations, and Lisp is employed by many workers in artificial intelligence.

Basic is available in the Version 7 release, though one might well enquire why—when such a wide range of better languages exists. Perhaps the answer is that Basic is directly interpreted, truly interactive, and therefore simple to use for quick calculations. Much the same point might be made for the desk calculator simulators available under most Unix systems.

There is one language always available under any operating system, which is absolutely not transportable: the native assembler language of the host machine. Very little use need be made of it, since the great majority of user needs is covered by C. However, there do arise some occasions when use of machine instructions is essential, and for those occasions an assembler is absolutely imperative. Unfortunately, it is not practical to give full details of the assemblers for all the many machines on which Unix operating systems now run; the PDP-11 assembler is briefly mentioned here as an example.

Fortran 77

The Fortran language is supported under Unix in its most recent version, Fortran 77. Fortran was first introduced in the late 1950s and was brought into standard form ten years later, the nominal date of the standard being 1966. The need for another revision became obvious some time thereafter, and led to the creation of Fortran 77, a new standard. Almost all of the old Standard Fortran (Fortran 66) is included as a subset of the Unix dialect of Fortran 77, so that the majority of ordinary Fortran 66 programs should be usable without any difficulty.

Because Fortran is well known, no attempt is made here to describe the Fortran language itself. People not acquainted with Fortran but interested in learning about it are well advised to begin by reading one of the many excellent introductory textbooks on this language.

The **f77** Fortran 77 Compiler

The normal Fortran language compiler available in most Unix systems is **f77**, which implements the new standard.

It is interesting to observe is that **f77** does not translate Fortran directly into assembler language for the machine in question. Instead, it produces C intermediate code. This approach to compilation implies that many features of C which are not considered part of Fortran under the standard rules become acceptable automatically. For example, recursive subroutine calls are not permitted in standard Fortran, but they are accepted in **f77** Fortran. All the library subroutines and system calls available through C become available through Fortran also. Compiling Fortran into C intermediate code further implies that procedures written in the two languages may be intermixed; Fortran programs can use C functions as if they had been written in Fortran, and C functions can call Fortran subroutines equally well. Indeed the intermixing extends to any other language, past or future, whose compilation passes through C intermediate code.

In Unix Fortran 77 there are also some variations from the Fortran standard which are not easily explained in terms of C-dependence. Few compiler writers have ever created Fortran compilers true to the published standard; there are usually a few added features, a few extensions, and some improvements. **f77** is no exception; it does accept (almost) any correct Fortran 77 program, subject to a few relatively minor exceptions, and it does provide some additional features not part of the Fortran 77 standard. There are only a few rather minor violations of the Fortran 77 rules by **f77**. The enhancements and added features are rather more numerous. Both the enhancements and the exceptions will be treated in some detail below.

Running Fortran Programs

The compilation, loading, and execution of a Fortran program under any operating system is quite a complicated affair, involving a sequence of processes. Fortunately, there is no need for most users to see the complexities because the commands needed to run simple jobs are pipelined and appear to the user as a single command. To run a Fortran 77 program stored in file **fortprog**, it suffices to enter the command

   $ f77 fortprog

When the shell prompt **$** next appears, an executable object program called **a.out** will be found in the user's current directory. It contains the machine-language code corresponding to **fortprog**. It can be moved to a more sensible name if desired; in any case, it can be executed. A more sensible name, say **newfile**, can also be specified in the command itself, following the option flag **-o**, which signifies that the output file will be named. For example,

   $ f77 -o newfile fortprog

There are various other options which the user may request. Those most directly concerned with program debugging are probably **-onetrip, -u, -w,** and **-C**. The **-onetrip** option makes all **do** loops execute at least once; i.e., it arranges for the index to be checked at the end of the loop. The **-u** option makes all variables undefined as to type at the start, thus forcing the programmer to declare each and every variable explicitly (as one would do in an Algol or Pascal program). Many subtle programming errors can be caught in this way. Warning messages are suppressed by the **-w** option. Very useful in mathematical work, **-C** causes all array subscripts to be checked during program execution to ensure that they do not exceed array bounds.

Like any good compiler, **f77** permits a very wide variety of further options. These are shared with the C compiler, the assembler, and the loader through a unified structure of option names and letters. Details will be found below, in the section on compilation and linking.

Textual Extensions to Fortran 77

Numerous extensions to Fortran 77 are accepted by **f77**, but many of them affect only a small minority of users. Those likely to prove of general interest involve formatting of program text, extensions to data types, and some rule relaxations on input and output.

Program form in standard Fortran 77 continues the tradition of the 80-column punch card: Fortran text must be placed in columns 7 to 72. Statement numbers, if there are any, belong in column positions 1 to 5, and any character in column 6 means that the statement in the previous card is being continued on a second or subsequent card image. **f77** is much more tolerant than the standard in such matters. Lines may be of any convenient length and may be typed anywhere in the available space. Continuation lines must contain an ampersand (the **&** character) in the first column position, with Fortran text following anywhere thereafter. Statement numbers are separated from statement text by a tab character.

While the Fortran 77 standard recognizes only the 26 uppercase alphabetic characters, one might well expect **f77** to share the Unix software designers' general addiction to lower case. In an attempt to achieve compatibility, **f77** expects lower case as a matter of course and normally translates all uppercase characters to lowercase (except in character constants). It is possible, however, to suppress this translation; in that case, uppercase characters are regarded as distinct from their lowercase brothers, so that **sum** and **Sum** become distinct variables. Fortran keywords are only recognized in lowercase form, so that when character translation is suppressed,

> **a = sin(b)**   is considered normal,
> **A = sin(b)**   is abnormal but acceptable,
> **A = sin(B)**   is all right, but different,
> **A = SIN(B)**   is simply unacceptable.

Within character string constants, both upper case and lower case are acceptable.

In program text, the Hollerith character construction of Fortran 66 may be employed for character string constants and for initializing noncharacter variables in data statements, even though the Fortran 77 standard does not care for it. For example, one may communicate a string of 23 characters by

```
23hthis ´ is an apostrophe
```

or analogously for uppercase characters. Such usage is particularly convenient where the string contains the apostrophe character, which Fortran 77 uses to delimit strings. f77 allows an alternative way of handling the apostrophe problem, through the provision of two standard quote characters, ´ and ". A character string may be started with either, and is considered terminated at its second occurrence. Hence

```
"this ´ is an apostrophe"
```

will also work nicely. The Hollerith construction was standard in Fortran 66; so its inclusion in f77 makes for program compatibility.

To strengthen compatibility with C, f77 also recognizes certain character combinations beginning with a backslash to be single special characters, not the two-character combinations that they seem to be. These are:

\n   new line
\t   tab character
\b   backspace character
\´   apostrophe ´
\f   form feed (new page)
\0   null character
\\   backslash \
\"   quotation mark "

The existence of these combinations provides yet a third solution to the apostrophe problem:

```
´this \´ is an apostrophe´
```

which may be a little less elegant than those above, but it works.

Extensions to Language Scope

The Fortran accepted by f77 includes two data types not wholly standard, and one entirely unheard of. The declarations

```
integer*2 j
double complex z1
```

are accepted by f77. Experienced Fortran programmers will no doubt guess that the first reserves only two bytes (a half-word) for variable j in byte-oriented machines. The second declaration makes variable z1 both double precision and complex, thus occupying four times the storage allocated to an ordinary real number. The standard Fortran functions applicable to complex numbers, such as `cabs(z1)` and `cexp(z1)`, cannot be used with the double complex data type. To cope, it has been necessary for the `f77` designers to introduce functions applicable to complex data in two parallel families, exactly as the original designers of Fortran provided real functions in both single- and double-precision versions. Function names beginning with `c`, such as `csqrt(z1)`, are used with single-precision complex numbers, while functions whose names begin with `z`, like `zsqrt(z1)`, are used with double complex arguments. Happily, it appears to have been possible to construct `f77` so that a similar double family of functions is not required for long and short integers; one can write, for example, `iabs(ij)` without worrying about whether `ij` is long or short. In other words, type mixing works just fine in integer functions.

A new data type, which is perhaps a bit less obvious, might be best introduced by the declarations

```
implicit undefined (a - z)
integer ij; real a1, bnx
```

The first declaration invalidates the Fortran convention that any symbol beginning with the letters `i` to `n` is an integer and any other symbol a real number; it says that no variable will be considered acceptable unless it has been explicitly declared as to type. The next two declarations (typed on *one* line!) then create the specific variables `ij, a1, bnx`. It is conventional in Algol, Pascal, C, and some other languages to require that each and every variable must be declared explicitly; the same rule can be imposed on the Fortran programmer by declaring everything to be undefined to start with. As one might expect, no operations of any kind are permissible with undefined data.

Initialization of variable values may be accomplished through data statements. In `f77`, bit strings may be specified in a data statement for any variable declared logical, real, or integer. The bit strings may be given in one of three notations: binary, octal, or hexadecimal, as in

```
data a, b, c /b´10010´, o´477´, z´2f´/
```

If both long and short integers are used, care must be taken to specify only as many bits as there actually are in the variable.

Finally, a very useful nonstandard feature of `f77` is the `include` statement. In normal usage, it takes the form

```
include textfile
```

where *textfile* is the name of a file containing Fortran statements. `f77` does not translate this statement; instead, it asks for a file *textfile* to be found and causes its contents to be copied into the Fortran program so as to replace the `include` statement. Blocks of Fortran text which need to be duplicated in many subroutines, such as array dimensions, `common` statements, and `equivalence`s, can be placed in a single file and then included in numerous places in a Fortran program (e.g., at the head of each subroutine) using this facility. An immense amount of debugging and editing labor can be saved during program development, since changes in array dimensions or variable declarations will be carried through all program segments automatically if they are changed in just the single file `included` in every program segment.

Fortran 77 Input and Output

In principle, all Fortran input and output operations are directed to logical input-output units identified by numbers. `f77` recognizes logical units 0 through 9 as being valid. Three unit assignments are made at the start of any program run, and remain in force unless changed by the program:

Unit 5 is the standard input, usually the keyboard.
Unit 6 is the standard output, usually the screen.
Unit 0 is the standard error output, usually the screen.

The remaining seven Fortran logical units are automatically connected to seven formatted sequential files when program execution starts. Unit 1 is connected to file `fort.1`, unit 2 to file `fort.2`, and so on. These files are located in the user's current directory (default directory) at the time the program is run. In fact, files `fort.1, ..., fort.9` will only be created and retained if they are used, so that users need not bother to open them or to remove them if they were not used.

Fortran logical unit assignments to files can be altered at any time using the Fortran 77 `open` and `close` statements. In their simplest form, these are

```
open (2, file = 'filename')
close (2)
```

The `open` statement attaches a file to a Fortran logical unit. In the normal course of events, the file could be a special file if input or output from a specific physical device (e.g., the keyboard) is expected, or it could be an ordinary file. The file name must be encased in apostrophes to satisfy the rules of Fortran, but in all other respects it is a normal file name in accordance with Unix file-naming conventions. If the unit was previously attached to another file, that file is detached automatically before the new attachment is made. The `close` statement detaches whatever file was attached to a logical unit and leaves the logical unit free.

Fortran files may be formatted or unformatted (binary), and they may permit either sequential or direct access. The Unix system supports all four types of file, handling them all as ordinary files. *Newline* characters are written at ends of records, and *newline* characters are expected as record terminators on input. Internally, direct access files are handled by moving the file pointer in accordance with the known record length. Consequently the record length must be declared (in bytes) when a direct access file is opened. For example, the Fortran statement

```
open (unit = 2, file = `phonebook´, form = formatted,
& access = direct, recl = 60, status = old, err = 999)
```

opens **phonebook** as an already existing formatted direct access file with a record length of 60 bytes, and connects it to logical unit 2.

Sequential files have their pointers positioned at their ends when they are first opened, so that writing can be done naturally by appending to the already existing file content. Attempts to read, on the other hand, will produce an end-of-file indication. To read a file, it is therefore necessary to rewind it first.

When reading numeric input, **f77** takes a somewhat more relaxed attitude to formatting than the Fortran 77 standard prescribes. The standard **format** statement is framed in terms of card images (column counts in **format** statements), while **f77** attempts to preserve its orientation to the screen display terminal. Commas are therefore accepted as separators between numeric fields, overriding the field widths shown in the **format** statements. For example, the format specification **2f12.0** will be quite satisfied by the character string

1.2758, 3.7

despite its failure to respect the format specification. This relaxed attitude is unfortunately only applicable to numeric data. There is no convenient way to extend the same leniency to character string variables, because the comma itself could be a legitimate part of a character string.

Fortran 77 Rule Violations

There is very little specified by the Fortran 77 standard not implemented in **f77**. The exceptions include

(1) The treatment of double precision variables which appear in **common** or **equivalence** statements.
(2) The treatment of character-valued variables when passed as subroutine arguments.
(3) The treatment of tab (absolute tab and leftward tab) format control codes is nonstandard for sequential files or devices.

Happily, the rules are violated only in cases which most ordinary programmers never run into, so that they are usually quite unaware the violations exist. The rarity of any malfunctions makes the shock doubly great when violations do occur, hence the warnings given here.

The first exception only arises on computers where the hardware requires all double-precision variables to start at even word locations. If there is any problem, a diagnostic message is issued; unwelcome surprises are rare. Unfortunately, the fact that only some machines have such a requirement means that f77 cannot be made totally machine independent.

The second exception results from the way character variables are handled by f77, which in turn results at least partly from a desire to remain compatible with C. Again, a warning message is issued if there appears to be any difficulty. Problems of this kind can always be cured by a few external declarations.

The third exception arises from a logical inconsistency in Fortran 77 or rather from inclusion in the standard of assumptions about how the language is implemented. Backing up (which is implied by a left tab) is clearly not possible on any truly sequential device or file. The Fortran 77 standard seems to assume that the input or output of any sequential device is sufficiently buffered to allow backing up at least within the current record, but the Unix dialect of Fortran does not make a similar assumption about genuinely sequential devices (e.g., a terminal display screen). Attempts to back up where Unix will not allow it lead to execution-time error messages.

Ratfor: A Rational Fortran

Ratfor is an extended form of Fortran. It includes many of the control structures around which Pascal and C have been built. Initially introduced as part of the Unix system, Ratfor has recently found wider acceptance. Several other operating systems now have Ratfor preprocessors available.

The ratfor Preprocessor

The Fortran language has long been the language favored by scientific programmers, for a large number of reasons, including its almost universal acceptance. Computer scientists generally consider it an unattractive antique because it contains neither the linguistic niceties that make for clean program structure nor the ability to structure data that Pascal, Ada, and other newer languages provide.

Short of redefining the Fortran language, there is not much to be done about its paucity of data types. However, syntax rules lend themselves to treatment by means of language enhancements through preprocessors. The Ratfor language represents a fairly successful step in this direction. In contrast to many other extended Fortran dialects, Ratfor text is never actually compiled, only translated into standard Fortran. Ratfor is therefore locked to the Unix system only to the extent of the Ratfor-to-Fortran conversion; from there on, the programs will run anywhere that a Fortran compiler can be found. Using the normal Unix language translators, the sequence from Ratfor to executable code thus passes through four intermediate forms, of which two or three (depending on one's taste for C intermediate code) are human-readable languages:

Ratfor	*translates to*	Fortran,
Fortran	*translates to*	C intermediate code,
C intermediate	*translates to*	assembler language,
assembler	*translates to*	relocatable object code,
relocatable code	*translates to*	executable object code.

The multiplicity of intermediate forms implies that program segments originating in other languages or created at other times can be grafted on to the structure easily and naturally. On the other hand, all the necessary processes are usually pipelined together; thus the average user need never even know what intermediate stages existed.

Program Text Formatting in Ratfor

Ratfor strikes the newcomer at first glance as being a free-format version of Fortran. Statements may be placed anywhere on a line and may be continued on as many lines as desired. Continuation characters are not needed. The `ratfor` preprocessor will justify statements to begin in column 7 and will supply continuation characters in column 6 where necessary. Multiple statements on one line are permitted. In general, the semicolon (the ; character) is used to separate statements. Semicolons are of course essential if several statements are to appear on one line, but they are optional if a statement ends at a line end. `ratfor` does make an effort to spot incomplete statements, and assumes that continuation across a line end is meant if a line ends with any one of the characters that imply arithmetic or logical operations to follow:

$$+ \; - \; * \; = \; , \; | \; \& \; (\; -$$

The underscore (the _ character) can be used to force `ratfor` to understand that a continuation is meant. Underscore characters are not reproduced in the Fortran output. Semicolons and underscores can always be used to avoid and dispel confusion about statement ends and continuations.

Statement numbers may be entered anywhere in a Ratfor line, but of course they must always precede the statement itself. In fact, wherever a line begins with a number, `ratfor` assumes that the number is a statement number and arranges it to be placed in columns 1 to 5 of the Fortran output. However, the structure of Ratfor is such that very few statement numbers are likely to be used in the Ratfor text in any case.

The comparison operators generally used to form Fortran logical expressions are replaced in Ratfor by symbols a little closer to their mathematical origins. They are subsequently translated by `ratfor` into their usual Fortran equivalents:

$==$ *becomes* `.eq.`	$\langle$ *becomes* `.lt.`	$!=$ *becomes* `.ne.`
$\rangle$ `.gt.`	$\langle=$ `.le.`	`&` `.and.`
$\rangle=$ `.ge.`	`!` `.not.`	`	` `.or.`

While experienced Fortran programmers may find expressions like `x .gt. 0` to be quite natural, many people would prefer `x > 0`.

Ratfor is deliberately designed so that the `ratfor` preprocessor need not understand any Fortran. There are occasions on which it seems desirable to prevent `ratfor` from even attempting to read Fortran lines, and for this purpose the percent mark (% character) at the beginning of a line is used. Any line that begins with the % character is copied into the Fortran output unaltered except for removal of the % sign itself. In Ratfor jargon, the % character when so used is called the *transparency operator* to indicate that it makes every such line pass through `ratfor` entirely unseen and unprocessed.

Statement Groups and **if** Statements

Ratfor control flow strongly resembles that of Algol or Pascal, indeed it is quite surprising how little translation is required to produce standard Fortran out of programs that hardly look like Fortran at all. A basic Ratfor idea is to allow Fortran programmers to use statement groups (like Pascal compound statements) where Fortran ordinarily allows only single ones, thereby making most statement numbers unnecessary. A statement group is exactly what the name says: a group of statements which logically belong together, and which may be inserted in Ratfor wherever the Fortran rules would allow a single statement. Statement groups are identified by enclosing them in braces **{ ... }**. To give a simple example, the Fortran **if** statement permits conditional execution of just one statement, while Ratfor allows several actions to be requested in one statement group:

```
if (x < 0) {call errmsg; answer = 0.0; return}
```

In ordinary Fortran, the equivalent would read

```
      if (x .ge. 0) go to 100
      call errmsg
      answer = 0.0
      return
100 continue
```

Very few statement numbers and very few **go to** statements, are needed in Ratfor. Many of the inverted **if** constructs of Fortran are also eliminated: Ratfor makes it easy to say "if x is negative, do this ..." rather than "if x is not negative, don't do this ..." as in the Fortran example above.

Ratfor allows an **if – then – else** construct to be used with statement groups, in the natural form

```
if (x < 0) then {a = res; j = -1} else {a = -res;
    j = 1}
```

This form is cleaner and tidier than its ANSI Fortran equivalent, which requires at least one inversion (below, left). It is much less verbose than its Fortran 77 equivalent (below, right) and distinctly easier to read than either:

```
      if (x .ge. 0) go to 10      if (x .lt. 0) then
      a = -res                    a = res
      j = 1                       j = -1
      go to 20                    else
   10 a = res                     a = -res
      j = -1                      j = 1
   20 continue                    endif
```

Ratfor **if – then** and **if – then – else** constructs can be nested. Intermixing the two in nested constructs could lead to ambiguities because it may not always be clear to which **if** an **else** belongs; every **if** does not necessarily require an **else**. The ambiguity is resolved by a simple rule: an **else** belongs to the most recent preceding **if** not matched by another **else**.

Program Loops in Ratfor

Ratfor provides a much richer set of looping constructs than Fortran. There are in fact four, which all permit one statement group to be repeated in accordance with some criterion. Pascal programmers will recognize them instantly; for others, they are perhaps best introduced by examples:

```
do i = 1,10 {... statements ...}
for (i = n; i > 0; i = i-1) {... statements ...}
while (x > 0) {... statements ...}
repeat {... statements ...} until (x > 0)
```

Unlike the Fortran **do**, the Ratfor **do** statement does not require a range ("from here down to statement number so-and-so") to be defined because its range is always exactly one statement group. Otherwise, it is similar to an ordinary Fortran **do** loop. In fact, **ratfor** translates the Ratfor **do** statement into just a Fortran **do** loop, so all the rules concerning validity of loop indexing are precisely those of the Fortran compiler which will be used after **ratfor**.

The **for** loop provides a very flexible looping structure. Like the **do** loop, it is guided by an integer loop index. The index is initialized at some value when the loop is first entered. During each trip around the loop, it is examined to see whether it meets some condition, and is then altered according to some rule. The initial value, condition, and rule are listed in the parentheses following the keyword **for**. The initializing and alteration may be performed by any one Fortran statement, and the condition may be any valid logical expression. Since "any one Fortran statement" includes a subroutine call, progression through a **for** loop can take place in infinitely many ways. The **ratfor** preprocessor creates Fortran code which tests for loop completion first, and performs the index alteration only after loop completion. Thus the loop indexed **for (i = 10; i<0; i = i + 1)** will not be executed at all. Looping backward or looping through chains of pointers can be accomplished easily with **for** loops.

The **while** loop and **repeat – until** loop are essentially index-free loops. Both merely examine a logical condition, and continue if it is met (**while** loop) or not met (**repeat – until**). The condition must be a single valid Fortran logical expression, but this rule is not very constraining, since the expression may involve a call to a separately defined logical function. The **while** loop tests for the condition before executing the statement group, so it is possible that the statement group will not be executed at all. The **repeat – until** condition is tested afterward; the associated statement group will therefore be executed at least once.

Ratfor allows two additional statements, **next** and **break**, to be embedded in the statement groups controlled by loops. Any statement group in any one of the four types of loop can be cut short by the Ratfor statement **next**. Unconditional exit from any type of loop is caused by the statement **break**. The **next** statement simply skips the remainder of the statement group. What happens next depends on the type of loop; in the case of a **for** loop, the index is incremented, but the other three loop types will proceed to test the loop terminating condition.

Text Insertions and Substitutions

Ratfor includes two further statements, which permit text substitutions; **define** and **include**. The **define** statement permits a character string value to be assigned to a name:

```
define long 500
```

Wherever the name **long** appears in subsequent Ratfor text, the character string **500** is substituted. Calling **long** a name implies that the character string **long** is recognized as such only if it is immediately preceded and followed by characters which are not alphanumeric. Thus the program segment

```
define long 500
dimension xarray(long); oblong = x + 27.5
```

will become on translation

```
dimension xarray(500)
oblong = x + 27.5
```

because the string **long** has nonalphanumerics fore and aft in the **dimension** statement and therefore constitutes a name in the foregoing sense; but **long** is preceded by the alphabetic character **b** in the subsequent arithemetic assignment, so it is not a name. The **define** statement is useful for achieving much the same effects as the **parameter** statement of Fortran 77. However, it is much more powerful because the name may stand for any character string whatever (e.g., a subroutine call), it is not required to denote a single numeric value.

The **include** statement of Ratfor is similar to the corresponding statement of Fortran 77:

> **include** *filename*

causes the file *filename* to be found and copied into the program text, replacing the **include** statement. It is very convenient for inserting multiple copies of the same text, e.g., of **common** blocks or globally applicable parameter definitions, while maintaining only one actual copy of the text. Any editing changes in the master text then automatically appear everywhere.

Ambiguity and Duplication

A fundamental principle of Ratfor design is that **ratfor** should not understand or for the most part recognize Fortran language. A few potential difficulties may arise from this fact.

In Fortran, keywords are not reserved and may be used as variable names, subroutine names, **common** block labels, etc. Thus

```
call call
```

may look a bit curious, but it is perfectly valid Fortran. The compiler will sort out that the first **call** is a Fortran keyword, the second a subroutine name. However, **ratfor** cannot do the same, since it does not know Fortran. Ratfor keywords are therefore reserved. It is not permitted to use **call** as the name of a subroutine nor **if** as the name of an integer variable.

One way of handling dubious lines is to prevent `ratfor` from reading them, by placing a % sign in the first column of the line. The arithmetic `if` statement, for example, can be handled only in this way; otherwise, `ratfor` will spot the keyword `if` and attempt to process the rest as an ordinary logical `if` statement. Similarly, the `include` statement may be intended for action by `f77` at a later time; if so, it can be shielded from `ratfor` by the % sign. Since lines marked by the % sign are not processed at all by `ratfor`, the user must assume full responsibility for their correctness.

Using `ratfor`

`ratfor` can be invoked in two ways: by itself, or as part of an `f77` run. If Ratfor text is placed in a file whose name terminates with `.r` (for example, `text.r`), `f77` will automatically include `ratfor` as the first step in the Fortran pipeline. Thus the command

    $ f77 text.r

will cause the file `text.r` to be translated to Fortran, compiled, and loaded into an executable object file called `a.out`—provided that no errors were encountered in the various processing steps.

If only a translation to Fortran is desired, without compilation, the command `ratfor` will invoke the preprocessor on its own. Some quite straightforward options are provided with `ratfor`. If none are specified, output compatible with the `f77` compiler is produced, but Fortran text formatting agreeable to other compilers can be provided as an alternative.

Reverse Processing with **struct**

Fortran programs can be made easier to maintain by using the convenience features of Ratfor. To do so, it is necessary first to invert the translation process, i.e., to generate a Ratfor program from the Fortran source code. The **struct** program does precisely this, producing reasonable Ratfor from either Fortran 66 or Fortran 77 text.

Like the result of any reverse translation process, the inversion produced by **struct** is not unique. A number of options is therefore provided, in order to allow a measure of control over the Ratfor text produced by **struct**. Most **struct** options can be safely ignored, because their effects are relatively harmless; e.g., **break** statements might be tidier than **go to** statements, but neither will hurt. Nevertheless, there are a few possible pitfalls, such as the use of Ratfor keywords as Fortran variable names in the original source code. Conversion of a large program is therefore best done in several passes, first inverting the program using `struct` and then following up with `ratfor` to check whether the inversion ran into any snags.

The C Language

The language C is the prime language of the Unix system. The two were in fact developed concurrently and grew together; thus the needs of the system largely shaped the language. In many respects C represents a halfway house between true high-level languages (like Pascal or Algol) which strive to be machine independent and assembler languages keyed entirely to the structure of a particular computer. Since C recognizes various lower-level entities with which the system programmer often has to deal, it is considered by many an ideal language in which to write operating systems. C compilers are now available under several operating systems of widely varying character.

In this chapter, C occupies a position slightly different from Fortran and Pascal. Nearly all C programmers are already acquainted with the Unix system or another similar operating system; people often learn the language because they work with the system, rarely the other way around. On the other hand, many experienced Fortran or Pascal programmers are newcomers to both C and Unix. Consequently, this section is intended primarily for programmers already acquainted with other high-level languages. It describes the main characteristics of C, outlines how C is related to other languages, and hints at why its authors should have deemed a new language necessary at all. The discussion given here is not sufficient to learn programming in C; for that, the definitive book by Kernighan and Ritchie should be consulted.

The version of C available with the Version 7 Unix system is (by definition!) the authoritative version. Hence there are no peculiarities or deviations from the standard to be noted.

General Characteristics of C

The structure of C places it midway between Fortran and Pascal, but with the significant difference that C understands a number of machine-dependent facts of life which the other two languages ignore. Although the C language is sometimes said to be machine independent, C programs frequently are not. Unlike Pascal or Algol, C assumes a twos-complement binary machine of finite and fixed word length, which supports double- as well as single-precision variables (short and long integers, single- and double-precision floating-point numbers). It presupposes that characters are represented by single bytes or by word segments which resemble bytes. The set of available data types and operators is large, almost as large as one might expect in a machine language. Bit-level operations such as shifts and maskings, unions and intersections are almost as readily accomplished in C as in machine language. There are other constructs in C which one is accustomed to find in assembler languages but not in high-level languages: address values, indices, incrementation and decrementation operators.

Structure of C Programs

A C program consists of one or more *functions*, each possessing zero or more arguments. A C function is comparable in form and purpose to a function in Fortran or Pascal. Functions in C have names; the function `funct` is invoked by mentioning its name, with its arguments listed in parentheses:

```
funct (a,b,c);
```

Functions without arguments may exist, but the parentheses are required even if there are no arguments, e.g., `funct()`. A function is declared to exist by naming it, with a dummy argument list, and giving the set of C statements which define it. The set of defining statements is enclosed in braces, as in

```
funct () {... C statements ... }
```

A function generally involves computation with its arguments and also with variables purely internal to itself. Argument declarations for a function go between the end of the argument list and the left brace:

```
funct(x,y,z) int x; double y,z; { ... }
```

Semicolons are used as declaration terminators. Here and elsewhere in C, it pays to note the difference between terminators and separators: a terminator is required after the last declaration.

A function has a value, i.e., it appears in C statements in contexts where an arithmetic value is expected. By default, all functions are considered to return integer values. If desired, a function may return values which correspond to any other acceptable data type in C, but a type declaration must then precede the function name. Thus

```
double dfunct (x, ...) int x, ...; { ... }
```

defines a function `dfunct` which returns a double-precision value. Functions may also perform other activities, e.g., read a character or write a block to tape. Where the value is in principle not explicitly necessary, it is often used as a success flag. For example, a function that copies one file to another may return the integer value 1 if the operation was carried out successfully, the value 0 if not (e.g., if the file to be copied was not found).

There is no such thing in C as a "main program" in the Fortran sense; instead, there is one privileged function name, `main`. Execution of a C program always begins with `main`, which in turn must invoke any other functions required. Although `main` is privileged in this way, it is a function and its declaration must contain parentheses. An interesting feature of C is that any arguments presented in `main` are passed on to or from the operating system itself, so that communication between the Unix kernel and a user program becomes possible. A typical C program will have the form

```
main () { ... C statements ... funct1 (p,q,r) ...}
funct1 (a,b,c) ... {... C statements ... funct2 (h) ...}
funct2 (x) ... {... C statements ...}
```

The braces {...} are considered to turn the whole string of statements into a single compound statement, much like the Pascal **begin** and **end** brackets. Indeed the punctuation rules of C resemble those of Pascal, with semicolons used as statement terminators. The closing brace obviates the need for a semicolon just as **end** does in Pascal.

No special statement exists in C for defining a function, a fact which may seem strange to programmers accustomed to `function`, `subroutine`, or `procedure` statements. If the C compiler encounters a name which has not yet occurred, and if the name is followed by a left parenthesis, it is automatically taken to be a function. There does exist a `return` statement, but many programmers use it only when they need it to specify the function value to be returned. Program control is returned when execution logically reaches the closing brace, even without a return statement.

Recursion is permitted in a C function, i.e., a function may invoke itself. However, functions may not be defined within functions. A C program therefore resembles a Fortran program much more closely than the nested block structure of Pascal or Algol. This structural simplicity makes separate compilation of C functions relatively easy to arrange. Furthermore, the Unix C and Fortran compilers can share a substantial amount of program code. Both are translated into a common intermediate language and processed in an identical fashion thereafter. Fortran, C, and assembler-language programs may therefore be intermixed quite freely, so that different sections of a large program can be written in different languages chosen to suit each processing task.

All fundamental C variables are passed to functions by value, not by name. In effect, duplicate variables are created for a called function when it is called, and values are assigned to the duplicates. The function operates on the duplicates only, and therefore cannot affect the variables or constants in the function which called it into action. If modification of variables in the calling function is in fact desired, the equivalent of a call by name is possible in C through the mechanism of pointers.

The sequence in which C functions are called into play is controlled by program flow mechanisms which strongly resemble those of Pascal and

Ratfor: **if** statements have a similar form; a **for ... while** construct exists, the **case** of Pascal reappears with the Algol name of **switch**.

Constants, Variables, and Pointers

The C language has a very rich set of fundamental data types, each allocated a different amount of memory. The memory allocated depends on the machine word length and memory organization. Machine word lengths of 16, 32, and 36 bits are common, and the PDP-11, IBM 370, and Honeywell 6000 computers may be regarded as typical representatives of these. The data types available in C and the number of memory bits allocated to each are given in the table below.

Memory Bits per C Variable

Data type as defined in C		Machine word length		
Name	Characteristics	16	32	36
int	signed integer	16	32	36
char	single character	8	8	9
short	integer (short)	16	16	36
long	integer (long)	32	32	36
unsigned	nonnegative integer	16	16	36
float	floating point	32	32	36
double	double precision	64	64	72

Type **unsigned** is useful for indexing operations, e.g., for addresses where sign is not a consideration. All numerical operations on unsigned integers are done in straight (uncomplemented) binary arithmetic. The other integer types are stored in twos-complemented notation, and arithmetic is performed accordingly.

There is no type *logical* or *boolean* in the C language. However, logical operations are defined on integers. C considers any nonzero value to signify *true*, and zero to denote *false*. Each and every variable must be declared in a C program; a new variable may never be introduced by simply using it. This insistence on strong typing of variables is felt by some people to contrast strangely with the lack of a function declaration statement. However, it is a matter to which Pascal and Algol programmers are quite accustomed in any case. In C, the usual place for declarations is at the head of each function. A declaration consists of a type name, followed by a list of variables:

```
float a, b, c;
int i, j, k;
```

The scope of a variable is confined to the function in which it is defined; it is undefined outside. Variables can be made `extern` by declaring them outside any function, for example,

```
int x,y;
main () {int f,g; ... funct(a,b) ...}
funct (p,q) int p,q; {extern int x,y; ...}
```

`extern` variables are somewhat like Pascal variables declared in the outermost block. They permit global use of values, somewhat along the same lines as the Fortran `common` declaration, but they are neater and easier because variable identification is always by name, not by storage position in a `common` block. Mercifully, there is no precise analogue of the Fortran `equivalence`, which many programmers find a breeding ground for particularly difficult bugs.

Pointers are widely used in C, much like pointers in Pascal. The value of a pointer is the memory address of the variable to which it points. There is no declaration *pointer*; instead, they are declared implicitly by saying, e.g., "p is a pointer which contains the address of a floating-point variable":

```
float *p;
```

The asterisk operator implies "the variable to which p points." Its inverse is the ampersand, i.e., `&x` is the pointer to (the address of) the variable `x`. Pointers and variables are associated by means of assignment statements which tie them together implicitly. For example,

```
p = &x;
y = *p;
```

In pointer manipulation, the different word lengths associated with different variable types are taken care of automatically. Thus there are in reality several different kinds of pointers, one corresponding to each possible data type.

Arrays in C are in principle one-dimensional. They are established by means of a type declaration statement like

```
float a[5];
```

Indexing of arrays always starts at zero, so this declaration says that array components a[0] to a[4] inclusive exist. Two-dimensional arrays are declared as arrays of one-dimensional arrays. The declaration consists of attaching to an existing declaration the number of repetitions in square brackets. Thus

```
float x[5][3];
```

is equivalent to the Fortran declaration `real x(3,5)`. Array storage is by rows (Fortran programmers take note), i.e., the rightmost subscript varies fastest.

C knows about various constants: integer, floating, character, string. All floating constants are automatically taken to be double length; therefore the exponential E notation covers both single and double precision. Character constants are set in quotes, e.g. ´A´. They can be used in arithmetic; however, their numeric values vary from one installation to another. There also exists a set of character constants, principally used to represent nonprinting characters, which are denoted by two-character sequences. The main ones are \n (the *newline* character), \r (carriage return), \b (backspace), and \t (tab). Any desired bit pattern may be placed in a character constant as *nnn*, where *nnn* is an unsigned octal number of one to three digits. A string constant is a string of characters encased in quotes, e.g., "string constant". They can be placed into character arrays of the appropriate size.

Arithmetic and Logical Operations

As programming languages go, C recognizes and uses a very large set of operators. Operators come in four principal classes: unary, binary, relational, and assignment.

Unary operators are used as prefixes to values (variables, constants, or functions), as is customary in almost any programming language. For example, one writes

    x = !x

to indicate that a logical complementation (negation) of the variable x is desired. Other unary operators are used in a similar fashion. An exception is formed by the operators ++ and --, which increment or decrement the operand, respectively. These operators may be applied either before or after evaluation of the operand (including a single variable) to which they relate, and they are positioned either preceding the expression (if predecrementation is required) or following it (for postdecrementation or postincrementation). For example, ++ x indicates incrementation prior to evaluation, x + + indicates incrementation afterward. While predecrementation and postincrementation are notions familiar to most machine-language programmers, they are not frequently encountered in high-level languages. These operators are included in the full set of available unary operators in the table below.

OPERATORS USED IN C

Unary Operators	
*	indirection (compute the value associated with a pointer)
&	pointer creation (compute pointer associated with a value)
–	arithmetic negation (negative of the value)
!	logical negation (zero produces 1, nonzero produces 0)
–	bitwise (ones) complement of an integer variable
++	following operand incremented before evaluation (e.g. ++ x)

Unary Operators (*Continued*)

`--`	following operand decremented before evaluation (e.g. `-- x`)
`++`	preceding operand incremented after evaluation (e.g. `x + +`)
`--`	preceding operand decremented after evaluation (e.g. `x - -`)
`(type)`	type name in parentheses preceding operand converts type
`sizeof`	size (in characters) of following operand or type name

Binary Operators

`*`	multiply the two operands
`/`	divide, truncating if operands are integers
`%`	find remainder from integer division
`+`	add the operands
`-`	subtract
`<<`	shift first operand left the number of bits given by second
`>>`	shift first operand right the number of bits given by second
`&`	bitwise AND (boolean product) of the two integral operands
`↑`	bitwise exclusive OR of the two integral operands
`|`	bitwise inclusive OR of the two integral operands
`&&`	logical AND (yields 1 if both operands nonzero, 0 otherwise)
`||`	logical OR (yields 1 if either operand nonzero, 0 otherwise)

Relational Operators

`<`	less than
`>`	greater than
`< =`	less than or equal to
`> =`	greater than or equal to
`==`	equal to
`! =`	not equal to

Manipulative binary operations in C also make up an unusually rich set. They all employ infix notation, so that the operator **op** connecting variables x and y always appears in C expressions in the form x **op** y. The relational operators are similar to those in other high-level programming languages. The full set of both manipulative and relational binary operators is shown in the table. Despite the large variety provided, not everything imaginable is included; for instance, there is no exponentiation operator.

   C also contains an unusually large number of assignment symbols. The equal sign = is used in its Fortran sense, but it may be augmented by a binary operator sign to indicate an operation on the variable itself. For example,

```
x += 2;   means   x = x + 2;
x -= 2;   means   x = x - 2;
```

and similar meanings apply for the `* =`, `/ =`, `% =`, `<< =`, `>> =`, `& =`, `=`, and `! =` operators. So far as the underlying bit manipulations are concerned, the precise meaning of an operator is further affected by the data types on which it operates. For example, the symbol **+** placed between two unsigned integers does not lead to the same manipulative operations as **+** placed between two real (type **float**) variables.

Structures

C permits use of entities called *structures*, denoted by **struct**, to simplify data handling. A structure is a set of data objects (not necessarily of the same type) identified by a common name. It closely resembles a **record** in Pascal. For example, a structure may be defined by

```
struct day {int date; char month [9]; int year;} x, y;
```

Henceforth **x** and **y** are understood to have the structure described in the declaration. Once the structure has been defined, other variables of the same type may be created by a simple declaration

```
    struct day birthday;
```

without repeating the details of what the structure must contain.

Two operations are permitted on structures: (1) setting a pointer to the address of a structure with the **&** operator, e.g., **&birthday**, and (2) accessing one of its members. Fetching (accessing) uses syntax similar to that in Pascal: the generic structural component name is suffixed to a specific variable name. The two are separated by a dot. For example,

```
    x = birthday.year;
    birthday.year = y;
```

However,

```
    birthday = another;
```

is not permitted in C, because structures cannot be passed or copied directly, nor can they be made into function arguments. This restriction is not nearly so severe as it might seem, for much the same effect can be achieved by equating or manipulating pointers to structures.

Input and Output with C

In principle, C has no input and output statements as such; but there does exist a library of standard functions which includes both primitive (character level) and formatted input and output. It may be requested through the loader, by means of the **-l** option, as for example in

```
    $ cc filename -lS
```

Here **S** indicates the standard library. The standard library relies on various macros and external variables; they are included in a C program by means of

```
    #include ⟨stdio.h⟩
```

The angle brackets instead of quotation marks indicate that the file in question is system supplied, not a user file.

For formatted output, the `printf (...)` function is invoked. Its arguments may include character strings containing text to be output, variables, and possibly conversion (formatting) control. Output can be produced as signed or unsigned decimal, octal, or hexadecimal integers; real numbers in plain decimal or exponential notation; or as characters. The field width to be occupied, whether left or right justification is desired within the field, and the number of digits to be printed for each variable, are matters controllable by appropriate arguments. Formatted input uses the `scanf (...)` function and follows much the same rules, with one significant exception: `scanf` requires pointers to variables named as its arguments, not the variables themselves.

The C Preprocessor

Before they are translated into lower-level code, C programs are passed through the C preprocessor. The preprocessor looks for lines beginning with # signs and, ignoring all other lines, regards these as instructions. Preprocessor instructions include conditional compilation and direct substitution.

There are two kinds of substitution: `#define` and `#include`. The preprocessor instruction

   `#include "`*filename*`"`

(where the quotes actually have to appear) will read file *filename* and copy its contents in place of the `#include` statement. When an inclusion is made, preprocessing restarts at the beginning of the included file. Therefore an included file may have other `#include` statements in it. Of course, circular references, in which file **A** contains `#include "B"` and file **B** contains `#include "A"`, must be avoided.

Another preprocessor instruction `#define` replaces a string of characters by another string of characters. The replacement technique is quite sophisticated; for example, it is possible not only to replace a function name but to have arguments substituted at the same time.

The C preprocessor allows declarations of structures, array sizes, variable definitions, utility functions, and various other useful program segments to be placed in separate files and to be copied into other programs where desired. It thus becomes possible to arrange source code so that definitions and parameters which must be the same in various program segments (e.g., array sizes) actually appear only in one place. Program alteration is thereby made easy, since a change in a single place will automatically propagate to wherever it is needed, through `#include` and `#define` statements. Similar facilities are provided to the Ratfor and Fortran 77 programmer.

Compiling, Assembling, and Loading

High-level languages supported under Unix systems are commonly compiled in a multistep process involving generation of C intermediate code. The C language itself is compiled in two steps, from C proper to C intermediate code, then from C intermediate code into assembler language. Other languages, in particular Fortran 77, are processed by partial compilers which produce C intermediate code also. The translation of intermediate code into relocatable object code and subsequent loading of the object code are tasks carried out by a set of programs common to all languages in this family. The benefits of this structure are many. Construction of additional compilers is simplified, since they only need to go as far as C intermediate code; procedures written in different languages can often be intermixed; subroutine libraries can be shared; and system calls can be equally accessible from all. Best of all, there need exist only one version of the machine-dependent parts of the system.

The ld Loader

The loader program ld produces executable machine-language programs by combining relocatable object modules. Relocation amounts to final translation of relocatable object code into absolute, executable machine code. A number of modules must usually be combined even when the source program consists of only a single text file such as a Fortran program, because the Fortran program commonly employs various library subroutines and system calls for such tasks as doing floating-point calculation, reading files, and sending characters to the screen. Typically, a Fortran or C program of only a few lines, say to read the keyboard input and echo it to the screen, will require combining dozens of individual program segments. The task of ld is to locate all the program segments, to link them together in the correct manner, and to write the resulting machine-language text into a file. The loader is invoked by the command

$ ld *file1* *file2* ... *file*n

The files named in the command must be relocatable object programs produced by the assembler or the names of object program libraries. The output is placed into a file named a.out unless the command is made to specify otherwise, e.g.,

$ ld -o outfile *file1* *file2* ... *file*n

Libraries normally provided as part of the operating system do not have to be named in the command; they are considered to be included automatically. User-supplied libraries, on the other hand, must be named explicitly.

In addition to the −o (name the output file) option, ld provides a large number of other options, all of interest only to advanced programmers.

The ld program is used by most programmers without realizing that they are using it, because the loader is included as the final process in a number of process sequences. In these, translator program output is automatically piped to the loader. cc and f77 are two such command sequences.

The cc and f77 Commands

The Fortran and C compilers usually provided in Unix systems are f77 and cc, respectively. Both produce output in the same language, the so-called *C intermediate code*. This code is translated to the assembler language of the machine in use by another program called (for historical reasons) "the second pass of the C compiler", its actual name is usually /lib/c2. C intermediate code is not implementation dependent, it is the same for every installation. On the other hand, the assembler-language text is necessarily different for every hardware configuration, for it reflects the machine instruction set on a line-for-line basis. The text thus obtained from the C second pass is finally translated by the assembler into relocatable object code, machine instructions in final and absolute form except for assignment of the actual memory locations where the program is to reside at execution time.

When the command cc is issued, a pipeline is created which comprises the first and second phases of the C compiler and the loader. The pipeline is in fact half a dozen programs long because the individual phases of C compilation involve several processes each. Indeed the assembler itself is part of the pipeline. On issuing the command

$ cc *filename*

the program sequence is executed, and the output is placed in a file called a.out. This default file name has nothing to do with the C compiler, rather it reflects the fact that the final program in the pipeline is ld. The exact structure of the pipeline, and whether any intermediate files are teed off, depends on the options included with the command.

The manner in which cc is set up permits a large number of options. Their number is in fact about twelve (most of which are of little interest), but it appears to be much larger because options and arguments are passed downstream to other processes in the pipeline if they are not recognized. Option names are chosen so that the C compiler phases and the loader all recognize different ones, so that, for example, the −o (output file name specification) option may be given with the cc command; it is not used by the C compiler itself, but is passed on down the pipeline until it is finally recognized by the loader. Thus

    $ cc -o outfile *filename*

produces the output in file outfile for the same reason as the above example placed it in a.out: the -o is passed downstream until it reaches the loader. The full set of options is shown in the table below.

Table of Language Compiler Options

Option	Process	Effect of Option
-c	*cc2*	Compile to object file, but do not load.
-d	*ld*	Define common storage in spite of -r flag.
-e	*ld*	Next argument is entry point of program.
-i	*ld*	Separate text and data address spaces.
-f	*cc2*	Use floating-point interpreter (no hardware).
-lx	*ld*	Abbreviation for /lib/libx.a, x = string.
-m	*f77*	Use M4 preprocessor ahead of ratfor.
-n	*ld*	Produce reentrant code.
-o ⟨*name*⟩	*ld*	Name the output file *name*, not a.out.
-onetrip	*f77*	Do loops are tested after loop execution.
-p	*cc2*	Produce profile file for program statistics.
-r	*ld*	Relocation bits to be generated in output.
-s	*ld*	Strip symbol table and relocation bits.
-t *sffx*	*cc1*	Limit compiler pass substitution (see -B).
-u	*f77*	All variable names undefined by default.
-u	*ld*	Tabulate next argument as undefined.
-w	*f77*	Suppress compiler warning messages.
-x	*ld*	Put only external symbols in symbol table.
-B ⟨*file*⟩	*cc1*	Find substitute cc passes in *file*.
-C	*f77*	Include subscript bound check in code.
-D ⟨*name*⟩	*cc1*	Define *name* to C preprocessor.
-D	*ld*	Next argument is the data segment size.
-E	*cc1*	Run only C macro preprocessor; do not compile.
-E ⟨*strg*⟩	*f77*	Use *strg* to pass EFL options.
-F	*f77*	Produce *.f files from *.r; do not compile.
-I ⟨*dir*⟩	*cc1*	Insert directory in file search chain.
-O	*cc2*	Optimize object code.
-O	*ld*	Overlay file.
-P	*cc1*	Run C macro preprocessor; produce *.i files.
-R ⟨*strg*⟩	*f77*	Use *strg* to pass Ratfor options.
-S	*cc2*	Produce assembler output in files *.s.
-U ⟨*name*⟩	*cc1*	Remove initial definition of *name* (see -D).
-X	*ld*	Save all local symbols not starting with L.
-	*as*	All undefined symbols are taken as global.

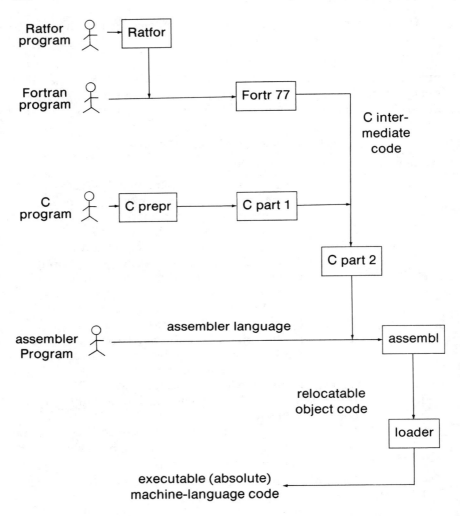

The **f77** command launches a process sequence similar to that of **cc**, but it uses the Fortran 77 compiler instead of the first phase of the C compiler to get started. In fact, it may even include **ratfor** as the starting process. Again, the number of options is vast but in reality much smaller than it seems, because unrecognized option symbols are passed downstream until they are understood by some other program. In principle, the sequence is thus **f77**, second phase of **cc**, **ld**. The entire process then runs as shown in the diagram above.

Additional high-level languages can be added to such a structure relatively easily; it suffices to devise a translation program to convert the high-level language into C intermediate code. Since C intermediate code is not machine dependent, this translator will not be machine dependent either. Additional languages can thus be added to the system in a reasonably simple fashion, and they can become available on all hardware implementations almost at once.

The Process Option Hierarchy

Because options are passed downstream, most option names are unique in the entire suite of compiling, assembling, and linking programs. There are about 30 options altogether, so that both uppercase and lowercase letters must be used. In fact there is some duplication of option names, but where it does occur, the option symbol will clearly be caught and processed by the first program to recognize it. In general, duplications occur only where simultaneous use of both meanings does not make much sense.

A comprehensive table of options applicable to the Fortran 77 and C compilers, the assembler, and the loader appears above. In the table, the various options are shown along with the processes which recognize them; *cc1* and *cc2* denote the first and second phases of the C compiler. The table is complete as given, and for that very reason it includes a whole lot of options that most users are very unlikely to need. Details on the more useful options may be found in the command descriptions. The Unix system manuals should be consulted for the full set, should it ever be required.

Program Archives

Although the Unix file structure permits large numbers of files to be marshaled conveniently, there is still a need for grouping together archives (also called libraries) of subroutines. A typical high-level language program may use several hundred system-provided routines such as mathematical functions, input-output services, and data conversions. Many of these are quite short, but each one must take up at least one block of file space (512 bytes) when stored in individual files. Further, searching for so many separate files would slow operation considerably even if file space and directory clutter were not a consideration. For this reason, the Unix system allows so-called library files to be built. These contain internal directories, which can be searched for the required routines.

Certain libraries exist in permanent form on every Unix system, but users may also build private libraries of frequently used functions. Libraries are maintained by the **ar** (archivist) program. It permits insertion, extraction, and moving of individual modules within a library, or between a library and other files. It also permits cataloguing libraries.

When loading programs, some system-provided libraries are automatically included (e.g., Fortran mathematical routines). Others, including all user-created libraries, must be explicitly named to the loader. Apart from this fact, there is no distinction between system-provided and user-created libraries.

Berkeley Pascal

Of the several Pascal compilers now available under the Unix operating system, Berkeley Pascal is very probably the most widely used version, at least on PDP-11 and VAX-11 computers. Initially built during 1976–1978 and subsequently maintained at the University of California, Berkeley, it is mature, well debugged software. A particularly valuable feature of the Berkeley Pascal subsystem is its ability to permit both interpretation and compilation.

Structure of the Pascal System

The whole Berkeley Pascal system consists of six commands, `pi`, `px`, `pix`, `pc`, `pxp`, and `pxref`.

   `pi` is a translator which turns the Pascal source code into an interpretive (intermediate) code, and `px` is an executive program that reads the intermediate code and interprets it. That is to say, `px` translates the intermediate code commands into binary machine instructions, one command at a time, and executes them immediately. `pix` is essentially a pipeline comprising `pi` and `px`.

   The `pc` compiler can be used to produce executable modules, or it may be employed to create assembler-language programs. These can be linked with other programs, possibly originating from other languages. Normally, `pc` expects to work on complete Pascal programs. However, incremental compilation is also possible.

   `pxp` and `pxref` are utilities which support Pascal program development. `pxp` is an execution profiler which monitors the execution of a program and indicates how many times each statement was executed. It can also be used to reformat Pascal source programs into readable form. `pxref` is a symbol cross-reference generator, useful in tracing variable names in large programs.

   The Berkeley Pascal system introduces a few conventions of its own, which it is well to adhere to. File names ending in `.p` are taken to be Pascal source files. The file name `obj` is reserved for interpreter output, and the name `a.out` for executable code.

Interpreted Pascal

The simplest manner of actually running the Berkeley system is via the interpreter pipeline. If file **source.p** contains a Pascal program, then

        $ pix source.p

causes the source program to be translated into intermediate code by **pi** and to be interpreted by **px**. The next screen response should therefore be whatever output the program **source.p** may produce. Alternatively, the user may wish to do the job in two steps; the sequence then is

        $ pi source.p
        $ px obj

since **pix** is essentially the Unix pipeline composed of **pi** and **px**. The interpreter **pi** places its output into file **obj** by default. Of course, it is possible to move this file to a different name, in which case the new name would have to be substituted for **obj** in the **px** instruction. The two-step procedure is useful for development of large programs, where there is not much point in retranslating sections already known to work.

The code produced by **pi** may be stored in files and executed by **px** at a later time. To the user, files produced by **pi** appear to be executable. In keeping with the usual Unix shell conventions, the file **obj** can therefore be executed either by the command **px obj** or by **obj**. Further, in the absence of any file name **px** assumes that **obj** is the desired file, so that simply typing **px** will have the same effect. **pi** is very convenient and easy to use, but it may place some restriction on program size since everything has to be in memory at once. On a PDP-11 with the usual 64K-byte limit on user memory, about 1000–2000 lines of source code can be handled.

The interpretive Pascal subsystem consisting of **pi** and **px** allows a number of options to be specified in a style consistent with the Unix shell; i.e., the command may be followed by a minus sign, a string of option letters as appropriate, and the file name or names which are to be operated on. The available options are

-b$\langle n \rangle$ Set output buffer to $\langle n \rangle$ blocks (output buffer = one line).
-i   List **include** files in full (**include** statements only).
-l   Source program listing to be generated (no listing).
-p   Postmortem error backtrace and dump omitted (trace is done).
-s   Standard Pascal language check (no checking is done).
-t   Subrange bound testing is suppressed (tests are performed).
-w   Warning diagnostics are suppressed (warnings are issued).
-z   Profile counters are set up for later **pxp** run (no counters).

All the options (except for **b**) are toggles; they reverse whatever their previous settings may have been. The values given in parentheses are those assumed by default, to be reversed if desired. Options may also be invoked in the program itself by including in the program text a special comment line. However, when used in a program, the options no longer act as toggles; they must be assigned firm ON or OFF values. Ordinary comments may follow the option resetting in the same comment brackets, permitting the user to retrace his program logic at a subsequent date. For example,

```
{$s + Standard Pascal checking turned on here}
 . . . . . .
{$s - Standard Pascal checking turned off here}
```

The **l, s, t, w** options are probably self-explanatory. A few brief comments on the others may be in order.

Berkeley Pascal permits sections of program text to be included via **include** statements, somewhat in the manner of C. The statement

```
#include "filename.i";
```

will be replaced at translation time by the text contained in *"filename.i"*. The included files must have names ending in **.i**. They are not normally fully listed in the program listings; only the **#include** statement will be shown. The **i** option causes them to be printed instead of the **#include**, if requested.

Since the interpreter is most useful for program development, an error backtrace (also called a postmortem dump) facility is provided. It counts the number of statements executed, indeed limits the number so as to prevent infinite loops. It also clocks the execution time and to some extent identifies run-time errors. If no backtracing is desired, it can be turned off with the **p** option.

The **z** option may be employed to turn on counters that subsequently allow execution profiles to be produced by **pxp**.

Ordinarily, Pascal output is buffered by print lines, i.e., output characters are saved up until an end-of-line character is encountered. The buffer size can be changed by the **b** option, or the output can be unbuffered; it is unlikely that any but expert users will need to make much use of this facility.

Compiled Pascal

The **pc** compiler produces executable object code or, if preferred, assembler-language code. It is thus possible to link Berkeley Pascal programs with programs originating in other languages at the assembler level. Program loading and execution follow the procedures as given above in connection with C and Fortran 77, with a few differences that arise from the idiosyncrasies of Pascal language structure. The procedures involved are similar to those of Fortran 77; pc may be imagined to feed into the second pass of the C compiler (*cc2* in the above).

The pc compiler is primarily intended for use where programs have been more or less thoroughly debugged with pi. Hence the options available are aimed primarily at yielding good-quality object code, with provision of debugging information (at the system integration level) a secondary goal. Fewer facilities are provided in pc than pi for finding programming errors.

The set of options provided with pc is wider than with pi. The options, with default values in parentheses, are

$-b\langle n\rangle$	output buffer $\langle n\rangle$ blocks (buffer = one line)	
$-c$	compile partial program (full program expected)	
$-C$	subrange bound test (no tests are performed)	
$-g$	log debugger information (none logged)	
$-i$	list all include files (include statements only)	*pi*
$-l$	source program listing generated (no listing)	*ip*
$-o\langle name\rangle$	output file *name* to be $\langle name\rangle$ (a.out is used)	*ld*
$-O$	object code optimizer to be used (not used)	*cc2*
$-p$	profiling counters for prof (none generated)	*cc2*
$-s$	standard Pascal check (no checking is done)	*pi*
$-S$	assembly language output (object code is produced)	*cc2*
$-w$	warning diagnostics (warnings are issued)	*pi*
$-z$	profile counters for later pxp run (no counters)	*pi*

Options marked *pi* are identical in effect to the corresponding options available with pi and will not be discussed further. Those marked *cc2* or *ld* have the same effect as discussed earlier in connection with the C compiler cc or the loader ld.

The subrange bound test option C is similar to that provided by pi except that the default is set the other way around, i.e., unless the user asks for it, no checking is done. This reversal will be seen to be consistent with the general approach of pc: good object code comes first, debugging second. The g option provides for logging the information required by the Unix symbolic debugger.

It is possible to compile parts of programs (e.g., individual procedures or functions) separately and to use the resulting relocatable object code later. The c option informs pc that a partial compilation is intended. Because Pascal allows considerable flexibility in creating data types, partial compilation is not quite so easy to arrange as in Fortran; similar data types must be similarly defined across the boundaries of separately compiled files. This problem is resolved in Berkeley Pascal through the use of included files containing the necessary definitions. For details of partial compilation, the Berkeley Pascal manuals should be consulted.

Error Flagging

The interpreter **pi** and the compiler **pc** flag source code errors by drawing a line across the source program listing, with an identifying label showing the nature of the error, and (where appropriate) an arrow to show the error location. For example, a missing **do** in a **for - do** loop is flagged by displaying

```
    37 for i := 1 to n begin
e  ------------------------>----------- Inserted keyword do
```

meaning: in source line 37, there exists a nonfatal error, which **pi** has attempted to cure by inserting the missing **do**. The label at the left of the ruled line indicates that the error is one **pi** has been capable of correcting well enough to allow execution. There are three categories of error flaggings: warnings **w**, nonfatal errors **e**, and fatal errors **E**. Warnings may be suppressed if there are many fatal errors in a program, on the reasonable supposition that many major errors are unlikely to be cured in one attempt. In any case, quite a few warnings usually arise through secondary effects of major program errors, and just as commonly they disappear all by themselves when the errors are cured.

The error messages issued by Berkeley Pascal generally take the form of quite readable English text, so that no book of error codes is required to decipher them. However, clear messages are not necessarily correct messages. All that **pi** can tell with certainty is that something has gone wrong; its guess as to what has gone wrong may quite easily be incorrect. In the above simple example, **pi** assumed that **do** should precede **begin**; it could not correctly guess that the user, in a moment of absentmindedness, had typed in the word **begin** when he really meant **do**. The incorrect guess will presumably manifest itself in the absence of an **end** to match the **begin**.

Execution Profiling

The **pxp** execution profiler lists the Pascal program specified in the command and shows the number of times each statement was executed. Such operation counts are useful in at least two important ways. First, program segments with zero execution count clearly have not been tested at all, suggesting that the test data should be altered, or else that program logic needs checking. Secondly, execution counts permit the programmer to identify those (usually very few) segments of the program which account for the great majority of execution time. Those and few, if any, others deserve to be reexamined with a view to code optimization. The profiling options available with **pxp** are

- **-a**   all routines to be included in the profile (omit if unused)
- **-t**   tabulate procedure and function calls (no table given)
- **-z**   profile named **included** files, or all (no profile at all)

Note that if neither the **t** nor the **z** option is specified (i.e., neither a detailed profile nor a table is asked for), no profiles will be given; all that results is a listing of the program text.

Profiling by **pxp** may include only those routines which were actually executed, but with the **a** ("all") option it will also produce a listing of those which were part of the program file but were not actually run. The execution count for these will naturally be zero. However, it is often useful to have them included in printout. Profiling can also be made selective, by requesting the **z** option, which permits a number of **.i** files to be named; only the named files will then be profiled. If no **.i** file names are given, the **z** option is understood to ask for everything to be profiled. The **t** option requests a summarizing table of procedure and function calls.

Program Tidying

When **pxp** is run without requesting any profile information, it will produce a program listing only. There are quite a few options through which **pxp** can be guided to produce pleasing and readable output. They are

- **-d**   suppress listing of declarations (all source text listed),
- **-e**   substitute text for **include** statements (statements only),
- **-f**   full parentheses for mathematics (minimal parentheses),
- **-j**   left justify everything (nested blocks indented four spaces),
- **-s**   strip comments in listing (comments are fully listed),
- **-_**   underline keywords in listing (keywords are listed plain),
- **-⟨n⟩**   indent nestings ⟨n⟩ spaces (default value is four spaces).

In producing listings, Berkeley Pascal works in lower case except for any literally included text (e.g., text to be printed out). Keywords are thus reduced to lower case, as are variable names.

The various options are probably self-explanatory, with the possible exception of **f**. When analyzing mathematical expressions, **pxp** generally reduces the number of parentheses to the least possible, consistent with preservation of the meaning of mathematical expressions. In other words, the rules of operator precedence are exploited to minimize the number of parentheses. Under the **f** option, sufficient additional parentheses are included to enforce the correct order of computation without reference to the rules of precedence. The mathematical meaning of each expression is then preserved even if the precedence rules of operators are ignored.

Listings produced by **pxp** contain date and time in the header. It should be noted that these do not show the time at which the listing was produced but do constitute a version date-stamp of the program—in other words, they show the time of the most recent modification of the program file.

Basic

Unix systems support a variety of interpreted as well as compiled languages, with **bas**, a dialect of Basic, included as part of the Version 7 release. Basic is a simple, interpreted, programming language whose major advantage is immediate execution—every statement can be executed, and its results can be known, on the spot. Like standard Basic, **bas** is not generally well suited to "serious" computation, where Fortran, Pascal, and C have a strong edge. However, it serves very well for occasional calculations, in the role of a super-powerful desk calculator. Because it is assumed that Basic will normally be used only in a desk calculator role, **bas** lacks many of the refinements which some other versions of Basic possess.

Only a very brief description is given here. It is intended to highlight the major features of **bas**; the reader is assumed to be is familiar with Basic itself.

Expressions, Names and Statements

As might be expected, **bas** works in lower case. Aside from this fact, its statements generally resemble those of standard Basic. Variable names in **bas** may be of any length and are composed of a letter followed by letters and numbers. Although long names are permitted, only the first four characters are actually used. Hence **voltage** and **volts** would both be considered identical to **volt**. Numeric values may be written in any of the notations acceptable to the **f77** compiler.

Expressions are formed by combining operators, names, and numeric values. The admissible operators are the usual arithmetic and relational ones, as well as the logical operators **&** (and) and **|** (or). Precedence rules for operators follow those of standard Basic, and precedence may be forced by means of parentheses.

A statement may consist of a single expression, which may include an assignment operator. A statement consisting of an expression without any assignment operator (i.e., lacking an equal sign anywhere) is evaluated, and the result is immediately displayed. This fact makes **bas** very convenient and useful as a high-powered desk calculator. Most standard Basic statements are acceptable to **bas**.

A statement in **bas** may be prefixed by a line number, as is usual in Basic. Lines prefixed by numbers are stored in order of line numbers and are only executed in response to the **run** statement. The internal (numbered) statements may be examined with the **list** statement.

Running **bas**

When **bas** is invoked, a file name may be passed to it as an optional argument. This file will be read as input; when the file is exhausted, input is taken from the keyboard. One possible use of this arrangement is to load filed programs for execution with the **run** statement, but other uses—for example, automatic partial execution of some calculation—can be devised. No other options are provided with **bas**.

Internal statements in **bas** can be edited using the **ed** editor, which can be reached by way of the **edit** statement in **bas**. This statement reaches out of **bas** to the shell and requests the **ed** editor to be run. The file edited is always the file named in the **bas** command to the shell. In other words, if **bas** was set running with the command

$ bas *progrm*

then **ed** will edit the file *progrm*; there is no choice. Editing and debugging is thus possible with the full power of **ed**, without any need for a separate editor to go with **bas**. The internal statements may be listed at any time with the **list** statement, and the internal statements may be saved on file with the **save** statement. Both **list** and **save** permit one, two, or no arguments, i.e., they may be issued in any one of the forms

```
list
list 20
list 20 40
```

In the first form, the entire file of internal statements is listed; in the second, only statement 20; in the third, all statements from 20 to 40 inclusive. The **save** statement works in the same way. If **bas** was invoked giving a file name, internal statements are saved in the named file; if no file name was given, they are saved in file **b.out**.

The mechanism provided in **bas** for reading external data is through a built-in function called **expr()**. Whenever this function is employed, it reads one line from the input and evaluates it as an expression. In other words, the statement

```
answ = data * expr()
```

will cause an expression (which could of course be simply a number) to be read from the input and to be used as if it had been written into the statement itself.

Assembler-Language Programming

Assembler language has long been the traditional choice for operating systems programming. Since assembler language addresses machine registers directly, it gives the programmer direct and complete control over exactly what action will be taken and how. Program efficiency, measured in terms of operation counts to accomplish any particular task, can therefore be maximized. For exactly the same reasons, assembler-language programs are totally machine dependent and cannot be moved from one computer to another.

The **as** Assembler

Within the Unix family of operating systems, the C language has largely replaced assembler language. Very little can be done in assembler language that cannot be done in C, though that little is very important. A residual need for programming at the machine level will therefore always remain.

Since C does nearly everything necessary for system programming, there is little need for elaborate macro assemblers under any operating system that supports C. For the PDP-11 family of computers, Unix systems employ the **as** assembler, which has very much the same general characteristics as the Digital Equipment Corporation PAL-11 assembler. In other words, **as** is a simple, straightforward assembler suitable for writing small programs. In principle, small machine-language programs are all that it should ever be necessary to write!

Chapter 9

A Selected Command Set

Any command in the Unix system is merely the name of a program, which can be executed in response to the command. In a strict sense, it is therefore not possible to catalogue the available commands, any more than one can give a list of all programs. However, there does exist a set of system-provided commands, i.e., a set of programs provided as part and parcel of the standard system release. These can be listed, and indeed the *Unix Programmer's Manual* does so in full detail. What follows in this chapter is a selection from that rather daunting list, augmented by a few other commands found on many Unix systems but not "official" in the sense that they are not part of the Version 7 system release.

Definitions of Commands

All currently valid standard commands supplied by the system are fully defined in the *Unix Programmer's Manual*, a copy of which is part and parcel of every Unix installation. For the novice user, and even for many practiced users who are not primarily system programmers, that book is at best heavy going. Although well enough written and nicely laid out, it often tells much more, and in much greater detail, than most users really want to know. Besides, the very volume of that encyclopedic tome prevents ready reference; it is over four inches thick in its typeset form as distributed, and it consumes the better part of half a box of paper when it is produced on the line printer. Most users therefore actually consult the full manual from their terminals, in its magnetically stored form, by means of the **man** command. The following brief summary of the major system-provided commands is not intended to compete with the definitive system documentation, but it will be easier to consult as a quick reference for most users.

The various commands are listed here in alphabetical order. For each, a brief description of its action is given, as well as a summary of the command syntax and of the major options and qualifiers available. In most cases, the lists of options are not complete, and many of the subtleties are omitted. For a complete and full description of each command, the user should turn to the manuals; the object here is to present enough material to satisfy most users most of the time. The following summary listing gives the commands treated in this chapter, and indicates for each in which chapter of this book further descriptive material about it may be found. For brevity, the chapter titles have been reduced to single keywords; and where a command is discussed in several chapters, only the chapter containing the fullest discussion is indicated.

ar	archivist	*Languages*
as	PDP-11 assembler	*Languages*
at	execute commands at set time	*Utilities*
bas	Basic interpreter	*Languages*
cat	concatenate files	*Utilities*
cc	C compiler	*Languages*
cd	change directory	*File*
chmod	alter permissions on a file	*File*
cmp	compare two files	*Utilities*
comm	common lines of two files	*Utilities*
cp	copy file	*Utilities*
date	display date and clock time	*Utilities*
diff	differences between two files	*Utilities*
df	display free space on disk	*Utilities*
du	show disk space used	*Utilities*
echo	echo command arguments	*Shell*
ed	line-oriented text editor	*Text*
file	determine file type	*File*
find	find file(s)	*File*
f77	Fortran 77 compiler	*Languages*
grep	find lines containing a string	*Utilities*
kill	stop a running process	*Kernel*
ld	loader	*Languages*
ln	create synonym for file name	*File*
login	log in another user	*Start*
lpr	line printer spooler	*Utilities*
ls	list directory contents	*File*
mail	send or receive mail	*Utilities*
man	display/print system manuals	*Utilities*
mesg	permit or deny messages	*Utilities*

mkdir	make a new directory	*File*
mkfs	make file structure (format)	*File*
mount	mount a file system	*File*
mv	move (rename) file	*File*
neqn	nroff equation preprocessor	*Text*
nice	run process at preset priority	*Kernel*
nroff	text formatter	*Text*
passwd	change user password	*Start*
pc	Pascal compiler	*Languages*
pi	Pascal interpreter	*Languages*
pix	Pascal interpret and execute	*Languages*
pr	display and paginate file	*Utilities*
ps	process status	*Kernel*
pwd	pathname of working directory	*File*
px	Pascal execution monitor	*Languages*
pxp	Pascal reformatter/profiler	*Languages*
ratfor	Ratfor preprocessor	*Languages*
rm	remove (delete) file	*File*
rmdir	remove (delete) directory	*File*
sh	shell (command decoder)	*Shell*
sort	sort alphabetically	*Utilities*
spell	spelling checker	*Text*
struct	Fortran–Ratfor translator	*Languages*
stty	set terminal parameters	*Shell*
tbl	troff table preprocessor	*Text*
tee	divert copy to second file	*Shell*
time	time execution of a command	*Utilities*
tr	translate characters	*Text*
troff	phototypesetter program	*Text*
tty	display terminal name	*None*
umount	unmount a file system	*File*
uniq	delete adjacent duplicate line	*Utilities*
vi	Berkeley screen editor	*Text*
wc	count words in file	*Utilities*
who	display who is logged in	*Start*
write	send message to logged-in user	*Utilities*

There are of course many more system-provided commands; the above list in fact covers far less than half of the over 150 commands listed in the seventh edition of the *Unix Programmer's Manual*. It is very likely, however, that these are precisely what users most frequently need.

A Selected Command Set

Commands are listed in alphabetical order in the following. In the descriptions, optional items are always shown enclosed in square brackets, in the form [item]. That is to say, items thus shown may be included in a command line, or omitted. Items not enclosed in square brackets are mandatory. The ellipsis ... indicates that the immediately preceding item may be repeated as many times as desired. For example,

> cat [option] ⟨file⟩ ...

indicates that the command verb **cat** may be followed optionally by some option qualifier; it must be followed by at least one file name ⟨file⟩ or several file names.

Words in angle brackets are to be understood as indicating a generic identifier, i.e., a name of a particular kind of entity, in a form comprehensible to the shell. Thus ⟨file⟩ means a file name, ⟨user⟩ means a user login name, and so on. The most frequently occurring identifiers are probably ⟨file⟩ and ⟨directory⟩.

Program function: Maintains archives and libraries.
Command syntax: **ar** *key* [⟨oldfile⟩] ⟨archive⟩ ⟨file⟩ ...
How and why used: The archivist is used to insert, remove, or replace files in libraries. Its major use is to update libraries used by the linker in making up executable program modules. One of the characters **dmpqrtx**, possibly followed by one or more of **abcluv**, constitutes *key*; ⟨archive⟩ is the archive file, and ⟨file⟩ is the name(s) of the constituent file(s). Replacements or additions may be specified to occur either before or after the constituent file ⟨oldfile⟩; if unspecified, they are placed at the end of the archive. The most important initial characters in *key* are

d deletes named files from the archive.
m moves named files to the end of the archive.
p prints the named files as they are in the archive.
q (quick) appends to end of archive without checking position.
r replaces the named files by new ones; allows repositioning,
t tabulates (lists) constituents of the archive.
x extracts named files from the archive.

The most important second characters, following those above, are

a put ⟨file⟩ in archive after item ⟨oldfile⟩.
b put ⟨file⟩ in archive before item ⟨oldfile⟩.
c (create) suppress message issued for a new ⟨file⟩.

ι local directory (most archives are in directory /temp).
υ update (with r) replace only files newer than exisitng ones.
ν verbose (i.e., with complete reporting of actions).

Program function: Assembler, similar to PAL-11 for the PDP-11.
Command syntax: **as** [-] [-o ⟨objectfile⟩] ⟨file⟩ ...
How and why used: **as** assembles programs, and produces object code executable after loading with the loader **ld**. The loader is automatically invoked. If the - option is specified, all undefined symbols in the source program are treated as global. The **-o** option allows the output to be put into the file ⟨objectfile⟩; otherwise, it is put into a file called **a.out**. It should be noted that **as** is very similar to PAL-11 but requires different treatment of **;** and **/** in addition to being addicted to lowercase characters.

Program function: Executes command file after a given time.
Command syntax: **at** ⟨time⟩ [⟨day⟩] ⟨file⟩
How and why used: Causes the commands listed in the command file ⟨file⟩ to be executed at or after the specified time. Time may be given in the 24-hour notation or most other reasonable formats, e.g., 8 am, 7 pm. The day, if included, can be given as a day of the week (sun, mon,..., sat) or as a date (jun 12). Exactly when the file is executed depends on the frequency with which the local system checks its clock for such processes; delays of minutes are not uncommon.

Program function: A Basic language interpreter.
Command syntax: **bas** [⟨file⟩]
How and why used: A dialect of Basic is interpreted. If the optional file name is given in the command, this file is read as input before the terminal keyboard. The dialect has a number of peculiarities which fit it into the general framework of the Unix system. In part they result from the view that there exist much better, and better integrated, languages than Basic for writing programs, but Basic will be employed by many users as a sort of powerful desk calculator.

Program function: Concatenates, then displays, files.
Command syntax: **cat** ⟨file⟩ ...

How and why used: Several files can be joined into a single output stream, unlike under the **pr** command, which only deals with one. If the output is sent to a file, as with **cat** *file1 file2* **>** *file3*, then the destination file is cleared out first. Thus, the command **cat** *file1 file2* **>** *file1* first destroys *file1* and thereafter copies *file2* into a new file called *file1*. Caution is necessary: the file destruction really is performed first, so that the erstwhile content of *file1* is simply lost in this case. If no file names are given in the command, the standard input and output files are used.

Program function: C language compiler, followed by loader.
Command syntax: **cc** [*option*] ... ⟨file⟩ ...
How and why used: Programs in the C language are compiled and loaded for execution. Valid options include all loader **ld** options except **-D** and **-O** and a number of options belonging to **cc** proper. The most important among the latter are

-c compile and assemble only (produce object file); do not load.
-S compile only; leave assembler text in **.s** file.

The files to be compiled should have their names end with **.c** if compilation is needed; assembler-language files may also be included, provided their names end in **.s**. If loading is suppressed, output files with similar names but ending in **.o** are produced. If suffixes are not used, an output file name can be specified via the loader **-o** option; if none is specified, the resulting executable module is placed in file **a.out**.

Numerous other options are listed in the *Unix Programmer's Manual*. Caution: Uppercase as well as lowercase characters are used in the options, with different meanings.

Program function: Changes the working directory.
Command syntax: **cd** ⟨directory⟩
How and why used: The current directory is abandoned, and ⟨directory⟩ is made the current directory, provided of course that it exists and that the user has execute (i.e., search) permission for it.

Program function: Change file access permissions.
Command syntax: **chmod** ⟨permission⟩ ⟨file⟩ ...

How and why used: Permissions are granted to read, write, or execute (r, w, or x), to the user who owns a file, the group of users he belongs to, or others (u, g, or o). The ⟨permission⟩ can be specified in the command in two ways. It can be set absolutely, by choosing an appropriate combination of the following numbers and adding:

	user	group	other
read	0400	0040	0004
write	0200	0020	0002
execute	0100	0010	0001

For example, chmod 0710 secret permits the program secret to be openly accessed by the owner, to be executed but not read by members of his user group, and not to be accessed at all by others.

Alternatively, ⟨permission⟩ in the command may be given symbolically, in the form [who] ⟨opr⟩ ⟨permit⟩ where [who] identifies the users (one or more of u, g, o; a may be substituted for ugo); ⟨opr⟩ is the operation to be performed (+, − or =), and ⟨permit⟩ is any combination of the permissions r, w, x. chmod examines the symbolic argument string and does the computation indicated above. The symbol + indicates that the new permissions are added to what is already there, − indicates subtraction, and = requests replacement of what is already there. Note that addition and subtraction refer to permissions, not purely arithmetic operations; adding a permission where it already exists produces nothing new. For example, if after execution of chmod 0710 secret another chmod command is issued, with the argument string indicated below, the following results could be obtained:

ug + r produces 0750 (permission 0040 added).
ug − r produces 0310 (permission 0400 removed).
ug = r produces 0440 (0400 and 0040 replace everything).

Several permission changes can be placed in the same command line, separated by commas but without intervening blanks, as in u = rwx,g = x to produce 0710.

Program function: Compares two files.
Command syntax: cmp [*option*] ⟨file-1⟩ ⟨file-2⟩
How and why used: The differences between files are noted by displaying the byte and line numbers where the differences occur. If the files are identical, no action is taken. Two mutually exclusive options may be used:

−l show decimal byte number and differing bytes.
−s show nothing; return exit codes only.

Exit codes: 0 means identical, 1 means different; 2 says there were some errors in the files.

comm

Program function: Finds and outputs common lines in two files.
Command syntax: comm [*option*] ⟨file-1⟩ ⟨file-2⟩
How and why used: The two files, which should first have been ordered in ASCII sequence (e.g., by sort) are read, and the lines in them sorted into three columns: those occurring (1) only in ⟨file-1⟩, (2) only in ⟨file-2⟩, and (3) in both files. The option may be given as any combination of the digits 1, 2, 3, preceded by a minus sign; each digit suppresses the corresponding column in the output. Two input files must always be specified; a minus sign instead of a file name means the standard input file.

cp

Program function: Copies a file.
Command syntax: cp ⟨file-1⟩ ⟨file-2⟩

  cp ⟨file⟩ ... ⟨directory⟩

How and why used: In the first form, makes a copy of ⟨file-1⟩ and calls it ⟨file-2⟩. In the second form, copies one or more files into the specified directory, with their file names as they are. A file cannot be copied onto itself.

date

Program function: Displays current date and clock time.
Command syntax: date
How and why used: Some people forget to keep their watches set to the correct time. Others don't carry a calendar. If its output is redirected to a file, this command can record the time and therefore can be useful for determining when some particular event happened.

diff

Program function: Finds the differences between two files.
Command syntax: diff [*options*] ⟨file-1⟩ ⟨file-2⟩
How and why used: The two files are compared on a line-by-line basis. Differences between the two files are listed in such a form as to exhibit how

they could be made the same. The available options are characters, preceded by the usual minus sign:

-b ignore trailing blanks in lines being compared.
-e produce **ed** script.
-f produce backward **ed** script.
-h hurried job; compare only a few neighboring lines.

The **-e** option is very useful; it can be used to keep a whole trail of file versions very compactly. One need only store the root file, plus a set of successive **ed** scripts that will change one to another. The reverse script unfortunately can only be read by eye; **ed** does not know how to operate backward.

Program function: Shows amount of free disk space.
Command syntax: **df** [⟨filesystem⟩ ...]
How and why used: Shows the amount of unused disk space remaining on the specified file systems. If no file system is named, free space on all the accessible and mounted systems is displayed. For most users, handy to determine remaining space on small external media such as floppy disks.

Program function: Shows the amount of disk space used.
Command syntax: **du** [*option*] [⟨directory⟩ ...]
How and why used: The amount of file space tied up by all files listed in ⟨directory⟩ and its subdirectories is determined. If no directory name is given, the current directory is assumed. Without options, all subdirectory names are listed and totals for subdirectories shown. Two options:

-a all file sizes (not just subdirectories) are listed.
-s summary only: no names are listed, only the grand total.

Only one option character may be given, preceded by a minus. The disk space is always listed in blocks of 512 bytes each.

Program function: Echoes arguments
Command syntax: **echo** [-n] arguments
How and why used: Useful for checking exactly what arguments the shell will employ, in situations where argument strings get complicated. Particularly handy where wild-card constructions are used, since these are fully

expanded. The **-n** option suppresses the *newline* character which is normally appended to the output of **echo**.

Program function: The standard Unix text editor.
Command syntax: **ed** [-] [⟨file⟩]
How and why used: All the usual program preparation, documentation, and text preparation functions. The − (minus sign) option suppresses character counts. If ⟨file⟩ is given in the command line, the relevant file is read in for editing; otherwise, **ed** begins with an empty editing buffer. There are many commands in **ed**, with various options and variants; in point of fact, **ed** is an interactive subsystem within the Unix operating system. More information will be found in the chapter *Text Processing and Preparation*.

Program function: Determines file type.
Command syntax: **file** ⟨file⟩ ...
How and why used: A series of tests is performed to try classifying what type ⟨file⟩ is—object, source, or whatever. If it is a text file (i.e., if it only contains valid ASCII characters), **file** tries to determine in what language. It is not always successful in that attempt.

find

Program function: Finds a file, or files of a particular kind.
Command syntax: **find** ⟨directory⟩ ... *filespec* ...
How and why used: The directory or directories specified in the command and all their subdirectories are searched in hierarchical order to locate all files that satisfy the specification *filespec*. Names of all files found are written to the standard output. Over a dozen different forms of file specification are possible; each is given as a keyword preceded by a minus sign, possibly followed by a parameter. The most important keywords are

-atime *n*   all files accessed within the last *n* days.
-group⟨*group*⟩   files belonging to a specified *user group*.
-mtime *n*   all files modified within the last *n* days.
-name⟨*file*⟩   specific name(s); * and ? are taken as wild cards.
-newer⟨*file*⟩   files newer than the file ⟨*file*⟩.
-type*t*   *t* = *d* or *f* (directory or plain files).
-user⟨*user*⟩   specific user; ⟨user⟩ may be login name or number.

The various kinds of file specification can be combined logically. The logical intersection (AND) is understood if two or more specifications are given in a row; **-o** is taken to mean logical union (OR); the exclamation mark **!** is used to mean negation. For example, **!atime 30** requests all files not used within the past month. Logical combinations can produce quite complex searches and can find the desired files even over a very large set of directories. Few users are likely to do so as a steady diet. Details may be found in the system manuals.

f77

Program function: Fortran 77 compiler
Command syntax: **f77** [*option*] ... ⟨file⟩ ...
How and why used: Compiles Fortran 77 text and, unless prevented by options, pipelines the resulting code to the loader **ld** so as to produce an executable module. Valid options include all options accepted by **ld** except **-u** and **-O**, all options accepted by the second phase of the C compiler, and some options applicable to **f77** only. The most important among these are

-onetrip	**do** loops execute at least once (check at end of loop).
-u	make all undeclared variables undefined (debugging).
-w	suppress all warnings.
-w66	suppress all warnings about Fortran 66 compatibility.
-C	subscript-out-of-bounds check done at execution time.
-F	Translate Ratfor to Fortran, do not proceed farther.
-R *string*	Pass *string* to **ratfor** as option for ***.r** files.

f77 expects Fortran text, unless the file name has a suffix which implies otherwise: **.r** for Ratfor, **.c** for C, **.s** for assembler. The **.f** suffix may be used to identify Fortran. Each file is compiled and/or assembled according to its suffix. The loader output is placed in file **a.out**, unless a file name is specified (see **ld** options), or unless files were identified by suffixes; in the latter case, the output is placed in a file by the same name, but with the **.o** suffix.

f77 implements a practically full Fortran 77, with some desirable extensions. Sufficiently legible diagnostics are produced to obviate any need for a book of error codes.

grep

Program function: Filters input lines, looking for a pattern.
Command syntax: **grep** [*options*] [character string] ⟨file⟩
How and why used: **grep** reads one or more files, looking for a specific character string in each line. If no options are specified, all input lines containing the specified string are copied into the output. Only one file name is permitted in the command, but numerous files will be read if the name contains wild-card characters. Options are, as usual, one or more

characters preceded by a minus sign. The main options possible are

−c Prints only the number (count) of lines with matches.
−e Exceptional character string (one that begins with -).
−n Number lines with line numbers from input file.
−v Output the lines *without* character string matches.
−y Ignore case (lower- and uppercase alphabetics match).

grep must be one of the least obvious command names and one of the most forgettable; even after finding out that it stands for *global regular expressions print*, one never remembers.

Program function: Halts (aborts) a currently running process.
Command syntax: kill ⟨process⟩
How and why used: Any currently running process may be halted by giving its process identification number ⟨process⟩ as the argument of this command. The process identification number is shown whenever a background process is set running; alternatively, process identification numbers can be determined by means of the ps command.

ld

Program function: Linking loader.
Command syntax: ld [*option*] ⟨file⟩ ...
How and why used: Links together several object programs with any necessary libraries, producing an object module. The object module may be executed, or (if used with the −r option) it may be used later as a component in another run of ld. The output is left in a file named a.out unless a file name is given in the −o option.

The files specified may be relocatable object code or libraries. They are concatenated in the order they are named. If libraries are included, it is important to note that ld will search each library exactly once as it proceeds from left to right through the list of files. Only those library programs are loaded which are required by the files listed ahead of the library. Program order within libraries is therefore important; calling programs must precede the programs they call. "Backward" references among library modules are not possible and will be left unresolved.

The loader permits a variety of options, expressed by character strings with a preceding minus sign. Among these the following are the most useful:

−d Define common storage area even if −r option is present.
−i Load text and data into separate address spaces.
−n Make the text section pure text (shareable among users).
−o If a name follows −o, it is used as the output file name.
−r Generate relocatable code (for further ld operations).

-s Strip debugging aids from object code, to save space.
-O Generate an overlay file.

Note that options use both lower and upper case; it is important which is typed.

Several language compilers within the Unix system pipe their output to ld automatically. In such cases, options can usually be passed through from the compiler command to ld.

Program function: Adds a further directory entry for a file.
Command syntax: ln ⟨file1⟩ [⟨file2⟩]
How and why used: Creates entries in directories referring to an ordinary file ⟨file1⟩. An additional entry may be created in a directory by giving the name ⟨file1⟩, following the usual pathname rules of Unix files, and optionally another name ⟨file2⟩. If ⟨file2⟩ is omitted, the ordinary file is placed in the current working directory, taking the last component of ⟨file1⟩ as its name. The old and new names of the file being referenced have equal validity for all further work; there is no "real" or "original" name. ln only creates synonymous names for files, it does not copy files. Creation of synonymous names across file systems (i.e., to removable volumes) is forbidden.

Program function: Logs in a new user.
Command syntax: login [⟨user⟩]
How and why used: A new user can log in without the old user explicitly logging out. If no user name ⟨user⟩ is given in the command, the system asks for it. A password is always required to log in and is asked for except if the user password has been set to blank. A blank user password is often set by system managers when authorizing new users, so as to allow each user to choose his own password.

lpr

Program function: Line printer spooler.
Command syntax: lpr [*option*] ... [⟨file⟩ ...]
How and why used: The files named are queued for printing on the line printer. Options are given by a character string prefixed by a minus sign. The most important option characters are

-c Copy the file immediately so any later changes do not print.
-m Report by mail when the print job is complete.
-r Remove (i.e., delete) the file after placing it in queue.

Note that the −r option removes the file after queueing it for printing, not after printing it. Thus some time may elapse during which there exists no printed copy as yet and no file any longer.

Program function: Lists contents of directories
Command syntax: ls [*options*] ⟨file⟩ ...
How and why used: Every directory file named in the command has its contents displayed; every nondirectory file named shows information as specified by the options. If no name is given, the current directory is listed. Options may be combined, and must be preceded by a minus sign. The most important ones are

−d List only the names for directory files, not their contents.
−l Long form: permissions, number of links, owner, size, etc.
−r List in reverse order (alphabetic, or time if **t** given).
−s Give size of files in terms of blocks.
−t List in chronological order, not alphabetically.
−u Use time of last access, not modification, with **t** and/or **l**.

Under the −l option, each file is classified by a character identifier as follows:

b or **c** block or character special file
d   directory file
−   ordinary file

The next three characters show read, write, and execute permission, for the file owner; the next three, permissions for users in the same group; and the next three, for everybody else. The characters **r**, **w**, **x** are used; the − character means no permission.

Program function: Sends mail to others, or reads mail.
Command syntax: mail ⟨user⟩ ...
                mail [*option*]
How and why used: To send mail, the addressee ⟨user⟩ is named; all subsequent input on the standard input file is considered to be the message, up to the next occurrence of a line containing only a period (. character), or up to the next control-D. The message is prefixed by the sender's name and time of transmission and left in the addressee's mailbox.

mail without an addressee's name is used to read mail. Messages are read with the most recent one first. As each message is displayed, the user is asked how to dispose of it. Valid responses are

d   Delete this message, go on to the next one.
m [⟨user⟩] Mail the message to ⟨user⟩ (default: same user).
p   Repeat display of this message.
q   Quit reading mail, leave unread mail in mailbox.
s [⟨file⟩]   Save this message in ⟨file⟩ (default: **mbox**).
w [⟨file⟩]   Save message, as with **-s** but without header.
x   Exit without changing the mailbox file.
-            Repeat display of previous message.
?   Display a summary of valid responses.
!*comm*   Execute the shell command *comm*, then continue.
newline   (RETURN key) go on to next message.
EOT   (control-D) quit, same as **q**.

The mail reading form of this command permits four options to be specified:

-f ⟨file⟩ read the ⟨file⟩ as if it were the mailbox file.
-p   display mail without pausing for disposal instructions.
-q   quit **mail** immediately on an interrupt (DELETE key).
-r   examine mail in reverse order, old mail first.

Options can be concatenated and must be preceded by a minus sign. While messages are being displayed, the display can be halted with an interruption (DELETE key).

   Program function: Display or print the *Unix Programmer's Manual*.
   Command syntax: **man** [*option*] [⟨chapter⟩] ⟨section⟩ ...
   How and why used: The *Unix Programmer's Manual* is searched for the requested ⟨section⟩ or sections. The search is confined to a particular chapter if a chapter number is given; otherwise, the entire manual is searched, and all sections with the specified name are output on the standard output file. Options may be specified as a character string preceded by a minus sign. The most useful options are

-n output using **nroff**.
-w show pathnames of the manual sections, but display no text.

If no options are given, the effect is that of **-n**; either an already formatted text is output, or (if there is no such) **nroff** is used to format it.

   Program function: Blocks incoming messages.
   Command syntax: **mesg** [*option*]

How and why used: Without option, the present state of the message switch (yes or no) is reported. To turn off incoming messages ("do not disturb"), or to accept them again, the command is used with the option n (no) or y (yes). *Note*: No minus signs prefix the options for this command.

mkdir

Program function: Makes new directories.
Command syntax: `mkdir` ⟨directory⟩ ...
How and why used: Creates new directories, provided the user has write permission in the parent directory. New directories are set up with read, write, and execute permissions granted to everybody; it is up to the user to protect his files if he wishes.

mkfs

Program function: Makes a file structure.
Command syntax: `/etc/mkfs` ⟨specialfile⟩ ⟨prototype⟩
How and why used: Mostly used to format previously unused magnetic media (disk packs, floppy disks) or to reformat them. Anything previously on the volume (disk or tape) is destroyed irretrievably. The device is accessed through its special file ⟨specialfile⟩.

In the simplest form of `mkfs`, ⟨prototype⟩ is simply a decimal number which specifies how many blocks of file space the new file structure is to cover. More generally, ⟨prototype⟩ is a file containing a string of instructions to define the new file structure. The flexibility provided by this command is enormous; almost any conceivable file characteristic may be specified in ⟨prototype⟩. The destructive power of `mkfs` is also enormous, for it can destroy whole diskfuls of files at a single blow.

In the standard Version 7 Unix system, `mkfs` is restricted to the system manager, and is located in directory `/etc`. Numerous other system versions and compatible systems have user-accessible, but often slightly different or restricted, `mkfs` commands.

mount

Program function: Mounts a file system.
Command syntax: `/etc/mount` ⟨directory⟩ [-r]
How and why used: Connects the file directory of a disk, tape, etc., volume to the Unix file system by attaching the volume root directory as ⟨directory⟩. The latter must previously exist and must be empty. The file volume must have a Unix file structure; if it does not, using `mount` will often cause a system crash. If the `-r` option is specified, the volume is mounted for reading only. This command may be issued without any directory name; it will then display what devices are currently mounted.

In the standard Version 7 Unix system, **mount** is restricted to the system manager and is located in directory **/etc**. Some other system versions and other systems have user-accessible **mount** commands, slightly different or with different access restrictions.

Program function: Moves (i.e., renames) files.
Command syntax: **mv** ⟨file-1⟩ ⟨file-2⟩
             mv ⟨file⟩ ... ⟨directory⟩

How and why used: In the first form, the name of ⟨file-1⟩ is altered to ⟨file-2⟩. If there already existed a ⟨file-2⟩, it is removed (destroyed) first. In the second form, the specified ⟨file⟩s are moved to the ⟨directory⟩ named. **mv** cannot be used to destroy a file by moving it onto itself.

Program function: Mathematical typesetting
Command syntax: **neqn** [-d⟨x⟩⟨y⟩] [⟨file⟩ ...]

How and why used: **neqn** is a preprocessor for driving **nroff**, capable of being used with terminals. There is another program **eqn** which is preferable for use with **troff**, although **neqn** may be used. Input is read from the specified files or from the standard input if no files are shown in the command. Output is directed to the standard output. All input is passed to the output unmodified except for (1) lines delimited by the command lines **.EQ** and **.EN** and (2) character strings encased in two delimiter characters ⟨x⟩ and ⟨y⟩, if such are set by including the proper option in the command line. The lines to be modified are processed by including such **nroff** or **troff** commands as appropriate to reformat the equations or mathematical expressions, so far as the hardware device (phototypesetter or terminal) is capable of forming mathematical expressions.

Program function: Run a task at reduced priority.
Command syntax: **nice** [⟨priority⟩] command [arguments]

How and why used: To keep a background job from interfering with terminal work, it can be made to run at reduced priority. If no ⟨priority⟩ is specified, the priority that would otherwise be assigned to the command is incremented by 10 (high numbers mean low priority). If ⟨priority⟩ is given, it must be a number preceded by a minus sign. Priority numbers can be raised up to 20 using **nice**. Only the system manager is entitled to improve the priority of a command, normal users can only push it farther into the background.

nroff

Program function: Text formatter
Command syntax: `nroff` [*options*] [⟨file⟩ ...]
How and why used: Text files are reformatted in accordance with commands embedded in the text itself. These set margins, justify and fill lines, indent paragraphs, number and title pages, and otherwise provide text formatting services. A large number of options is allowed. Each option must be individually preceded by a minus sign; all the options must be listed before any of the files. The main options are

`-m`⟨*name*⟩	*Use macro library* `/usr/lib/tmac/tmac.`
`-n`⟨*n*⟩	Number the first page ⟨*n*⟩.
`-o`⟨*n1-n2,n3,n4-n5*⟩	Print only pages *n1* to *n2*, *n3*, and *n4* to *n5*.
`-s`⟨*n*⟩	Stop every ⟨*n*⟩ pages to allow paper changing.
`-T`⟨*name*⟩	Use terminal of type ⟨*name*⟩.

The ⟨file⟩s listed are processed in the order given; if no files are listed, the standard input is used. A single minus sign will also be understood to signify the standard input. The standard manuscript-preparation macro library is located in `/usr/lib/tmac/tmac.s` and is (in accordance with the above) accessed by `-ms`.

passwd

Program function: Changes password, or installs one.
Command syntax: `passwd`
How and why used: The user is asked for both old and new passwords, and the new one is installed. Passwords are refused if they are too short (fewer than four characters). If the current password is blank (which counts as no password at all), the `passwd` command is used to install a new one. Blank passwords are often assigned by system managers to newly authorized users.

pc

Program function: Berkeley Pascal compiler.
Command syntax: `pc` [options] ⟨file⟩
How and why used: Compiles Pascal, producing either assembler code or object code, as specified by the options. `pc` may be considered to feed into the second pass of the C compiler, so that options not recognized by `pc` will be passed on to the assembler and the loader `ld`. The Pascal accepted is close to the ISO standard. The input file name must terminate in `.p`, so that `pc` may recognize it as a Pascal source file.

The compiler `pc` is intended for compiling programs debugged with the interpreter `pi`, which provides more facilities for finding program errors.

The set of options provided with **pc** is wider than with **pi**, and is biased toward yielding good object code. Options are specified by giving a string of option letters, preceded by a minus sign. Option letters may be concatenated into a single string. Both upper and lower case characters are used in **pc** options; they are not interchangeable. The available options are

−b⟨*n*⟩	output buffer ⟨*n*⟩ blocks	(buffer = one line)
−c	compile partial program	(full program expected)
−C	subrange bound test	(no tests are performed)
−g	log Unix debugger information	(none logged)
−i	list all **include** files	(list **include** statements)
−l	source program listing generated	(no listing)
−o ⟨*name*⟩	output file name to be ⟨*name*⟩	(**a.out** is used)
−O	object code optimizer to be used	(not used)
−p	profiling counters for **prof**	(none generated)
−s	standard Pascal check	(no checking is done)
−S	assembly-language output	(object code is produced)
−w	suppress warning diagnostics	(warnings are issued)
−z	profile counters for later **pxp** run	(no counters)

If options are not specified, actions or values given in parentheses are assumed.

Parts of programs (e.g., individual procedures or functions) may be compiled separately, the resulting relocatable object code being linked and loaded later. For details of partial compilation, the Berkeley Pascal manuals should be consulted. **pc** is part of the Berkeley Pascal system; it is not part of the standard Version 7 Unix software.

Program function: Berkeley Pascal interpreter.

Command syntax: **pi** [*options*] ⟨file⟩

How and why used: Interprets Pascal, producing intermediate code which can be executed by means of the **px** execution monitor. The code produced is placed in a file named **obj**. The Pascal accepted is close to the ISO standard. The input file name must terminate in **.p**, so that **pi** may recognize it as a Pascal source file.

pi options are stated in the usual style. The command may be followed by a minus sign, a string of option letters as appropriate, and the file name or names to be operated on. The available options are

−b⟨*n*⟩	set output buffer to ⟨*n*⟩ blocks	(buffer = one line)
−i	list **include** files in full	(list **include** statements)
−l	source program listing to be generated	(no listing)
−p	postmortem error backtrace and dump omitted	(trace is done)

-s	standard Pascal language check	(no checking is done)
-t	subrange bound testing is suppressed	(tests are performed)
-w	warning diagnostics are suppressed	(warnings are issued)
-z	profile counters are set up for later **pxp** run	(no counters)

The option values given in parentheses are those assumed by default, to be reversed if desired. Options may also be invoked in the program itself by including in the program text a special comment line.

pi is often used to debug programs which, when finished, are compiled into executable binary code with **pc**. In general, **pc** produces better optimized, faster running programs with lower memory requirements, whereas **pi** runs quicker and provides better debugging aids.

Program function: Berkeley Pascal interpreter and executor.

Command syntax: **pix** [*options*] ⟨file⟩

How and why used: Interprets and executes Pascal. **pix** is the combination of the **pi** interpreter and the **px** execution monitor; command descriptions for these should be consulted for details.

Program function: Prints files.

Command syntax: **pr** [*option*] ... ⟨file⟩ ...

How and why used: Listings are produced in the standard output file (usually the terminal screen) of one or more named input files. Each file starts on a new page. The page starts with a header including date and file name. Options for **pr** are listed separately, each with its proper preceding plus or minus sign; the characters are not concatenated. The main options of importance are

-l⟨*n*⟩	sets page length to be *n* lines (default = 66).
-m	lists all files simultaneously, one per column.
-⟨*n*⟩	produces *n*-column formatted output.
+⟨*n*⟩	begins printing at page *n*.
-w⟨*n*⟩	sets page width to be *n* characters (default = 72).

The right number of columns should be set up if the **-**⟨*n*⟩ option is given, i.e., ⟨*n*⟩ should be the number of files, or an integer multiple of it, or an integer submultiple. *Note*: During the running of **pr**, interterminal message passing is disabled.

Program function: Displays process status.

Command syntax: **ps** [*options*] [⟨process⟩ ...]

How and why used: Gives status information about the currently active processes. If a process identification number ⟨process⟩ is given, information is furnished about the named process(es). Three options are allowed,

a   all processes associated with a terminal
l   long form
x   all processes not associated with a terminal

It should be noted that, contrary to most commands, **ps** does not require minus signs in front of the options. If a long form listing is requested, a whole lot of information is tabulated. Of likely interest to users are the state of each process (s), the user identification number (UID), the process identification number (PID), the identification number of the parent process (PPID), the event that will trigger a process if it is sleeping or waiting (WCHAN), the terminal controlling the process (TTY), the cumulative execution time (TIME), and the command that initiated the process (CMD). The state reports give single characters with the following meanings:

I   intermediate   T   stopped
O   nonexistent   W   waiting
R   running   Z   terminated
S   sleeping

In short form (without the l option) **ps** shows only part of the information, but usually quite enough.

Program function: Pathname of working directory.
Command syntax: **pwd**
How and why used: Displays the full pathname of the working directory at the terminal. Some users with many files do occasionally lose track of where they were and where they are going; but more often **pwd** is useful for finding out where in the Unix file structure the current working directory is located.

Program function: Berkeley Pascal execution monitor.
Command syntax: **px** [⟨file⟩]
How and why used: Executes Pascal intermediate code produced by **pi**. If no file name is given, **obj** is assumed. **px** is most often used as part of the **pix** command, which is a combination of **pi** and **px**.

Program function: Berkeley Pascal reformatter and profiler.
Command syntax: **pxp** [*options*] ⟨file⟩

How and why used: Produces an execution profile of a Pascal program, i.e., shows how many times each source line was executed. The execution count is shown on a reformatted program listing, so that by suppressing the execution information, **pxp** may also be used as a program reformatter/beautifier. The input file name must terminate in **.p**, so that **pxp** may recognize it as a Pascal source file.

Options available with **pxp** are communicated in the normal style, i.e., each option is specified by a single option letter, and options may be concatenated into a letter string. A minus sign must precede the string. Two classes of options apply with **pxp**: those concerned with profiling and those concerned with formatting the listings. The options are

−a	all routines included in the profile	(omit those not used)
−d	suppress listing of declarations	(all source text listed)
−e	substitute text for include statements	(statements only)
−f	full parentheses for mathematics	(minimal parentheses)
−j	left-justify everything	(nested blocks indented 4 spaces)
−s	strip comments in listing	(comments are fully listed)
−t	tabulate procedure and function calls	(no table given)
−z	profile named included files, or all	(no profile at all)
−_	underline keywords in listing	(no underlining)
−⟨n⟩	indent nestings ⟨n⟩ spaces	(4 spaces)

If options are not specified in the command line, action will be taken as shown in the parentheses above. If neither **t** nor **z** is specified (i.e., neither a detailed profile nor a table is asked for), no profile will result, only a listing of the program text. All listings produced by **pxp** contain in the heading the date and time of most recent modification of the program file (not the time at which the listing was produced). Listings are produced in lower case except for any literally included text (e.g., text to be printed out). Both keywords and variable names are reduced to lower case if they were not so already.

ratfor

Program function: Translates Ratfor to Fortran.

Command syntax: **ratfor** [*options*] ⟨file⟩ ...

How and why used: Translates the files named in the command, which must be Ratfor language text, into Fortran. The resulting output is deposited in the standard output file. Options available with **ratfor** are prefixed with a minus sign; they are

−h	quoted strings are given as Holleriths, like Fortran 66.
−c	comments are copied to output, and neatly reformatted.

-6c   c in column 6 for continuation line (otherwise **&** in column 1).

ratfor can also be invoked under **f77**; in that case, any options must be passed via the -R option of **f77**.

Program function: Removes files from the system.
Command syntax: **rm** [*options*] ⟨file⟩ ...

How and why used: Removes (i.e., deletes) the named files from the current working directory, provided the user has the appropriate permissions. Confirmation is asked, by a **y** from the terminal, for every file without write permission. Options are characters, which may be concatenated, prefixed by a minus sign. They are

-i   asks for a **y** response before removal of *any* file.
-r   asks for **y** for every entry if removing a directory file.
-f   forces removal without any questions asked.

Program function: Removes directories.
Command syntax: **rmdir** ⟨directory⟩ ...

How and why used: Removes directories from the system. Directories are not removed unless they are empty. Otherwise, operation is similar in principle to the **rm** command. No options are available with this command.

Program function: Command decoder.
Command syntax: **sh** ⟨file⟩

How and why used: **sh** is the standard Unix command decoder; in fact, it is the decoder which receives and understands all the commands listed in this chapter. Its standard input is from the keyboard. Files of commands to the shell, including a complicated set of conditional execution constructs and symbolic arguments, may be built and set running as in the syntax shown above. There are many advanced ways of invoking the shell, with various options, for which the manual **man** should be consulted.

Program function: Shows object file size.
Command syntax: **size** [⟨file⟩] ...

How and why used: Handy for determining file size. The decimal number of bytes of each of the three portions of an object file is shown, as well as the total size. The file name may be omitted; **a.out** is then understood.

| sort |

Program function: Sorts the lines in one or more files.

Command syntax: **sort** [*option*] [[+*pos*] [-*pos*]] ... [-o *outfil*] [⟨file⟩] ...

How and why used: The lines in the file(s) ⟨file⟩ are sorted and written to the standard output or to *outfil* if that option is specified. If no ⟨file⟩ is given, the standard input file is assumed. By default, the lines are sorted in ASCII sequence. Two forms of options exist. The alphabetic character options, always preceded by a minus sign, are very numerous; the most important are

-b   Blanks at the start of a line are ignored.
-c   Check that file is sorted as specified, no output if it is.
-d   Dictionary sort (only letters, digits, and blanks count).
-f   Forget case differences (i.e., consider **A = a**).
-i   Ignore everything but ASCII 040–176 in nonnumeric sorting.
-m   Merge files only; the files are already sorted.
-n   Numeric strings at line starts, sorted by arithmetic value.
-r   Reverse the sorting order.
-tx The field separator character is defined to be x.
-u   "Unique", i.e., discard extra copies of duplicate lines.

The column options [+*pos*] and [-*pos*] restrict the sort to consider the field from the first (+) to the second (-) position. A position has the form *f.c* where *f* is the field number and *c* is the column number in that field. In addition, each position may be qualified by the alphabetic options **bdfinr**. Thus multiple sort keys, modified sort keys, and various suboptions are possible.

| spell |

Program function: Tries to find spelling errors.

Command syntax: **spell** [*options*] [⟨file⟩ ...]

How and why used: ⟨file⟩, or in its absence the standard input file, is read to find all the words in it. These are compared against a spelling dictionary. Three options, concatenated characters preceded by a minus sign, are available:

-b   British spellings are given preference (*colour, recognise*).
-v   verbose: anything slightly dubious is listed in detail.
-x   lists every plausible stem for doubtful words.

Spellings are checked but syntax is ignored. For example, no message is issued if *its* replaces *it's*. Further, misspellings can be identified only if they are close; *dq5* is not recognizable as *cat* even though it is *cat* typed with the left hand shifted one row of keys. **spell** may vary a good deal between installations.

struct

Program function: Translates Fortran to Ratfor.

Command syntax: **struct** [*option*] ... ⟨file⟩

How and why used: Translates the ⟨file⟩ named in the command, which must be Fortran language text, into Ratfor. The output goes to the standard output file. The translation is not unique and may be guided by options, the most useful of which are

-a maps sequences of **elseif**s into a (non-Ratfor) switch.

-b avoids multi-level break statements; uses **go to**'s.

-i does not map computed **go to**'s into switches.

-n avoids multi-level next statements; use **go to**'s.

-s expects standard card-image (not free formatted) input text.

struct can be confused by some of the more esoteric (and badly structured) constructions available in Fortran 77, such as multiple subroutine entry and return points.

stty

Program function: Sets expected terminal characteristics.

Command syntax: **stty** [*option*] ...

How and why used: Establishes the expectations of the Unix kernel software, so as to make them match the actual characteristics of the terminal. This matter is complicated, for one might also set up the terminal to match the expectations of the kernel. The number of options verges on the incredible; those shown are likely to be useful for ordinary screen terminals. Two separate groups can be identified: settings and toggles. Settings simply pick some setting. Toggles can be used with a preceding minus sign or without; one undoes the other. For example, **echo** causes all typed characters to be echoed to the terminal, **-echo** asks for no echoing.

Toggles:

even allows (- disallows) even parity.

odd allows (- disallows) odd parity.

echo echo every input character to screen.

lcase map capital letters to lowercase.

tabs preserve tabs (- replaces with blanks).

Settings:

ek set erase and kill characters to **#** and **@**.

erase *c* set erase character to *c* (mostly BACKSPACE).

kill *c* set kill character to *c* (usually **@**).

300 1200 etc., are baud rates for communication.

For many terminals, special commands set all the various options; e.g., **tty33** sets up everything right for a KSR 33 Teletype, and **tek** does likewise for a Tektronix 4014.

When setting up a terminal, it is very important to make sure that all the option switches on the terminal are set to correspond to the settings made by **stty**. Note that on many terminals the switches actually set input bits for a microprocessor. It may be necessary to turn the terminal off and then on again after a few seconds so as to force the microprocessor to read the bit settings.

Program function: Table formatter
Command syntax: **tbl** [⟨file⟩ ...]
How and why used: **tbl** is a preprocessor for **nroff** or **troff**. All input text is taken from the named files or from the standard input if no files are named in the command. The input is passed through to the standard output except for lines encased in the command lines **.TS** to **.TE;** the latter are preprocessed by writing **nroff** or **troff** commands.

Program function: Pipe fitting in Unix pipelines.
Command syntax: **tee** [*option*] ⟨file⟩ ...
How and why used: The standard input is transcribed to the standard output, with an extra copy deposited in ⟨file⟩. There are two useful options, each of which must carry its own minus sign (if both are used):

-a   Append to ⟨file⟩; do not overwrite.
-i   Ignore any interruptions while transcribing.

Program function: Times execution of a command.
Command syntax: **time** ⟨command⟩
How and why used: Useful for finding out how much time a program takes to run; ⟨command⟩ may be any valid command understood by the shell. The elapsed time, processor time, etc., are displayed, in seconds. *Caution*: Timings can vary quite a bit depending on what other jobs are running on the system.

Program function: Character translation.
Command syntax: **tr** [*options*] ⟨string-1⟩ ⟨string-2⟩

How and why used: The standard input file is transformed and written into the standard output file, with every character in ⟨string-1⟩ removed and replaced by the character in the corresponding position in ⟨string-2⟩. The only generally useful option is −d, which deletes (rather than transforms) every character listed in ⟨string-1⟩. Primarily useful for changing uppercase to lower case characters, and similar character-for-character transformations.

Program function: Phototypesetter-based text formatter
Command syntax: troff [*options*] [⟨file⟩ ...]
How and why used: Text files are reformatted in accordance with commands embedded in the text itself, and are transmitted to the phototypesetter. troff functions similarly to nroff except that the range of options is wider because the output hardware device is more flexible.

Program function: Displays the terminal name.
Command syntax: tty
How and why used: Sometimes useful for determining the pathname of the terminal special file. More often useful for checking whether the system is healthy; a fast and harmless way to make the system do something and produce a little output. In shell files, a way of identifying from what terminal input originated.

umount

Program function: Unmounts a file system.
Command syntax: /etc / umount ⟨directory⟩
How and why used: Disonnects the root directory of a disk, tape, etc. volume from the Unix system. ⟨directory⟩ is released and returned to whatever use it had before the corresponding mount command.

In the standard Version 7 Unix system, umount is restricted to the system manager and is located in directory /etc. Numerous other system versions and systems have user-accessible, but often slightly different or restricted, umount commands.

uniq

Program function: Finds repeated adjacent lines in a file.
Command syntax: uniq [*options* [+*n*] [-*m*]] [⟨infile⟩ [⟨outfile⟩]]
How and why used: The input file ⟨infile⟩ is read and copied to ⟨outfile⟩; if no names are given, the standard files are used. Adjacent lines

are compared while copying. If no options are given, all second and further copies of repeated lines are discarded. Specifying some number m in -m causes m fields to be skipped in each line before comparing begins; giving +n causes n characters to be ignored in the first field examined. Options are concatenable characters preceded by a minus sign:

-c   Count repetitions of each line, and display their number.
-d   Copy over only the duplicated lines, one copy of each.
-u   Copy over only the unduplicated lines.

The utility **sort** must be used first if the files in question are not already sorted.

Program function: Screen editor for text preparation
Command syntax: **vi** ⟨file⟩
How and why used: Screen editor with variable and independently controllable screen window size and placement, with cursor-controlled editing functions. **vi** is a very powerful editor with a large command set and is often used in place of **ed** for text preparation. ⟨file⟩ is opened for editing when **vi** is invoked; it may be overwritten with edited text when exiting.

Program function: Counts characters, words, and lines in files.
Command syntax: **wc** [*options*] [⟨file⟩ ...]
How and why used: Used to assess size of text files. If several files are named, both individual and cumulative totals are shown. All three entities are counted if no option characters are shown; otherwise, any one or combination of the three may be selected by the option characters **c**, **w**, **l**. If used, the option characters may be concatenated and must be preceded by a minus sign. If no file name is given, the keyboard is taken as the default input device, and the typed input is counted until a control-D is sent.

Program function: Shows who is on the system.
Command syntax: **who** [am I]
How and why used: Without option, displays the terminal pathnames, user identification names, etc., of everybody currently on the system. **who** should be employed, prior to using the **write** message-passing facility, to determine whether the intended message recipient is logged in. With the [am I] option, information is displayed for the requestor only, a convenience

for author identification in shell files. Useful as a harmless activity to check whether system is alive; also good for amnesia sufferers.

Program function: Sends immediate message to specified user.

Command syntax: `write` ⟨user⟩ [⟨terminal⟩]

How and why used: The command line causes the intended recipient ⟨user⟩ to be alerted that a message impends. All lines typed at the keyboard after the `write` are immediately transmitted to the recipient, interrupting whatever else he may have been doing (with a few exceptions). A terminal name may also be given, and this is useful if the recipient is currently logged in at several terminals. Transmission is terminated when a control-D is typed. Two-way communication can be set up, provided some form of agreed "over-and-out" protocol is used to avoid both parties sending or listening at the same time.

Chapter 10

Bibliography

The literature now available on the Unix operating system includes several books as well as a substantial number of articles and technical papers. Many of the technical papers will prove to be of little interest to the system user whom this book is intended to serve, because they deal with specialized internal details. On the other hand, textbooks and handbooks are likely to be of greater importance. An attempt has therefore been made to cover the textbook and monograph material rather thoroughly, while listing only a small fraction of the periodical literature.

Books

Bell Telephone Laboratories, Inc.: *Unix time-sharing system: Unix programmer's manual*. Revised and expanded version. New York, N.Y.: Holt, Rinehart and Winston, 1983. ISBN 0-03-061742-1 (Vol. 1), 0-03-061743-X (Vol. 2). xvi + 425 pp. (Vol. 1), vii + 616 pp. (Vol. 2).

This book is the openly published version of the 7th edition of the Unix system documentation, somewhat amended and revised. Its original version, edited by B. Kernighan and M. D. McIlroy, has been the authoritative support manual for the Unix system as used at Bell Laboratories since 1979. A machine-readable version of this pair of large quarto (22 cm by 28 cm) volumes is furnished as part of the normal Unix system itself. It is available at almost every installation in an edited and altered form, so as to bring it into line with the software actually installed there. Hence it exists in various versions, applicable to different system configurations. It is indispensable for system maintenance and a valuable reference for the average user, but it is not very useful as a beginner's book for learning to use the system. Most users employ it as an encyclopedia, to look up specific details from time to time. Few users ever possess a copy, but extract the appropriate pages from the machine-readable file as necessary.

Gauthier, Richard: *Using the Unix system*. Reston, Virginia: Reston Publishing Co. (A Prentice-Hall Company), 1981. ISBN 0-8359-8164-9. xiv + 297 pp.

Gauthier's book can be read by the novice, but it can be quite difficult going for anyone who does not possess a good deal of prior experience with interactive computer systems. Oriented to system managers and users rather than to system programmers, it contains little internal detail but does give a substantial amount of information on how to set up, manage and maintain a Unix system installation. Most of the text is directed at the system (in the narrow sense), so that many of the programs commonly wanted by users (e.g., nroff) are not covered, and languages used in computing (e.g., Fortran) are not even mentioned. While examples are given for almost all the material treated, the level of the material varies from very elementary to very advanced. A set of review questions is provided for each chapter, with suggested answers at the back of the book.

Thomas, Rebecca, Yates, Jean: *A user guide to the Unix system*. Berkeley: Osborne/McGraw-Hill, 1982. ISBN 0-931988-71-3. xi + 508 pp.

This book is intended to serve the end user at the terminal, rather than the system manager. It covers only a small portion of the available Unix system utilities, but gives examples of all the commands which it does treat, in a beautifully clear form. Occasionally, however, the examples are so lengthy and extensively detailed as to verge on the boring. A very useful summary short list is given of those commands that do appear in the book. But the user is assumed to be interested only in the treatment of text files through basic system utilities, so that programming language support (C, Fortran, ...) does not even rate a mention; and the quite strong text processing facilities which Unix software includes, such as nroff, appear tantalizingly in marginal notes but are never treated as working tools. Thomas and Yates thus provide the neophyte a very good introduction, but do not accompany him very far in learning to use the system.

Bourne, S. R.: *The Unix system*. Reading, Mass.: Addison-Wesley, 1982. ISBN 0-201-13791-7. xiii + 351 pp.

Written by a member of the original Unix software team, this book deals extensively with the shell, with document preparation, and with a selection of utility programs. It contains a chapter on the C language and gives much useful detail on system programming. Although beginning users will find it readable, this well-written book really addresses itself to the experienced system programmer without previous Unix experience.

Banahan, M., Rutter, A.: *Unix—the book*. Wilmslow, Cheshire: Sigma Technical Press, 1982. vi + 265 pp. (Distributed by John Wiley). ISBN 0-905104-21-8.

A comprehensive description of the Unix operating system, containing a great deal of detailed material in very brief form, this book is of reference value to anyone prepared to live with its two shortcomings. It is written in a distinctly unfunny style presumably intended to be humorous, which quickly becomes wearying for the reader; and it has a glue binding of poor quality, which begins shedding pages almost before leaving the bookstore. The text processing facilities and utility programs that form part of Unix software are covered in detail; so is the C language. But curiously, other more common programming languages barely rate a mention. System startup and shutdown, and system maintenance occupy a chapter. All in all, a good reference book for the experienced programmer willing to accept gratuitous insults from the authors, but not an easy book for beginners.

Christian, K.: *The Unix operating system.* New York: John Wiley, 1983. ISBN 0-471-87542-2. xviii + 318 pp.

This well-organized book is subdivided into two parts suitable for beginners and advanced programmers respectively. The beginners' part occupies the first 138 pages, covering about the same subject matter as most other introductory books: shell, login procedures, file management, text processing, etc. The advanced programmers' part occupies about 120 pages. It is mainly devoted to the facilities available for applications software development (rather than to the needs of the system manager). The book is well-designed and produced, but relatively expensive.

Lomuto, A., Lomuto, N.: *A Unix primer.* Englewood Cliffs, N.J.: Prentice-Hall, 1983. ISBN 0-13-938886-9. xvi + 240 pp.

A very simple book directed at people with no computing experience whatever. Its content is largely confined to using Unix files and the **ed** editor. The book contains little cartoons to break the tedium of reading, and it provides plenty of white space for readers to doodle in.

McGilton, H., Morgan, R.: *Introducing the Unix system.* New York: McGraw-Hill/Byte (McGraw-Hill Computer Books), 1983. ISBN 0-07045001-3. xx + 556 pp.

The main strength of this book is its detailed treatment of text processing (editing, formatting, and manipulation), to which over two-thirds of its text is devoted. The remainder of the book consists principally of four or five introductory chapters, which are suitable for beginners, and a useful chapter directed to system managers. There is also a short chapter on the Berkeley Unix System. In contrast to most other books, no summarizing chapter of system commands is provided. The book is very rich in examples, and therefore probably better for initial study than for use as a reference work.

Waite, M., Martin, D., Prata, S.: *Unix primer plus.* Indianapolis, Ind.: Howard W. Sams, 1983. ISBN 0-672-22028-8. 414 pp.

Written for the true beginner, this book contains a general description of Unix structure, an introduction to text editing, and a brief mention of the programming languages available. Like the Lomuto and Lomuto book, it is designed not to overstress its audience. Little if any computing experience is expected of the reader, while frequent changes in writing style, cartoons, and two-color printing all contribute to easing understanding.

Thomas, R., Emerson, S., Yates, J., Campbell, J.: *A business guide to Unix*. Reading, Mass.: Addison-Wesley, 1983. ISBN 0-201-08848-7. 488 pp.

Thomas, R., Emerson, S., Yates, J., Campbell, J.: *A business guide to Xenix*. Reading, Mass.: Addison-Wesley, 1983. ISBN 0-201-08847-7. 488 pp.

Prince, V.: *Le systeme Unix*. Paris, France: Editests, 1983. ISBN 2-86699-003-X. 128 pp.

This first book on Unix to appear in the French language gives a well-organized overview of the major commands, and includes introductory chapters to help the beginning Unix user to get started. It attempts to cover too large a number of commands in too little detail; but this shortcoming may be forgivable, indeed desirable, from the point of view of readers unable to make good use of the English-language literature on the subject.

Kernighan, B. W., Plauger, P. J.: *Software tools*. Reading, Mass.: Addison-Wesley, 1976. ISBN 0-201-03669-X. iii + 338 pp.

The major utilities (and a few kernel-level functions) provided in the Unix system are described by giving the underlying processing algorithms, and developing `ratfor` programs to implement them. Full of examples, program segments, and avuncular advice on good programming practices. The book is fairly easy to read right through, but harder to dip into for bits and pieces, because chapters tend to build upon each other. A `ratfor` translator is included as part of the book.

Kernighan, B. W., Ritchie, D. M.: *The C programming language*. Englewood Cliffs, N. J.: Prentice-Hall, 1978. ISBN 0-13-110163-3. x + 228 pp.

The definitive (and only) book on C. Well written and illustrated with a profusion of examples. Indispensable for anyone intending to construct Unix system programs, but very much optional for the casual user.

Articles

Barak, A. B., Shapir, A.: Unix with satellite processors. *Software Practice and Experience*, vol. 10, no. 5, pp. 383–392, May 1980.

Reports on an extension of the Unix system to handle a network of processors including several small computers and one large computer. Such networks are likely to become important in the future.

Bourne, S. R.: Unix time-sharing system: The Unix shell. *Bell System Tech. Journal*, vol. 57, no. 6, pt. 2, pp. 1971–1990, July–Aug. 1978.

This clearly written article describes how the Unix shell appears to the user. It is a little lacking in detail, and too compact for reference, but the description is good and the summary of commands very useful.

Cherlin, E.: The Unix operating system: portability A plus. *Mini-Micro Systems*, vol. 14, no. 4, pp. 153–154, 156, 159, Apr. 1981.

The Unix system is transportable, but still requires at least the writing of device drivers, parts of the kernel, and a C compiler. It has served as a model for several operating systems for 8-bit machines. The greatest portability difficulties arise in interrupt handling and memory management.

Feldman, S. I.: Make—a program for maintaining computer programs. *Software Practice and Experience*, vol. 9, no. 4, pp. 255–265, April 1979.

`make` is a Unix utility for keeping track of the course of development of programs of significant size, and for cataloguing the parts that make up the program. Its characteristics and use are described.

Greenberg, R. B.: The Unix operating system and the Xenix standard operating environment. *Byte*, vol. 6, no. 6, pp. 248–264, June 1981.

Historical origins of the Unix system, a review of its design goals and characteristics, largely from the viewpoint of microcomputer users.

Johnson, S. C.: Language development tools on the Unix system. *Computer*, vol. 13, no. 8, pp. 16–24, Aug. 1980. [16 refs.]

Software tools are described which make the writing of program generators relatively easy. (Program generators accept task specifications in user-oriented terms and produce programs in standard languages for performing the tasks).

Kernighan, B. W., Lesk, M. E., Ossanna, J. F., Jr.: Unix time-sharing system: Document preparation. *Bell System Tech. Journal*, vol. 57, no. 6, pp. 2115–2135, July–Aug. 1978. [20 refs.]

An overview of the text processing facilities standard under the Unix operating system: `troff`, `nroff`, `tbl`,..., and how they fit together.

Kernighan, B. W., Mashey, J. R.: The Unix programming environment. *Computer*, vol. 14, no. 4, pp. 12–24, April 1981. [38 refs.]

A survey article, well written and easy to read. Describes the principal system features and outlines the range of Unix software tools available. Of interest mainly to newcomers to the system, though some details may be news even to old hands.

Lions, J.: Experiences with the Unix time-sharing system. *Software Practice and Experience*, vol. 9, no. 9, pp. 701–709, Sept. 1979.

Describes the author's experience in a university teaching environment.

Manning, E. G., Howard, R., O'Donnell, C. G., Pammett, K., Chang, E.: A Unix-based local processor and network access machine. *Computer Networks*, vol. 1, no. 2, pp. 139–142, Sept. 1976.

General purpose time-sharing systems composed of small computers and a large mainframe are considered, with particular attention to making the entire system appear to the user through one command language. Of research interest.

Morgan, S. P.: The Unix system: making computers easier to use. *Bell Laboratories Record*, vol. 56, no. 11, pp. 308–313, Dec. 1978.

A very broad and general description, possibly of value to readers of this book, but certainly of interest to a broader audience.

Ritchie, D. M.: Unix time-sharing system: A retrospective. *Bell System Technical Journal*, vol. 57, no. 6, pp. 1947–1969, July–August 1978. [15 refs.]

An overview of the Unix system and of its early technical history. Well written and very readable, though no longer up to date.

Roome, W. D.: Programmer's Workbench: new tools for software development. *Bell Laboratories Record*, vol. 57, no. 1, pp. 19–25, Jan. 1979.

Programmer's Workbench is a set of Unix software tools larger than what is normally provided. Its content and characteristics are described.

Stiefel, M. L.: Unix. *Mini-Micro Syst.*, vol. 11, no. 4, pp. 64–66, April 1978.

A general description is given of the Unix operating system, noting that commercial versions are now available. The review is optimistic, and sees few flaws in the system.

Index

Numbers in italics indicate pages on which term is defined.